AUDIT IN A DEMOCRACY

Audit in a Democracy

The Australian Model of Public Sector Audit and its Application to Emerging Markets

PAUL NICOLL
Australian National Audit Office, Australia

ASHGATE

Published by

Ashgate Publishing Limited
Gower House
Croft Road
Aldershot
Hampshire GU11 3HR
England

Ashgate Publishing Company
Suite 420
101 Cherry Street
Burlington, VT 05401-4405
USA

Ashgate website: http://www.ashgate.com

British Library Cataloguing in Publication Data
Nicoll, Paul
Audit in a democracy : the Australian model of public sector audit and its application to emerging markets
1. Finance, Public - Auditing 2. Finance, Public - Australia - Auditing
I. Title
657.8'35'045

Library of Congress Cataloging-in-Publication Data
Nicoll, Paul.
Audit in a democracy : the Australian model of public sector audit and its application to emerging markets / by Paul Nicoll.
p. cm.
Includes bibliographical references and index.
ISBN 0-7546-4429-4
1. Finance, Public--Auditing--Law and legislation--Australia. 2. Legislative auditing--Australia. 3. Australian National Audit Office. 4. Finance, Public--Auditing--Law and legislation. I. Title.

KU2744.N53 2005
343.94'034--dc22

2005020471

ISBN 0 7546 4429 4

Printed and bound by Athenaeum Press Ltd, Gateshead, Tyne & Wear.

Contents

List of Tables and Figures

Preface

The origins of this book are in Azerbaijan. Azerbaijan was part of the former Union of Soviet Socialist Republics until its independence in 1991. In 2003, the World Bank provided funding for a project to reform the Azerbaijan Chamber of Accounts, which is the public sector audit agency. I was invited to participate in a bid for the project and prepared material, but did not participate in the bid because of a change in the project's direction.

Late in 2003, the Australian Government announced that, at the request of the Government of Papua New Guinea, it would provide additional assistance to ensure the stability of government and public administration. One focus of additional assistance was the Audit Office of Papua New Guinea. Papua New Guinea became independent from Australia in 1975. This additional assistance commenced in 2004.

In 2004 I was in Brazil, where I learned of a major project to modernise the Courts of Accounts in Brazil's states and at the national level. Brazil is a far larger nation than either Azerbaijan or Papua New Guinea, and its economy is far more diversified and complex than the economies of these two countries. The Brazilian Courts of Accounts are public sector audit agencies. Part of the project of particular interest was the scope for each of the more than 20 Courts of Accounts to appraise its public image, and to engage the public much more in supporting reform of public administration. In other words, the process of reform of the public sector audit function involved a more direct relationship between the public sector audit agency and the public.

I realised that issues in the reform of public sector audit in Azerbaijan were similar to issues being addressed in Papua New Guinea and Brazil.

The Brazilian experience echoed what I learned some years before while working for the Australian Parliament's Joint Committee of Public Accounts, (now the Joint Committee of Public Accounts and Audit). The Parliamentary Committee conducted the first major review since Australia's independence in 1901 of what is now the Australian National Audit Office. The Audit Office was established in 1901. The Parliamentary Committee gave itself the task of sorting out the Audit Office's confused identity, and resolving whether it was part of government, part of the legislature or something else. A smoothly operating audit office is essential for good government. The Committee consisted of Members of Parliament and Senators, few of whom knew where the Audit Office was in the national capital. It was premature to talk of a relationship between the Audit Office and Parliament if elected representatives had no idea of something as basic as the Audit Office's location. The Committee took some simple, first steps to develop its own understanding of the role of the Audit Office in the public sector. Those first steps became the basis for fundamental reform of the relationship between the Australian Parliament and the Australian National Audit Office.

When the Australian Parliamentary Committee reviewed the Audit Office, the Committee was struck by the public's limited knowledge of the latter. This was a surprise in light of the importance of the Office to the modern state. Since the Committee completed its work, there have been advances in public awareness of the Office's work.

For some years, a colleague Rod Nicholas and I have taught a graduate course in performance auditing and management review at the Australian National University in Canberra. We noticed that some concepts and ideas in the course, that we considered uncontroversial, were disturbing or unsettling to many in our classes. This appeared to be because of the analysis and exploration of concepts fundamental to public sector reform. Amongst those was the concept of accountability. There was uneven understanding of this concept in public administration. A course objective was to assist students to clarify definitions for their own countries. We learned that, at least in one language, the word 'accountability' did not exist, although the concept did. Consequently, we attempted to be even more sensitive in discussing concepts behind performance auditing and management reviews.

Private sector auditing is under scrutiny internationally because of public and media attention on the work of audit firms in several business collapses, notably in the United States, Italy and Australia. These collapses have raised fundamental questions about the role of private sector audit. It is only a matter of time before similar questions are asked of public sector audit. The material to follow anticipates a wider debate about the role of public sector audit in developing countries, especially those that are forming or strengthening market economies.

These experiences and views led me to realise that some of the material prepared for the World Bank project in Azerbaijan had wider applicability. I expanded the material, which became this book.

Paul Nicoll

Canberra, Australia

Acknowledgements

The views expressed are mine and not those of the Australian National Audit Office.

I am grateful to friends and colleagues within the Australian National Audit Office who commented on draft chapters. In particular, I would like to thank Gillian Gould, Jodie Machin and Rod Nicholas, colleagues from other organisations, who patiently read and commented on the draft manuscript.

The idea for this book came from Dr Maria Helena Horta Ludolf de Mello Nicoll. She identified the possibilities of an exploration of concepts used in public sector audit in Australia, and their application to developing countries.

Acronyms

ANAO	Australian National Audit Office
ASOSAI	Asian Organization of Supreme Audit Institutions
COA	Court or Chamber of Accounts
GAO	General Accountability Office
INTOSAI	International Organization of Supreme Audit Institutions
JCPA	Joint Committee of Public Accounts
JCPAA	Joint Committee of Public Accounts and Audit
SAI	Supreme Audit Institution
WTO	World Trade Organization

Introduction

A government has funded a hospital in a large city to provide health services to residents. The hospital delivers some but not all of the services for which it receives finance. Money set aside for specialist equipment disappears. Patients die because of poor service and inadequate equipment, even though the minister for health states that it is the best funded hospital in the country. Hospital administrators affirm their sound management of the hospital. The auditors have given an audit opinion on the hospital's accounts. Who is responsible for the poor service and inadequate equipment? Why did the auditors not find any problems in the accounts and management, even though patients have died? What went wrong?

A government telecommunications company provides telephone and Internet services to most of the population and to most businesses. It has much revenue since it dominates the market. However, the telephone system in parts of the capital and in large areas of countryside does not always function. The company's invoices for telephone and Internet services provided to the private sector are often incorrect and late. Company service is slow. The company's accounts are audited regularly, and the auditor does not report any problems. The public and the legislature ask what is happening.

These are examples of problems that can and do exist in many countries, including countries with well-developed economies and those where the economy is changing rapidly. They occur in societies where government has a stable role, and they appear where the role of government is evolving quickly. The problems are important since they affect the everyday lives of citizens. They must be addressed by government for the latter to retain popular support. In addition, the legislature will be concerned about what is happening, since the electorate may not support their representatives at the next election if these serious problems continue.

Electorates in all countries want good government and sound laws. They expect their legislatures to enact laws on the performance of government entities, such as public hospitals and telecommunications companies. They expect those laws to be implemented. They also expect to be informed where laws determining the behaviour and performance of government entities are not implemented. The electorate wants to know about mismanagement of public moneys that they have provided through the taxation and revenue system. Citizens tend to expect that audit will find things that are wrong, finding weaknesses and corruption. They are less accustomed to conceive audit as providing an assurance of good government although it can provide such an assurance. Already we can see that a compendium of popular expectations is part of the environment in which public sector audit works.

This book is not an audit manual. Rather, it searches for and identifies any role of public sector audit in cases such as those described earlier, as in the hospital where patients died perhaps prematurely, and in the telecommunications company that upset so many of its clients. It explores certain critical ideas in public sector audit, such as public sector audit's function in government and with the legislature. In particular, it introduces public sector audit's capacity to assess government agencies' compliance with the law and their management of taxpayer funded programs and services. The book starts with an account of the Australian model of public sector audit. This is a foundation for exploring the meaning of audit reform in developing countries' public sectors. Many developing countries are continually examining the role of the market. These states will have mixed economies, and the roles of the state and the market vary greatly within them. Ideally, a mixed economy will have both strong public and private sectors. A vital element for a strong public sector is community and business confidence in government. Audit is one tool that can reinforce confidence in government, or, where necessary, communicate authoritatively that confidence is misplaced. In other words, audit can be a tool for reform of the public sector, alongside other mechanisms for reforming the market sector and making it more efficient.

Public sector audit is not primarily responsible for resolving problems in a nation's public sector. However, because of the importance of public sector audit to good government and administration, it is always a participant. Sometimes its activities are visible, and at other times they are not. This introduction largely to legal issues in public sector audit will highlight when its work should be visible. Once its work is visible and, in turn, its role understood, then it becomes as accountable for its actions as management of the public hospital and telecommunications company. Careful definition of the role of public sector audit is a foundation for reform of public sector law. That definition separates the current role of public sector audit from what ought to be its role. Much of the discussion in the following chapters distinguishes between current and ideal characteristics of a strong and successful public sector function, inviting the reader to consider the strengths and weaknesses of audit in his or her country.

The approach is to raise and discuss critical issues in audit in general, and in public sector audit in particular. A point of view is often adopted in regard to the critical issues, which are put forward as bases for considering current audit law. It is written in the belief that it is up to citizens of developing countries to establish the role of public sector audit and to define the way in which public sector audit does its work. Therefore, while we have put arguments on critical issues, in this case, it is the task of citizens and their elected representatives to consider which of these issues are applicable to their country, and to find the best way or ways to address them. Probably, the best way will involve a review of public sector audit law where it exists, and consideration of the desirability of such law when there is none. If so, then this material will assist in such a review.

A common term used to describe a nation's public sector auditor is Supreme Audit Institution (SAI). This term has been adopted by the International

Organization of Supreme Audit Institutions (INTOSAI). INTOSAI comprises representatives of national public sector audit institutions from most countries. In 2004, the great majority of nation states were members of INTOSAI.

The issues raised apply to SAIs in economies in developing countries, whether most economic activity is in the public or private sector. All SAIs address the issues one way or another. SAIs in various developing countries have found different answers to challenges of the critical issues. Various responses to these challenges to public sector audit arise because of differences between nations in the role of the elected legislature and government. Public sector audit works with both the legislature and with government. Consequently, the relationship between them will influence strongly legislation surrounding the audit institution, for instance, in the extent of its legal powers. A starting point, then, for reform of public sector audit, and especially of the relevant law or laws, is to understand the current relationship between the legislature and government.

We are used to thinking about audit in its work with individual entities in the public and private sectors. In other words, we are most familiar with reading about audit opinions on this or that body. Audit appears as an activity with two participants, the auditor and the entity under audit, called the auditee. While true, this is an incomplete description of audit in both sectors. Possibly, we are not as accustomed to viewing public sector audit as a key element in a democracy. It is so because, as it will be argued below, public sector audit ideally is a creation of a national legislature. It is applied by the legislature to the activities of executive government. Therefore, it is inevitable that public sector audit has political implications. Those SAIs which have flourished for a long time have learned to live with the political implications of their work, and to meet the expectations of major participants in the political process. The major participants are government and its opposition – however the latter is formed.

Desirable conditions for survival of an SAI are legislation that permits it to do its work, and a relationship with both government and the legislature. This exploration of critical issues is intended to provoke thought and analysis about the components of legislation relevant to an SAI.

When preparing this material, I revisited earlier reviews of public sector audit law, notably in Australia. The most significant of these was a review of the Australian SAI by a committee of the Australian Parliament.[1] This was the first Parliamentary review of the Australian SAI since its foundation 88 years previously in 1901 when Australia became an independent country. A major task for the review was to find a way to remove ambiguity in the role of the Auditor-General, who was the head of the SAI. The ambiguity was because of a lack of clarity about who the Auditor-General was serving, leading to role confusion. The ambiguity was removed with the recommendation of the Parliamentary Committee

---

[1] Joint Committee of Public Accounts and Audit (1989), *The Auditor-General: Ally of the People and Parliament, Reform of the Australian Audit Office*, Report No. 296, AGPS, Canberra, Australia.

that the Auditor-General should be an officer of the Parliament. The Government accepted this recommendation, which became a crucial part of new audit law. A second major study revisited in preparing this document was a review of public sector auditing in an Australian state.[2] The report of that review commenced with an account of the constitutional setting for public sector auditing. These two examples of audit reviews are mentioned since they show the continuity of interest in critical issues in one country. Many other states that differ greatly from Australia in location, culture, political system, history and relative size of the market manifest a similar continuity of interest.

A characteristic of courts and chambers of accounts is that they are collegial and judicial. They may have jurisdictional power over the accounts, over the accountants or even over administrators. The International Organization of Supreme Audit Institutions, INTOSAI, reminds us that judgements and decisions that these institutions make are natural complements to the administrative audit functions with which they are charged. Their jurisdictional actions should be seen as part of the logic of the general objectives pursued by external audit and in particular those objectives that relate to accounting questions.[3] Where an SAI is structured in collegiate form such as in a court of accounts, INTOSAI points out that the final opinions and decisions represent the view of the organization as a whole, even if the action is taken or exercised in bodies differentiated by their composition but not their power.

A court of accounts can consist of legal specialists, such as advocates and court members who function as judges, as well as auditors. A characteristic that distinguishes courts of accounts from other kinds of SAIs is the co-existence of these two sets of specialists – one with legal training and the other with audit training. In some countries, courts of accounts have functions additional to audit. Examples are preparation of reports on the socio-economic circumstances of local governments, and confirmation of the level of retirement benefits of former government employees. This study addresses the audit functions of SAIs. It does not canvass these other functions, for which a separate study would be necessary.

The approach taken here is to introduce issues in the reform of public sector audit – and particularly of public sector audit law – as a series of questions, which are answered. This approach was adopted for its simplicity in presenting through an auditor's eyes complex matters of public sector reform. It will especially assist those readers with little or no previous engagement with public sector audit, and who find themselves involved in their countries in what can be a disorienting and confusing discussion of why and how to change the public sector auditor.

---

[2] Queensland Electoral and Administrative Review Commission (1991), *Report on Review of Public Sector Auditing in Queensland*, Electoral and Administrative Review Commission, Brisbane, Australia.

[3] INTOSAI (1992 and 1995), *Accounting Standards*, INTOSAI, Vienna, Austria, p.29, <www.intosai.org>

The book has four parts. Each part poses one principal question. These are:

- What is the Australian model of public sector audit?
- What is a Supreme Audit Institution (SAI)?
- What authority does the SAI need for its work?
- What are the next steps in reform of an SAI's legal framework?

The first question is the base that is analysed critically. The second question considers the SAI's role in the context of the roles of the legislature and executive government, exploring answers in addition to those in the Australian model. Sorting out the role of the SAI can only be done in this wider context, and no single or rigid model of public sector audit is proposed. The third question canvasses more operational issues that must be considered in audit law. The final question summarises the material in the first three questions and is a foundation for action.

In the Australian experience, there is limited understanding, and uncertainty and confusion about public sector audit. These conditions are evident within administrative circles, at the political level, within universities, amongst part of the media and society. One sign of this is the surprise of many persons when told that the Auditor-General conducts both regularity and performance audits. Others are startled to learn that the Auditor-General has no legal authority to require audited agencies to implement recommendations, and that there are strong reasons for such powers to be withheld by the legislature. It is possible that political, administrative, media and popular views of audit in developing countries are similar. The book was written to demystify certain erroneous or narrow views about public sector audit. It does so by posing fundamental questions about this function.

More research is warranted on the role of SAIs in both developed and developing countries. There is a special need for comparative research into the visibility of SAIs in different nations and societies. Research data would assist in exploring whether high or low profile SAIs have the greater impact in reform of public administration. The profile of an SAI is evident in political and societal knowledge about its role.

After reading this book, you may conclude that current law – where it exists – is relevant and sufficient. In this case, exploration of the critical issues will provide assurance about the foundations for the SAI's tasks, and it will not lead to change. However, it is likely that the need for at least some legislative change will become apparent after the ideas and concepts are considered. To reaffirm a statement made earlier, it is only the citizens of the developing nation and their elected representatives who can confirm the satisfactory nature of any current audit law or argue that it must alter. In addition, it is only those citizens who can affirm the pace of reform of public sector audit including creation of or change in the law. They will decide how much change they want and at what speed they want change to occur. Their decisions will depend on how many of the critical issues in this book they feel the need to address.

PART I

WHAT IS THE AUSTRALIAN MODEL OF PUBLIC SECTOR AUDIT?

What is the Australian Model of Public Sector Audit?

Part I addresses the following issues:

- The legislature and audit in Australia
- Why is there an Auditor-General?
- What standards does the Auditor-General apply?
- Money for audits
- The special case of performance audits
- What happens to audit opinions?

The final chapter summarises the Australian model.

Each of the above issues reveals a different aspect of the Australian model of public sector auditing, including the relationship with the Parliament and government, the reasons for auditing, audit finance and the uses or results of audits.

These matters are discussed more generally in later parts of this book, where their links, limits and effects are explored for countries where markets are emerging. For instance, the first three issues above are canvassed in Part II. Audit finance is discussed in Parts II and III. Performance audits and their differences with regularity audits are described in Part II. The last issue above, which is what happens to audit opinions, also is raised in Part II.

Chapter 1

The Legislature and Audit in Australia

The Australian model of public sector audit has changed since 1997 when new audit legislation was introduced. In order to understand why and how it has changed, it is necessary to portray the condition of the national Audit Office before then. Therefore, this chapter will describe what was the relationship between the legislature and the Auditor-General, including his Audit Office, before later chapters canvass what now is the relationship. First, however, there is a brief introduction to the Australian political system so that the role of audit within it can be understood.

Introduction to the Australian political system

Australia has a federal system of government. In addition to the Australian Government, there are six state governments that evolved from colonies existing before the nation's independence, and two territory governments, with powers generally similar to those of state governments. There are local governments in every state and territory. The Australian Constitution affirms that the Commonwealth or Australian Parliament can make laws for subjects including taxation, defence, external affairs, interstate and international trade, corporations, marriage and divorce and immigration.[1] State Parliaments can make laws on a wider range of subjects including education and criminal law. However, the Commonwealth Parliament can make laws for specific purposes that include those latter subjects.

There is an Auditor-General at the national level of government, and Part I is largely about that position and that of the Office. In each state and territory, there is an Auditor-General. Each Auditor-General in Australia is independent of the other, and each position is created by legislation. Therefore, there are nine separate laws for the nine Auditors-General. Where necessary to understand the role of the Australian Auditor-General, we will refer to the work of these other Auditors-General.

---

[1] Attorney-General's Department (2004), *Australia. The Constitution – as in force on 1 June 2003*, Attorney-General's Department, Canberra, <http://scaleplus.law.gov.au>

What was the relationship between the legislature and the Australian Auditor-General?

Australia became independent from Great Britain in 1901. The fourth act of Parliament was the *Audit Act 1901*, which defined aspects of the relationship between the legislature and the Australian Auditor-General.

Audit Act 1901

The Act stated that the Governor-General, who is the representative of the Queen of Australia, may appoint some person to be Auditor-General for the Commonwealth of Australia.[2] [3] The Governor-General was not required to consult with Parliament about the appointment, and the appointment could be made without involving it. The Act set out the basis for the Auditor-General's continuation in office. He could be removed if the Senate and the House of Representatives, which are the two Houses of Parliament, requested the Governor-General to remove him. The Governor-General could suspend the Auditor-General for physical or mental incapacity, incompetence or misbehaviour. If the Governor-General took such action, he was obliged to advise both Houses of Parliament within seven days. A suspended Auditor-General would be restored to office unless each House of Parliament within seven weeks requested the Governor-General to remove him. These legislative provisions gave the Governor-General the authority to appoint the Auditor-General. It was customary for the Prime Minister to advise and recommend a person to the Governor-General for appointment to the position. The Governor-General could temporarily suspend the Auditor-General, with the Parliament being the only authority to permanently remove him from office.

The Act mentioned Parliament in a few other places. For instance, the Act required the Auditor-General to report the results of audits of Parliamentary departments, such as the Department of the Parliamentary Library, to the President of the Senate and the Speaker of the House of Representatives. The Act also required the Auditor-General to provide a copy of any report on the aggregate financial statements (of the Commonwealth or Australian Government) to the Parliament.

Performance audits, which are also called efficiency or value-for-money audits, are relatively new to Australia. The Audit Act was amended in 1979 to permit the Auditor-General to conduct efficiency audits, later called performance audits. This was 78 years after he was given the authority to conduct regulatory audits. The Act did not give Parliament the power to request the Auditor-General to conduct efficiency audits of government departments or ministries. These would be conducted at the discretion of the Auditor-General. However, the law gave

---

[2] The Australian Constitution refers to the Commonwealth of Australia.

[3] Attorney-General's Department (2004), *Audit Act 1901*, Attorney-General's Department, Canberra, <http://scaleplus.law.gov.au/htm/histact/browse/TOCAU.htm>

Parliament the power to request the Auditor-General to conduct efficiency audits of all the operations of eligible incorporated companies. In general, these were government companies. Any Parliamentary request was required to be from both Houses of Parliament, which created an exceptionally strong and difficult condition. Significantly, a Minister could request the Auditor-General to conduct an efficiency audit of an eligible incorporated company. This provision was simpler than that required for a Parliamentary request.

The legislation permitted a Minister to request the Auditor-General to conduct an efficiency audit of an entity created through an agreement between the Australian Government and a state government, as long as the state agreed. The Act authorised the Attorney-General to issue to the Auditor-General a certificate that disclosure of certain information would be contrary to the public interest. This provision gave the Government some control over the Auditor-General's ability to report. More widely in regard to the latter, the Act stated that the Auditor-General may include the results of an efficiency audit in his report on financial statements which was made available to Parliament. He was not required to provide his efficiency audit reports to Parliament, with supply of such reports to that audience being optional.

Most of the *Audit Act 1901* was about financial administration and management. There were few references to the Parliament's authority to guide or direct the Auditor-General, and few other references to any requirement for the Auditor-General to report the results of his work to Parliament beyond those already mentioned here.

Parliamentary inquiry

The Auditor-General's annual report for the 1986–87 financial year[4] criticised the Department of Finance's funding of his office, and affirmed that the funding risked limiting the exercise of his statutory responsibilities. The report, written in unusually strong terms, triggered a Parliamentary inquiry into the then Australian Audit Office. The inquiry led to significant changes in public sector auditing in Australia, and contributed to development of the Australian model of public sector auditing. This part of the chapter will outline what the Parliamentary inquiry attempted, what it found, and what it recommended. It will help readers understand the evolution of the Australian model of public sector audit.

---

[4] Auditor-General (1987), *Annual Report of the Australian Audit Office 1986–87*, AGPS, Canberra.

What the Parliamentary inquiry attempted

Largely in response to the Auditor-General's report, the Joint Committee of Public Accounts, JCPA, announced the terms of reference for an inquiry.[5] These were to investigate whether:[6]

- the Australian Audit Office had kept pace with developments in regard to the public audit function in the states and territories and in comparable countries; and
- current arrangements guaranteed the independence and resources necessary for the Australian Audit Office to fulfil its role as determined by the *Audit Act 1901*.

The Committee's two objectives for the inquiry were:

- to revitalise the Office and redefine its role; and
- to increase debate about public sector auditing through removing its mystique.

The terms of reference and the inquiry's two objectives focused on the Audit Office, and not on the Auditor-General. However, it became apparent to the Committee that the role of the Auditor-General must be discussed prior to discussion of the Audit Office. That was because the Auditor-General was the only person with the legal authority to appoint persons to the Office. Therefore, the inquiry was as much an analysis of the role of the Auditor-General as it was of the Audit Office.

What the Parliamentary inquiry found

The JCPA reported a number of discoveries during its inquiry. The first of these was that the Audit Office had not been reviewed in part for many decades, and it had never been reviewed in its totality. A second discovery was that the Parliament and the executive were complacent about the Audit Office's condition, and a third was that audit legislation needed major change.

Looking more closely at the Audit Office itself, the Committee reported that the Audit Office:[7]

- had developed enormous expertise in public sector audit;

---

[5] The Joint Committee of Public Accounts, or JCPA, comprising representatives from both Houses of Parliament, was established by the *Public Accounts Committee Act 1951*. It was also known as the Public Accounts Committee, or PAC.

[6] Joint Committee of Public Accounts (1989).

[7] The following discussion refers extensively to the JCPA's 1989 report.

- had a reputation for integrity. This was a valuable asset which maintained community and political confidence in the Office;
- was a powerful deterrent on illegal behaviour by public officials. Existence of the Auditor-General and his Office was insufficient to stop illegal acts and wasteful decisions by public officials, but they would be more frequent without this deterrent role;
- was respected by Parliamentarians from all political parties because of the bipartisan way in which the Auditor-General and his Office performed their work. The Auditor-General's decisions were seen to be not political and to be politically neutral. The Committee looked for ways in which the political neutrality of the Auditor-General and his staff could be strengthened; and
- was a means by which executive Government was kept accountable to the legislature.

The JCPA heard and received some severe criticisms of the Audit Office. These were that the Office:

- asked the wrong questions. It was concerned with the pennies and not with the pounds. It focused on regularity auditing of individual items of government expenditure rather than on larger issues of budgeting and financial control;
- was intrusive because of its efficiency auditing of management decisions;
- was ill-informed. That was because staff did not have expertise in the various areas where they conducted efficiency audits, such as in engineering units, scientific institutions and the military;
- was out of date because staff were behind accounting and auditing practices in the private sector; and
- was unstable because of high levels of officer turnover. Consequently, there was little continuity in the Audit Office's staffing of annual regularity audits in the same agencies.

This book focuses on public sector auditing in emerging markets, especially those in developing countries, many of which are reforming their public sector. With this in mind, the Committee's analyses of changes in the financial environment are worth repeating since they started by referring to changes in the economy. The Committee reported how, in the decade before its inquiry:

- financial markets were deregulated and the currency floated. These initiatives required government trading enterprises to change their operations;
- the speed of technological change in management of financial and other resources had accelerated, placing greater demands on auditors;

- larger numbers of public sector bodies were required to operate on a commercial basis, with allied changes in their financial controls;
- stricter accounting and financial controls were introduced to the public sector;
- professional associations of accountants and auditors were more active, for instance, in setting professional standards;
- government companies formed more subsidiaries, sharpening questions over whether the public sector auditor should audit them;
- the machinery of government changed, with greater devolution of authority to the heads of government agencies; and
- new laws were introduced for the public sector.

Another Parliamentary committee was also interested in these changes. While the JCPA was reviewing the Audit Office, the House of Representatives Standing Committee on Finance and Public Administration was inquiring into central aspects of financial reform. Its report broadened Parliamentary interest in financial management reform in the public sector.[8]

The JCPA argued that public sector audits were conducted in a more complicated environment than before, which presented new challenges to the Auditor-General and his staff. A motive for these changes was to reduce public sector expenditure, and another was to increase the public sector's efficiency. The Committee was uncertain whether broader changes in the economy, such as the floating of the currency and more liberty for commercially oriented government entities, with government companies functioning with fewer controls, affected the accountability of executive government to the Parliament. The Committee did not put the case that these changes had increased the Government's accountability to Parliament. It perceived the above changes as contributors to a possibly reduced level of accountability.

It noted how new audit methodologies, including greater use of computers, had increased the Office's productivity and lowered audit costs. These changes took place when the number of government entities audited had increased substantially. The Committee noted appearance of the spectre of under-auditing, while taxpayers were demanding more efficient and better government, and when fraud had increased. Evidence for the possibility of under-auditing was in the time needed to conduct efficiency audits of all large and medium sized programs. There were 121 programs with annual expenditure greater than $100 million, and a further 229 programs with an annual appropriation between $10 million and $100

[8] This House Committee reviewed a range of matters crucial to financial management reform, including agency budgeting, agencies' commercial practices, reporting mechanisms, administrative law and human resource management: Parliament of the Commonwealth of Australia (September 1990), *Not Dollars Alone – Review of the Financial Management Improvement Program*, Report of the House of Representatives Standing Committee on Finance and Public Administration, AGPS, Canberra.

million. The Committee calculated that the Audit Office, with its current resources, would take 40 years to conduct an efficiency audit of each of these programs. It was doubtful if the public and the Parliament would wait that long when expectations of better government were increasing.

In its examination of audit costs, the Committee noted that expenditure on regularity audits was ten times that on efficiency or performance audits. The Office charged agencies fees for regularity audits, and also the proportion of its income from fees had increased very much over the previous twenty years. It did not expect agencies to pay fees for performance audits since the Government argued that these were not done at the request of those agencies.

The Office had few data on its audit costs, and it was unable to compare the focus, scope, methodology and duration of audits with those in the private sector. In other words, the Audit Office had inadequate data to demonstrate its efficiency. Also, audit fees were not published, which limited the Parliament's and the public's information about audit and about the reasons for any fees that were high. Significantly, a Government Minister approved the hourly rate of fees, and some commercially oriented government bodies could select an auditor other than the Auditor-General.

What the Parliamentary inquiry recommended

The JCPA upheld the importance of the Auditor-General having sufficient resources for audit. His capacity to conduct the types and numbers of audits he considered necessary was affected where there were insufficient resources. Importantly, the Committee argued that the Auditor-General should make such decisions about the numbers and types of audits, although he could be advised by the Parliament and Government.

The JCPA considered three models of resource allocation to a national audit office as follows:

- the audit office determined its own resources;
- the executive determined the audit office's resources; or
- the legislature set the audit office's resources.

It considered that Australia had the second model, wherein the Government controlled the Audit Office's resources. A conclusion was that the degree of Government control of the Audit Office affected the Auditor-General's independence from Government and his ability to scrutinise those Government actions and decisions for which he had a mandate. Since the Auditor-General was primarily a Parliamentary tool for executive government accountability, agencies' payment of fees to the Auditor-General was questionable. That was because their payment of fees suggested that the Auditor-General's work was primarily a service for them, rather than a service performed for the legislature.

The Government required agencies to pay audit fees because it argued that such payments were consistent with the user pays principle that the Government promoted to achieve efficiencies in resource distribution. However, the Committee found that, since the Auditor-General primarily worked for the Parliament, it was the Parliament that should pay for his services. Parliamentary allocation of resources to the Auditor-General for his work was a more consistent application of the user pays principle. In contrast, agency payment created the impression that the agencies were the Auditor-General's primary client, which they were not. It can be seen that the Committee accepted that the Auditor-General and his staff could have more than one client. The first was Parliament, and the second was the group of government agencies that were audited. In essence, the Committee criticised the Government's policy of agency payment of fees as a mistaken and misguided application of the user pays principle. The Government's policy had confused client with auditee, and reduced the Office's discretion.

The favoured model of resource allocation was where the Parliament accepted responsibility for determining the amount of resources it wished to allocate for public sector audit. This model was chosen for two reasons:

- to avoid previous conflicts whereby the Government set the Audit Office's resources based on advice from the Government's central budgetary agency, which was the Audit Office's most important auditee; and
- to strengthen the Auditor-General's accountability to Parliament.

The difficulty was that, historically, the Parliament had taken little interest in the funding of public sector audit. It was hoped that a mechanism to permit Parliamentary involvement in resource decisions would prompt greater Parliamentary interest. With this in mind, the Committee recommended that:

- Parliament consider the Audit Office's annual budget bid at the same time as it considered its budget requirements, and separately from its review of the Government's budget; and
- Parliament create an Audit Committee, comprising very senior Parliamentarians. This would result in even more Parliamentary attention to public sector audit, and to its service to the Parliament in assisting it to keep executive government accountable.

The Audit Committee would have a majority of Government members, which would maintain a disciplined interest in the Audit Office's resources.

In order to remove the ambiguity surrounding the role of the Auditor-General, the Committee recommended that relevant legislation state unequivocally that the Auditor-General was an officer of the Parliament. At that time, the Government appointed whomever it wished to the position of Auditor-General. Consistent with its belief that the Auditor-General was more properly a

Parliamentary servant than a government employee, the Committee recommended that, in future, the Prime Minister consult with Parliament before nominating a person to the position. A means for consultation was also proposed, involving the Chair of a Parliamentary Audit Committee, amongst other Parliamentarians including a representative or representatives of the Parliamentary Opposition. The Committee sought to remove Government control over the terms and conditions of employment of the Auditor-General's personnel. It recommended that the Auditor-General have authority to determine the terms and conditions of employment of his staff.

The Government permitted certain government trading entities to appoint their own auditors. A result was the risk that those auditors accepted that their primary client was management of those entities or the shareholders, of which the most important was the relevant Government Minister. Where commercially oriented government entities appointed their own external auditors, the latter worked under private sector audit legislation with fewer reporting requirements than public sector audit law. Consequently, the Parliament received less information about the financial performance and controls of those entities than if the Auditor-General had the mandate to review their accounts. Some government companies presented their accounts to the Auditor-General for review, but appointed private sector auditors to audit their subsidiaries. This made more difficult the task of obtaining whole pictures of the companies' accounts. Therefore, the practice of some commercially oriented government entities appointing their own external auditors was inconsistent with external auditors accepting that their primary client was Parliament. Accordingly, the Committee proposed that the Auditor-General be reinstated as the external auditor of those entities, including of their subsidiaries, but that, if he wished, he could contract a private sector audit firm to conduct the work on his behalf.

The Auditor-General was encouraged to employ private sector audit firms on contract when he had insufficient resources or where he needed additional skills, such as in auditing foreign exchange transactions. Then and now, many private sector audit firms perform other work for their auditees, such as advising on taxation and information technology. An effect was the possibility of private sector audit firms having conflicts of interest where those firms audited and provided other services at the same time, since they risked auditing their own advice. These conflicts of interest endangered the integrity of audit opinions. Thus, the Committee suggested that when the Auditor-General employed private audit firms, a condition of their contracts be prohibitions on other services to auditees during audits. This was a strong view on the need to avoid conflicts of interest. It anticipated by 13 years a concern of the *Sarbanes-Oxley Act of 2002* in the United States.

As indicated earlier, Australia is a federation comprising six states and two territories. The Australian or Federal Government funded services in those states and territories, where it also delivered programs directly. In some policy areas, such as health, housing, infrastructure and education, state and territory governments also funded services and delivered programs. Thus, more than one level of government was active within the same communities in the same locations. Federal Government agencies[9] set different financial and performance requirements for those communities and for state and territory governments in receipt of federal funds. Overall, the Federal Government's financial reporting requirements of other levels of government were confusing and inconsistent as well as being variable. For example, some Federal Government agencies expected the Auditor-General to audit state and territory government entities, for which he did not have a mandate. Other agencies required state and territory Auditors-General to provide audit opinions on their governments' use of Federal Government moneys. To address these issues, the Committee made a number of recommendations to the Federal Government and to the Auditor-General. The intention was to simplify the Federal Government's reporting requirements of other levels of government, increasing the likelihood of federal agencies receiving the financial and performance data they wanted. One of the proposals was to explore the possibility of joint audits between the Australian Parliament's Auditor-General, and Auditors-General in the states and territories. A consequence of such recommendations would be development of a more national approach to identifying the application of taxpayers' moneys spent by all levels of government.

The Committee explored and commented on several other areas including performance audits. It argued for a substantial increase in resources for performance audits, and more coherence in the Auditor-General's reports through including the findings of regularity and performance audits of the same agencies in the same reports to Parliament.

A major matter was the fate of audit recommendations. The Auditor-General's reports were submitted to Parliament but recommendations within those reports were addressed to audited agencies. Recommendations stood on their merits: agencies were and are not required to implement them. The Auditor-General could work according to the best professional standards, and make significant findings and forward-looking recommendations. But if recommendations were not implemented, then the audits were of little use. The Committee tried to sort out responsibility for consideration of audit findings and recommendations. It described the situation as follows:

- there was no single approach to considering implementation of audit findings and recommendations. Rather, there was a loosely connected set of approaches;
- many government and Parliamentary agencies were involved, with a necessary duplication and overlap of responsibilities;
- these agencies differed in assessments of the importance of various findings and recommendations; and

---

[9] The Australian Government is also called the Federal or Commonwealth Government.

- the Auditor-General followed up agency responses to regularity audits, but gave almost no attention to following up agency responses to performance audits.

The Committee made recommendations to get more attention to the need for third party interest in how well agencies addressed the management issues uncovered by audit.

Conclusions

In conclusion, the Committee argued that new legislation was necessary. The existing *Audit Act 1901* should be repealed and replaced by separate audit and financial management laws. New and separate legislation would clarify the Auditor-General's responsibilities and affirm the Officer's Parliamentary service and identity. It would also provide the Auditor-General with time to review the balance between the compliance nature of regularity audits and the need for more performance audits to reinforce the public's and the Parliament's expectations of efficient and effective government. Both kinds of audits were vital to good government and sound administration. Repeal of the *Audit Act 1901* would also provide the Government with the opportunity to draft new financial management legislation, which was warranted in light of major changes that had already occurred in the public sector and other changes that were foreshadowed.

Chapter 2

Why is There an Auditor-General?

This chapter will describe the purposes of public sector audit in Australia. It will introduce the Audit Committee of Parliament, the means of appointment of the Auditor-General, Parliamentary appointment of private sector firms to audit the Audit Office, the Auditor-General's mandate to audit budget-funded agencies and government companies and their subsidiaries, access powers, and the Audit Office's ability to advise government agencies. These matters involve the Auditor-General's relationship with the executive as well as with the legislature. The main focus will be on the relationship between the Australian Parliament and the Australian National Audit Office, ANAO, which is the current name for the Office of the Auditor-General, although it will refer to equivalent relationships in the Australian states and territories between their legislatures and audit offices.[1]

Seven years after the Public Accounts Committee's 1989 report on the then Australian Audit Office and as a response to the report, the Federal Government introduced new public sector audit legislation. This was the *Auditor-General Act 1997*. The following discussion draws on that Act.[2]

The *Auditor-General Act 1997*

The Audit Committee of Parliament

A starting point for understanding why there is an Auditor-General, or what are the purposes of public sector audit in Australia, is the Government's acceptance of the Joint Committee of Public Accounts' recommendation to establish an Audit Committee of Parliament. The Government amended the legislation which created the Joint Committee to give it the additional responsibility of functioning as the

---

[1] When the JCPA reported in 1989, the Office of the Auditor-General was called the Australian Audit Office. The Committee recommended that the Office change its name to reflect new audit law. Before the new law, called the *Auditor-General Act 1997*, was introduced, the Auditor-General changed the Office's name to the Australian National Audit Office, ANAO, which was the name proposed by the Committee.

[2] *Auditor-General Act 1997*, <http://scaleplus.law.gov.au/html/pasteact/browse/TOCAU.htm>

Audit Committee of Parliament.[3] It was renamed the Joint Committee of Public Accounts and Audit, JCPAA. Since the Committee had members from both Houses of Parliament and from Government, Opposition and minor parties, it could identify and express the audit interests of Parliament.

The duties of the Committee are to examine all reports of the Auditor-General including performance audits. This meant that the Committee's previous principal role of considering the results of regularity audits was matched by consideration of reports on the efficiency and effectiveness of government operations. Its other roles included considering and reporting to Parliament on the Audit Office's operations, resources, and reports of the Independent Auditor. It would make recommendations to the Parliament on the adequacy of the Audit Office's budget, determine the audit priorities of the Parliament and advise the Auditor-General on those priorities.

This legislative basis of the Audit Committee of Parliament gave a high status to its focus on audit matters. This new role complemented the Public Accounts Committee's earlier role with the Government's accounts. The Committee's role will be described in more detail later.

Appointment of the Auditor-General

Accepting the Committee's recommendation, the Government drafted the new Auditor-General Act to affirm that the Auditor-General was an independent officer of the Parliament. The Act also established an Audit Office that consisted of the Auditor-General and his staff.

The relevant Minister would recommend to the Governor-General a person to be appointed as Auditor-General. First, however, the Minister must consult with Parliament about the appointment. Consultation will involve the Minister referring the proposed recommendation to the Joint Committee of Public Accounts and Audit for approval, and only recommending an appointment to the Governor-General when the Committee has approved it. As pointed out earlier, since the Committee contains members from both Houses of Parliament and from Government, Opposition and minor parties, it is broadly representative of the main elected interests. This means of appointment, where the Parliamentary Committee must approve the Government's recommendation, will increase the role of Parliament in future appointments. That is because the Parliament had no role in the appointment under the previous legislation.

A Parliamentary role in appointment of the Auditor-General contrasts with its absence in appointment of Justices to the High Court of Australia. Before recommending the appointment of a new Justice, the Attorney-General must

---

[3] Attorney-General's Department (2004), *Public Accounts and Audit Committee Act 1951*, Attorney-General's Department, Canberra, <http://scaleplus.law.gov.au/html/pasteact/0/209/0/PA000120.htm>

consult with Attorneys-General in the states. The Attorney-General is not required to consult with Parliament.[4]

The current Auditor-General is the first to be appointed by the Government under the new system wherein the Parliament has a prominent role. Future research will reveal the impact of this method of appointment. The 1997 legislation sets strict rules surrounding removal of an Auditor-General. The Governor-General may remove the Auditor-General if each House of Parliament requests this because of the Auditor-General's misbehaviour or physical or mental incapacity. Note that if such conditions are met the Governor-General may remove, rather than be required to remove, the Auditor-General. This is the limit of Parliamentary authority. In addition, the Governor-General must remove the Auditor-General if the officer becomes bankrupt or has other specified financial difficulties. In sum, these conditions protect the Auditor-General from Government dismissal because of unfavourable audit findings.

That he or she is an independent officer of the Parliament is different from were he an officer of the Parliament. In the latter case, he would be subject to direction. Because he is both independent from the Parliament while being a Parliamentary officer, he has authority over what he chooses to do, and a certain level of Parliamentary protection of his decisions. The Act makes it clear that he is not subject to direction from anyone in relation to:

- whether or not a particular audit is to be conducted;
- the way in which a particular audit is to be conducted; and
- the priority to be given to any particular matter.

Notwithstanding, he or she is free to seek advice from the Parliament, while the latter can make suggestions to him on the above matters. He or she must have regard to the audit priorities of the Parliament as determined by the Joint Committee of Public Accounts and Audit. In 2002–2003, the ANAO completed one performance audit report requested by this Committee, and another performance audit report solicited by a Senate Committee.[5] These were a small percentage of the 47 performance audit reports tabled in the Parliament by the Auditor-General in that year.[6]

---

[4] Attorney-General's Department (2004), *High Court of Australia Act 1979*, Attorney-General's Department, Canberra,
<http://scaleplus.law.gov.au/html/pasteact/0/462/top.htm>

[5] ANAO (2003), *Annual Report 2002–2003. The Auditor*-General, ANAO, Canberra, pp.31–32. All ANAO reports are available on its website <www.anao.gov.au>

[6] ANAO (2003), p. 28.

Appointment of an Independent Auditor

Before explaining the Auditor-General's mandate, we will portray a special feature of the Australian model. This is the Parliament's appointment of an independent person to review the Audit Office.

Parliament requires an independent auditor to audit the Audit Office's annual financial statements and to conduct a performance audit of the Office at any time. The independent auditor must have regard to the Parliament's priorities as expressed by the Joint Committee of Public Accounts and Audit. The work of the independent auditor gives Parliament the opinion of another professional auditor, who so far has always been from the private sector, on the Audit Office's financial controls, financial reporting and efficiency and effectiveness. These opinions are public since they are released when the reports are tabled in the Parliament.

The mandate

The Auditor-General's mandate includes auditing financial statements of Commonwealth entities, where these include departments of state, statutory authorities, government business enterprises and government companies and their subsidiaries. Prior to such audits, the entities must prepare financial statements and make them available for audit. These are requirements of complementary financial administration laws, which were enacted at the same time as the *Auditor-General Act 1997*.[7] Simultaneous introduction of new audit and financial administration legislation was consistent with the Public Accounts Committee's 1989 recommendation to replace the earlier audit legislation with separate audit and financial administration legislation. Public sector audit had developed to the point where it needed its own law.

The audit legislation continued the Auditor-General's authority to conduct performance audits. He could conduct a performance audit of an agency, such as a government department, at any time. He could also conduct performance audits of other government bodies such as statutory authorities and certain kinds of government companies. There were other kinds of government business enterprises for which he did not have the authority to conduct performance audits. These were government business enterprises that were competing with private sector firms in industries such as telecommunications, postal services and health insurance. The Government did not legislate to give the Auditor-General the authority to conduct performance audits of these enterprises because it believed that these government

---

[7] There are two financial administration laws: The *Financial Management and Accountability Act 1997* for budget-dependent agencies such as departments of state, and the *Commonwealth Authorities and Companies Act 1997* for Commonwealth Government authorities, companies and their subsidiaries. Department of Finance and Administration (2004), Canberra, <www.dofa.gov.au/scripts/search.idq>

businesses, participating in markets, were subject to sufficient market forces to maintain and improve their services and efficiency and to reduce their costs.

There were other considerations as well. One of these was that private sector firms were not subject to performance audits. Therefore, to require performance audits of certain government businesses, with results probably reported publicly, would mean that those businesses were subject to more controls than their private sector competitors. A result would have been that the operating costs for these government businesses would have been higher than for their private sector competitors. As the Minister for Finance stated when introducing the legislation:[8]

> For bodies that are government business enterprises, in recognition of the fact that they are subject to the overlying accountability framework that requires them to pursue optimal market performance and to improve the return to the Commonwealth as shareholder, the Auditor-General would not subject them to performance audits unless requested by Parliament – through the Joint Committee of Public Accounts – or a minister. If the body concerned is a partially privatised Commonwealth company, however, it would not be subjected to a performance audit. In this regard, the Government has reflected on the need to continue the principle, as already accepted under the *Audit Act 1901*, of forbearance in consideration of the investment interests of private shareholders in such companies.
>
> Performance audits are an extra feature on the accountability landscape peculiar to public sector bodies. It does not follow, however, that the often high parliamentary profile given the reports of such audits would always be beneficial to the interests of the companies' private investors/shareholders. To avoid the claim that, through imposing this extra tier of performance auditing, the Commonwealth was, thus, 'oppressing' the minority private shareholders, the Auditor-General's surveillance over the operations of partially privatised Commonwealth companies is to be exclusively as the mandated external auditor of their financial statements.

In 1997 when the new audit law was introduced, successive Australian Governments were converting certain government agencies into businesses and selling them. An effect of the limitation on the Auditor-General's mandate to exclude some of these entities was to reduce the information publicly available on their management and performance. However, no evidence is available to suggest that this was an intentional effect. Prior to their partial or whole sale, if the Auditor-General had the resources and authority to conduct performance audits of these entities, then the market would have been more fully informed about their performance and capacity during the sales.

---

[8] Department of Parliamentary Services (1996), *House of Representatives Hansard*, Thursday, 12 December 1996, Canberra, pp.8342–8344.

The new law did not exclude totally the Auditor-General from performance auditing these enterprises. That was because he could performance audit them if the responsible Minister or the Joint Committee of Public Accounts and Audit requested him to do so. Also, the Auditor-General could suggest to these authorities that they invite a performance audit. There was no information available publicly on whether any Minister or the Joint Committee of Public Accounts and Audit requested the Auditor-General to performance audit these government businesses, and no information publicly available on whether the Auditor-General agreed to any request from them.

The Minister for Finance described performance audits as additional accountability requirements of the public sector not required of privately listed firms. After the new law was introduced, the Joint Committee of Public Accounts and Audit reviewed aspects of auditing in the private sector. The Committee's report proposed that the Australian Stock Exchange explore the costs and benefits and alternative methods of introducing performance audits in the private sector.[9] In 2004, the Federal Government reviewed the legislative requirements of private sector auditors, and it did not propose performance audits for the private sector.[10] Although performance audits of public sector entities generate additional work for those bodies in comparison with private companies, the benefit is that those audits produce information that otherwise would not be publicly available about the management of those government entities.

The Auditor-General's mandate extended to reviews or examinations of part or whole of the Federal Government. This gave him the authority to conduct cross-portfolio performance audits. Cross-portfolio reviews are an increasing percentage of performance audits. For instance, in 1997–98, 9 of 48 performance audits or 19 per cent were cross-portfolio;[11] and in 2002–2003, 14 of 56 performance audits or 25 per cent were cross-portfolio.[12] These cross-portfolio reviews were of a wide range of topics, including confirming that government agencies disclosed on the Internet the value of all contracts above a certain amount, internal audit, management of trust moneys, and government agency compliance with taxation requirements.[13] The reviews permitted the Auditor-General to

---

[9] Parliament of the Commonwealth of Australia (2002), *Report 391. Review of Independent Auditing by Registered Company Auditors. Joint Standing Committee on Public Accounts and Audit*, Parliament of the Commonwealth of Australia, Canberra, <http://www.aph.gov.au/house/committee/jcpaa/indepaudit/execsum.htm>

[10] Blake Dawson Waldron (2004), *The BDW Guide to CLERP 9. Practical Guide to the Corporate Law Economic Reform Program (Audit Reform and Corporate Disclosure) Act 2004*, Blake Dawson Waldron, Sydney, <http://www.bdw.com/frameit.asp?page=/news/clerp9guide.pdf>

[11] ANAO (1998), *Annual Report 1997–98. The Auditor-General*, ANAO, Canberra.

[12] ANAO (2003), *Annual Report 2002–2003. The Auditor-General*, ANAO, Canberra, pp.125–130.

[13] Other cross-portfolio audit reports tabled in 2002–2003 were of physical security, energy efficiency, management of guarantees, warranties and letters of comfort, reporting on

identify trends and patterns in public administration that would not otherwise be detectable. Publication of the results of these cross-portfolio reviews provides information and analyses for continued public sector reform.

The legislation added a new factor to the Auditor-General's decision-making authority. That was because it gave him the authority to enter into an arrangement with any person or body to audit its financial statements and conduct performance audits, with the option of charging for these services. The Auditor-General conducted a small number of audits under these arrangements, largely of the probity of agencies' contractual arrangements.[14]

Power to obtain information and access premises

The Auditor-General was given the power to direct a person to provide information that the Auditor-General required, to attend and give evidence before the Auditor-General, and to produce documents. He also received the power, at all reasonable times, to enter and remain on any premises owned by the Federal Government or one of its authorities and companies. In those places, he had access to any documents on the property, and he could copy and take extracts from those documents.

The purposes of public sector audit

We have seen that the *Auditor-General Act 1997* does not define the purposes of public sector audit. Rather, it defines the functions or services of the Auditor-General, which are to conduct financial statement and performance audits. The Act does not state why the audits are conducted. Therefore, we must look for other information to understand the purposes of public sector audit at the national level in Australia.

A primary information source is the Auditor-General's account to Parliament of why it should support his work. This information is in the ANAO's budget papers and annual reports. Parliament uses this information to decide whether it will continue to fund the Auditor-General and his Office. In 2004, the

---

ecologically sustainable development, staff management, management of staff absences from work, business continuity management, capitalisation of software, and end of financial year management of the accounts.

[14] Examples are ANAO (1998), *Evaluation Processes for the Selection of Hearing Devices. Department of Health and Family Services*, Report No. 49 of 1997–98, ANAO, Canberra; and ANAO (1998), *OGIT and FedLink Infrastructure. Office of Government Information Technology, Department of Finance and Administration*, Report No. 11 of 1998–99, ANAO, Canberra.

Auditor-General informed Parliament that his Office had two major purposes, which he expressed as desirable outcomes of the Office's work:[15]

- improvement in public administration; and
- assurance.

More completely, these two purposes were:

- independent assurance of the performance of selected Commonwealth public sector activities, including the scope for improving efficiency and administrative effectiveness; and
- independent assurance of public sector reporting, administration, control and accountability.

What is striking about these expressions is that they both emphasise the Audit Office's role in assuring Parliament about the financial and operational performance of government activities. This is the opposite of a common perception of audit as an activity focusing on the errors, mistakes and omissions of others. In other words, the Auditor-General's description of his role as provider of an affirmation of the sound performance of government entities contradicts the image of the auditor as fault-finder. His tools for providing an assurance are both regularity and performance audits. The two kinds of audits focus on the public sector's management.

Let us consider the implications of this assurance role. Where the Auditor-General provides an assurance about the public sector's sound performance, then the need for reform is reduced, and any change can continue at its current rate. But where the Auditor-General cannot provide an assurance about sound management, then the need for reform is sharper and the pace of change will be reviewed. Thus, the Auditor-General's opinion about the public sector's performance, which is also an opinion about management's performance, has the potential to influence the speed and direction of public sector reform. A later chapter will examine whether and how Parliament uses audit reports to effect reform or change.

At the state government level, the functions of state auditors-general are described, but there is less attention to the purposes of public sector audit. An example is the law governing the functions of the Auditor-General for the State of New South Wales. It states that the Auditor-General's functions include the following:[16]

---

[15] Department of Prime Minister and Cabinet (2004), *Prime Minister and Cabinet Portfolio. Portfolio Budget Statements 2004–2005*, Department of Prime Minister and Cabinet, Canberra, <http://www.pmc.gov.au/pbs_paes/2004-2005/docs/pbs_2004-2005.pdf>

[16] New South Wales Consolidated Acts, *Public Finance and Audit Act 1983*, S27B, <http://www.aaustlii.edu.au/au/legis/nsw/consol_act/pfaaa1983189/>

a. to audit the Total State Sector Accounts and any other accounts that the Auditor-General is required or authorised to audit by law,
b. to provide any particular audit or audit-related service to Parliament at the joint request of both Houses of Parliament,
c. to provide any particular audit or audit-related service to the Treasurer at the request of the Treasurer or to any other Minister at the request of that other Minister,
d. to report to Parliament as required or authorised by law,
e. to do anything that is incidental to the exercise of the Auditor-General's functions.

Of note is audit legislation for the State of Victoria. The purposes of the relevant state public sector audit law are the closest approximation to the purposes of public sector audit of any state or federal law. Therefore, they are quoted here:[17]

(1) The objectives of this Act are –
  (a) to determine whether financial statements prepared in the Victorian public sector present fairly the financial position and financial results of operations and authorities and the State;
  (b) to determine whether –
    i. authorities are achieving their objectives effectively and doing so economically and efficiently and in compliance with all relevant Acts;
    ii. Victorian public sector operations and activities are being performed effectively, economically and efficiently and in compliance with all relevant Acts;
  (c) To determine whether financial benefits given by the State or an authority to non-government bodies are being applied economically, efficiently and effectively for the purposes for which they were given;
  (d) To ensure that the Auditor-General is held accountable for his or her performance and the performance of the Office.
(2) It is the Parliament's intention that, in pursuing these objectives, regard is had as to whether there has been any wastage of public resources or any lack of probity or financial prudence in the management or application of public resources.

With the exception of audit law for the State of Victoria, legislators have not felt obliged to define the purposes of audit. Rather, they have been content to give attention to the functions or duties of the Auditor-General. Consequently, any assessment of how an Auditor-General and the related office perform requires an assessment of how well the Auditor-General has conducted audits. Standards of relevant professional bodies are guides to legislators assessing an Auditor-General's performance. These will be explored in a later chapter. Where an

---

[17] Auditor-General, Victoria (2004), *Version No. 043, Audit Act 1994. Act No. 2/1994*, Victorian Auditor-General's Office, Melbourne, Victoria, S3A.

Auditor-General determines his or her standards, then it is logical for a Parliament to assess the officer against those standards. This is a necessary but insufficient step in appraising the work of an Auditor-General and an Audit Office. A legislature's exclusive reliance on professional standards to assess an Auditor-General's performance, including when those standards are determined by an Auditor-General, removes some of the need for legislators to ask whether public sector audit is improving public administration, and the need to define improvements.

Perhaps in recognition of this, from time to time, some Auditors-General have reported data on their success in implementing legislated functions. A good example is the Auditor-General of Western Australia, who reported that:[18]

> All Key Performance Indicators had significant falls. The largest percentage fall (21 per cent) was in the belief that the Auditor-General was effective in achieving his desired outcome of informing Parliament on the accountability and performance of the public sector, which fell from 84 per cent to 66 per cent. However, there was no growth in the belief that the Auditor-General was NOT effective in achieving this outcome, which remained at two per cent.
>
> The only indicator to show an increase compared to last year was the belief that the services of the Office helped to increase public confidence in the public sector, which increased to 59 per cent. The responses to this question have shown a small but consistent improvement since 2001 (44 per cent).

The auditor as adviser

The Auditor-General and the ANAO have accepted the role of adviser to government agencies. Acceptance is based on the Act, which states how the Auditor-General may provide advice or information to a person or body relating to the Auditor-General's responsibilities if, in his opinion, it is in the Commonwealth's interests to do so.[19] The Auditor-General has used audit findings to develop guides to good management and administration, called better practice guides. They are developed primarily as bases for audits. That is because both regularity and performance audits use normative criteria to assess financial and operational management. By publishing those normative criteria, he has allowed agencies time to examine their management performance before the auditors arrived. For example, in one guide, he wrote:[20]

---

[18] Office of the Auditor-General for Western Australia (2003), *Annual Report 2002–2003*, Office of the Auditor-General for Western Australia, Perth, p.13.

[19] *Auditor-General Act 1997*, S23.

[20] ANAO (2001), *Internet Delivery Decisions. A Government Program Manager's Guide*, ANAO, Canberra, Foreword, <www.anao.gov.au>

> The Guide will be used by the ANAO as a basis for establishing audit criteria in reviewing agency performance in Internet service delivery. This was a major catalyst for our involvement in developing and coordinating its preparation.

In 2002–2003, the ANAO published five better practice guides, which cost less than $1 million in the agency's $53 million budget.[21] The Audit Committee of Parliament and government agencies have supported the ANAO's production of guides to good management. However, the ANAO risks auditing its own advice. In fact, following issue of a guide, and where the ANAO audits agency behaviour against what it defined in a guide as sound management, it is auditing its own advice.

There have been no objections to this so far, perhaps because of the low level of resources the ANAO allocated to these management guides. If the resources increased significantly and the number of guides rose, then there could be objections. Unlike in the private sector, the ANAO does not charge fees for its advice and does not benefit financially from it. Parliamentary and agency knowledge of the absence of financial incentives for ANAO to provide some advice on sound management has also led to acceptance of a limited ANAO role in this domain. In future, another factor that will affect the ANAO's decisions on the number, content and timing of its management guides is greater Parliamentary and public interest in private sector audit firms avoiding conflicts of interest.

For 2002–2003, two of the eight state and territory Audit Offices published guides to good management. The names of this kind of document varied, but they had similar functions of assisting agency management. In one state, the Office issued model financial reports for certain government bodies.[22] The other state published five sets of guidelines on various topics.[23] Resource shortages limited the capacity of other Audit Offices to prepare and publish guides. However, all Audit Offices gave some advice to their government's central agencies on

---

[21] The better practice guide topics were internal budgeting, a framework for managing learning and development of staff, managing Parliamentary workflow, goods and services tax administration, and model financial statements. ANAO (2003), *Annual Report 2002–2003*, pp.39–40.

[22] Auditor-General Victoria (2003), *Annual Report 2002–2003*, Auditor-General Victoria, Melbourne, p.30.

[23] The topics were:

- Guidelines for the Conduct of Audits of Performance Management Systems;
- Better Practice Guidelines for E-Business Environments;
- Checklist for Preparation of Financial Statements;
- IFRS Checklist for Public Sector Agencies; and
- Better Practice Guidelines for Non-Current Assets.

Queensland Audit Office (2003), *Annual Report 2003*, Queensland Audit Office, Brisbane, p. 86.

financial matters. For instance, a treasury department requested and received advice on model financial statements that were to be distributed to agencies.[24]

The Introduction to this book told how a common term used to describe a nation's principal public sector auditor is Supreme Audit Institution, SAI. The primary task of an SAI is to audit, but the Australian experience shows that, under certain conditions, there can be support for an SAI to allocate some resources to an advisory role. Those conditions include a legislative base for the role, modest resources in comparison with resources for audit, visible links between that advice and the SAI's capacity to assure the legislature on good management, and also links between the advice and improved management and agency performance.

Conclusions

Federal legislation specifies the functions of the Auditor-General. In general terms, they are to conduct financial and performance audits and to report to Parliament. The legislation is silent on the purposes of public sector audit. Therefore, in order to identify them we must look elsewhere. The Auditor-General has defined the purposes of audits as to provide an independent assurance to Parliament on public sector management, and to improve public sector administration. The Audit Committee of Parliament has accepted these as the reasons for the Auditor-General's services.

State and territory audit legislation gives more attention to the functions or duties of Auditors-General than to the purposes of public sector audit. Whatever the reasons for this situation, an effect is to reduce the need for legislators to define improvements in public administration, and to establish criteria, alongside those set by professional bodies of auditors, for determining whether Auditors-General have improved public administration while working within their legislation. In other words, in general, public sector audit law does not require Auditors-General to establish the nature of their effects on public administration.

There is some scope for the Australian Auditor-General to provide some advice to government agencies through guides to sound administration. Until now, publication of these guides has been accepted. With sharper distinctions in the private sector between audit and consulting roles, acceptance of the Audit Office's role in advising on better administrative practices may be questioned.

---

[24] Auditor-General Australian Capital Territory, (2003), *Annual Management Report for the Year Ended 30 June 2003*, ACT Auditor-General's Office, Canberra, p.9.

Chapter 3

What Standards Does the Auditor-General Apply?

This chapter outlines how the Auditor-General determines standards for his audits and the nature of those standards. It compares audit law for the public and private sectors in regard to standards. Since public sector administrative law is a critical part of the environment in which he works, the chapter describes the interaction between audit standards and the requirements of agencies as determined by administrative law. It also notes the Auditor-General's role within the public sector in the movement towards international harmonisation of auditing and accounting standards.

How audit standards are determined

The Act gives the Auditor-General the authority to set auditing standards for staff and for contractors appointed to assist him. It also requires him to publish, opening them to public and professional scrutiny. Openness of audit standards to review by interested or disinterested persons is a key means to obtain their acceptance. Their availability results in all Parliamentarians, the Government, its agencies and staff, the public and media having information to question or challenge them. General ease of access to auditing standards maintains confidence in the process of auditing, and contributes to confidence in audit opinions. Inevitably, the Auditor-General's standards are compared with those in the private sector, and to questions about whether they are the right ones.

The Auditor-General adopted for regularity and performance audits the standards of the Australian Auditing and Assurance Standards Board,[1] which, in turn, were derived on behalf of the main professional bodies of accountants. He explained the reasons as lying in recognition of responsibility of the professional associations of accountants in Australia for setting and maintaining auditing standards and practices for their members. He wrote that:

> These bodies have issued Australian Auditing Standards which set out the basic principles and essential procedures, together with relevant guidance, to be applied

[1] ANAO (2002), *ANAO Auditing Standards May 2002*, ANAO, Canberra, <http://www.anao.gov.au/WebSite.nsf/Publications/744C7F82DE39D37C4A256D6E0>

> to all financial report audits and as far as possible to all audits of other financial and non-financial information and all audit related services. …
>
> The Auditor-General recognises there is commonality in the auditing standards expected of the private and public sector auditing professions and wishes to conform to the greatest extent possible with the Auditing Standards promulgated by (the two main associations of accountants). The Auditing Standards are equally applicable as an expression of the minimum standard of audit work expected of auditors in the public sector as they are in the private sector. The Auditing Standards are consistent with the principles expressed in the INTOSAI Auditing Standards.
>
> The Auditor-General may issue additional directions or instructions to auditors to whom these Standards apply which expand on, or modify, the Auditing Standards where it is appropriate.

Adoption ensures a consistency of auditing standards between the private and public sectors, with an underlying equivalence of issues and approaches. Although not the primary intention of adoption, an effect is to simplify employment of audit firms and individual private sector auditors on contract, since they already use those standards. Also, the ANAO's staff who are members of professional accounting associations are required to apply Australian standards. As can be seen, the Auditor-General has the right to modify those standards where he considers it necessary.[2]

The alternative to adopting common standards was for the Auditor-General to develop his own. In that case, the starting position would have been the view that there were significant differences between auditing in the two sectors. Successive Governments have encouraged government agencies to learn from and adopt some private sector management and reporting practices. If those government policies have had some success, then the assumption of equivalence, or at least of strong similarities, between auditing in the two sectors has merit. It is important to note that regularity auditing refers here principally to financial statement auditing.

The Australian Auditing and Assurances Standard Board has developed 46 standards for application by both the private and public sectors, and two of these apply exclusively for performance audits.[3] Some standards for financial statement audits also apply to performance audits. An example is 'Quality Control for Audit Work', on policies and procedures of an audit firm regarding audit work generally; and for procedures delegated to assistants.[4] The overall ratio of

---

[2] Of note is the Audit Office's support for convergence of Australian Auditing Standards and International Standards on Auditing. ANAO (2004), *Opinions*, ANAO, Canberra.

[3] Some of these standards will be revised as part of convergence with international auditing standards issued by the International Auditing and Assurance Standards Board.

[4] AUS 206 sets out the responsibilities of an audit firm to implement quality control policies and procedures designed to ensure consistency with Australian Auditing Standards. AUS 206 also describes how an individual auditor should implement those quality control

standards reflects the relative involvement of private sector audit firms in the two kinds of audits. The first standard for performance audits[5] is called 'Performance Auditing', which defines the objective and general principles governing a performance audit. The second standard is 'Planning Performance Audits'.

These standards require that the performance audit would proceed only when the auditor and auditee agreed on the terms of engagement. This curious caveat on private sector external auditors means that they can proceed only when management of the audited firm agrees. There is no similar restriction on financial statement auditors in the private sector. The notion of an independent performance audit is weakened where the auditor can commence work only after the auditee's management agrees. The standards accommodate the public sector in recognising how legislated mandates give an auditor the discretion to determine the activity to be audited and the audit's scope. In this case, the auditor's notification of the legislative mandate, scope and focus of the proposed audit to the auditee would meet the standards' requirements. The Auditor-General has emphasised the importance of this part of the relevant standard on performance auditing.[6]

The ANAO conducts a higher proportion of performance audits than any private sector audit firm. Despite this greater involvement, the Auditor-General has not believed it necessary to develop additional standards for performance audits. Notwithstanding, due to the Audit Office's greater involvement in performance auditing than any private audit firm, the Auditor-General found it essential to develop an audit manual for his staff. The manual interprets Australian Auditing Standards for performance audits of public sector entities. The manual is the Commonwealth Government's intellectual property and it is not distributed outside the Audit Office. In contrast, the Audit Office purchases financial statement audit methodologies from the private sector because of the more obvious equivalence of audits in the two sectors, adapting those methodologies for the public sector to cover, for instance, compliance with legislation and budgetary requirements.

---

procedures, and it affirms that the standard's advice is consistent with the relevant International Standard on Auditing. Australian Accounting Research Foundation, (AARF) (2002), *AUS 206 Quality Control for Audit Work*, AARF, Melbourne, <www.aarf.asn.au>

[5] This standard, AUS 806, sets out the objective of performance audits, their general principles, provision of reasonable assurance, terms of engagement, planning, work performed by assistants, using the work of an expert, criteria, audit evidence, documentation, audit conclusions and reporting, and compatibility with International Standards on Auditing. The second standard for performance audits is AUS 808. It covers matters such as the audit mandate, audit objectives and scope, materiality and risk, criteria, evidence, planning and compatibility with International Standards on Auditing. AARF (2002), *AUS 806 Performance Auditing*, and *AUS 808 Planning Performance Audits*.

[6] ANAO (2002), ANAO Auditing Standards.

What is material to an audit opinion?

The issue of materiality is important to the audit opinion. Before exploring the meaning of materiality for the Audit Office, the latter's definitions of financial statement and performance auditing will be introduced since they are its bases. Keeping in mind that the Auditor-General has adopted Australian Auditing Standards, these define a financial statement audit as an audit of a financial report:[7]

> The objective of an audit of a financial report is to enable the auditor to express an opinion whether the financial report is prepared, in all material aspects, in accordance with an applicable financial framework.

They define the objective of a performance audit as:[8]

> To enable the auditor to express an opinion whether, in all material respects, all or part of an entity's or entities' activities have been carried out economically and/or efficiently and/or effectively. In the case of a direct reporting audit, the objective also includes the provision of relevant and reliable information about performance.

To understand materiality in the two kinds of audits, the first step is to understand the objectives of these audits. Now that the definitions adopted by the Auditor-General from Australian Auditing Standards as objectives for the two kinds of audits have been introduced, we can address materiality. In order to provide a sound and defensible basis for defining what is important to an audit opinion, the Australian Auditing and Assurance Standards Board defined materiality. Its definition is:[9]

> Information which if omitted, misstated or not disclosed separately has the potential to adversely affect decisions about the allocation of scarce resources made by users of the financial report or the discharge of accountability by the management including the governing body of the entity.

---

[7] AARF (2002), *AUS 202 Objective and General Principles Governing An Audit of a Financial Report.* This standard also states that 'the phrases used to express the auditor's opinion are "give a true and fair view" and "present fairly", in all material aspects, which are equivalent terms.'

[8] AARF (2002), AUS 806 Performance Auditing.

[9] AARF (2002), *AUS 104 Glossary of Terms.* The definition is repeated in *AUS 306 Materiality and Audit Adjustments.* Also relevant in *AUS 104* is the definition of misstatement as a mistake in financial information which would arise from fraud, error or non-compliance with laws or regulations.

The Australian Government has adopted Australian Accounting Standards for the Australian Government sector,[10] and the Auditor-General reviews agencies' compliance with them. The Department of Finance and Administration, which is the relevant central government agency, has deemed some disclosures in government accounts to be material.[11] The Australian Accounting Standards Board provided guidance on estimation of materiality. It stated that:[12]

> An amount which is equal to or less than 5 per cent of the appropriate base amount may be presumed not to be material unless there is evidence, or convincing argument, to the contrary.

The Auditor-General's adopted standards for performance audits apply to the latter the same definition of materiality as for regularity, financial report or financial statement audits. They explain how in assessing materiality and risk, the auditor would consider both quantitative and qualitative factors such as:[13]

a. the importance of the operations to achieving the entity's objectives;
b. the financial impact the operations have on the entity as a whole;
c. the nature of transactions, for example, high volumes, large dollar values and complex transactions;
d. the extent of interest shown in particular portions of the entity by, for example, the legislature or other governing body, regulatory authorities or the public;
e. the economic, social, political and environmental impact of the operations;
f. the extent of management's actions regarding issues raised in previous audits;
g. the diversity, consistency and clarity of the entity's objectives and goals;
h. the nature, size and complexity of the operations;
i. the complexity and quality of management information and external reporting;
j. the effectiveness of the internal control structure, including the level of internal audit coverage;
k. the nature and degree of change in the environment or within the entity; and management's effectiveness in a particular area.

---

[10] Department of Finance and Administration (2004), Finance Minister's Orders. Schedule 1: Requirements for the Preparation of Financial Statements of Australian Government Entities, Department of Finance and Administration, Canberra, Policy 1B, <http://www.finance.gov.au>

[11] These include budget appropriation disclosures (Policy 2C), special accounts (Policy 2F), and special payments such as acts of grace, ex-gratia payments and waivers (Policy 7A). Department of Finance and Administration (2004).

[12] Australian Accounting Standards Board (1995), *AASB 1031 Materiality*, Australian Accounting Research Foundation, Melbourne, 4.1.7; and AARF (1995), *AAS 5 Materiality*, AARF, Melbourne, 4.1.6.

[13] AARF (2002), AUS 808 Planning Performance Audits.

These definitions indicate how an auditor can determine that a matter is material because of the amount of money involved, or because of the nature of the material or issue. Financial and performance auditors can differ in their assessment of whether an accounting or management issue surrounding use of public moneys is material. An example follows. A financial statement auditor can decide that an accounting problem involving an agency's use of $10 million is material where that amount is greater than five per cent of the agency's expenditure or revenue.[14] In this case, the performance auditor would likely agree where the matter is a sign of imperfect, inefficient or ineffective agency management. However, where the $10 million is less than five per cent of the agency's outlays or revenue, then the financial statement auditor can decide that the related accounting issue is not material. Then, it would not necessarily be mentioned in the auditor's report. However, the performance auditor would remain interested in the matter if, as before, it was related to imperfect, inefficient or ineffective management. In this second scenario, the performance auditor would consider the matter to be of sufficient importance for the audit report, while the financial statement auditor would have concluded that there was insufficient reason to mention it since the matter did not affect the financial statement audit opinion.

The conclusions of both auditors are correct. That is because their stances are determined by the kinds of audits they conducted. Both auditors would base their conclusions on the Auditor-General's audit standards. The example demonstrates how the purposes of audit influence the definition of materiality.

The complication is when financial and performance auditors review a public sector agency at the same time. Then, the agency can receive different audit opinions also at the same time. In the above example, the financial statement auditors would not necessarily mention the $10 million accounting issue in their financial statement audit report because it had no effect on the financial statement audit opinion, while the performance auditor would raise it since it would reveal aspects of effective, efficient or other management. It can be confusing to an agency's management to receive two differing opinions from the external auditor on the same issue.

Extending the example further, the financial statement auditor could also consider that, although the $10 million was immaterial in financial terms, it was material by nature. Therefore, the auditor would report it. The performance auditor reviewing the agency also would report it, and the agency would receive two audit opinions consistent in their conclusions.

---

[14] The Australian Accounting Research Foundation provides this example. 'If an amount of $10,000 was selected as an appropriate benchmark for a quantitative evaluation of materiality in the financial report of a specific entity, then an amount of say $2,000 might be assessed as the materiality level appropriate for capturing and recording individual misstatements. However, the auditor may decide to document certain amounts below $2,000 if qualitative factors indicate that the misstatement could be material…' AARF (2002), *AUS 306 Materiality and Audit Adjustments.*

The ANAO is different from large private sector audit firms because of its higher proportion of performance auditors than in those firms. Therefore, with a large annual program of financial statement audits, and a large program of performance audits, the Office has a greater probability of differing financial and performance audit opinions than do the large auditing firms. There is no evidence publicly available that the Audit Committee of Parliament or the Federal Government has criticised the Auditor-General for differences between financial statement and performance audit opinions from audits conducted at the same times. Therefore, the ANAO has measures to ensure a consistency of approach between the two kinds of audits, and it has communicated to agencies the reasons why the two kinds of audits can reach different views of the skills of agency management.

Private sector audit law

Australia is a mixed economy, with separate audit legislation for the public and private sectors. As the *Auditor-General Act 1997* is the basis for the Auditor-General's authority over standards for his Office, there is a separate law for private sector auditors. This is the *Corporations Act 2001*. Notwithstanding the existence of different laws for the two sectors, there are similarities in requirements of auditors. As described above, the Auditor-General recognised this when he adopted the Australian Auditing and Assurance Standards Board standards. That is because they were developed under the aegis of the Corporations Act for private sector, largely financial statement, auditors.

The public sector audit law also authorises him to accept appointment under the corporations legislation to audit a subsidiary of a government authority, a government company, or any other company in which the Australian Government has a controlling interest. This means that the Auditor-General can audit under both public and private sector audit law. The Australian Government requires commercially oriented government entities to operate under the same legislation as private sector equivalents, including being bound, for instance, by the same taxation, reporting and audit requirements as private firms. That is the basis for the Auditor-General's authority to audit commercially oriented government entities under private sector audit law. In these instances, the authority is for financial statement not performance audits. The Australian Government requires its businesses to prepare financial statements for audits in the same way that private firms must do under their legislation.

Commercially oriented government entities have separate legislation for their establishment and operation. When the Auditor-General audits them under private sector audit law, he also audits compliance with their enabling legislation.

Are Australian Government agencies subject to stronger accountability requirements than private firms? If so, what are the implications for the public sector auditor?

This discussion leads to the question of whether the Australian model of public sector auditing has different requirements from those in the Australian private sector. The answer is yes because of the legislative requirements of the Auditor-General to:

- first, with the exception of government companies, conduct performance audits of particular kinds of government agencies when he thinks fit, and to report the results to the Government and to Parliament; and,
- second, report to Parliament on any matter.[15]

An earlier chapter explored the first of these points. Here we discuss the implications of his authority to report to Parliament on any matter relevant to financial statement audits.

Each year, the ANAO tables in Parliament a report of findings about internal control structures and procedures in major budget-funded government agencies. The report includes assessments of whether an entity's internal control environment assists sound agency governance. As such, the report includes information on each major agency's business operations, key business and financial statement risks, governance, information technology and financial reporting.[16] The report lists what the auditors expect in an internal control environment:

- a senior executive group which meets regularly;
- an audit committee;
- an effective internal audit function;
- a current corporate plan, business risk assessment and management plan, and fraud control plan;
- clearly specified systems of authorisation, recording and procedures;
- sound organisational business practices;
- financial and accounting skills commensurate with responsibilities; and
- a timely reporting regime.

The ANAO rates its findings on a risk scale, identifying matters that agencies should address urgently, and matters of moderate and minor risks. This report provides agencies, the Government, Parliament and the community with

---

[15] *Auditor-General Act 1997*, S25.

[16] ANAO (2004), *Control Structures as part of the Audit of Financial Statements of Major Australian Government Entities for the Year Ending 30 June 2004*, Report No.58 2003–2004, ANAO, Canberra.

detailed information about the adequacy of financial management in budget-funded agencies.

Until 1996–97,[17] the ANAO also reported publicly on the internal controls of major government businesses, such as in the telecommunications and health insurance industries. This practice of advising Parliament on the adequacy of the internal controls of government businesses ceased with introduction of the *Auditor-General Act 1997*. Since then, the ANAO advises majority shareholders, who would be the relevant Government Ministers, on the adequacy of internal control environments in government businesses. The advantage of the previous practice, wherein the ANAO advised the Parliament on the results of audits of internal controls of government business enterprises, was that Parliament was informed about sound management in commercially oriented entities. This could have appeared as a disadvantage to their boards of directors and chief executive officers since those ANAO practices provided more information to the public about their leadership and management than what was available on their private sector counterparts. Under the new arrangements adopted since introduction of the *Auditor-General Act 1997,* a significant disadvantage to individual shareholders in companies which have the Government as the major shareholder is that they have less information to inform investment decisions. With greater Parliamentary, public and shareholder interest in the performance of directors and management in Australian companies, Parliament may show greater curiosity in future about audit findings on the adequacy of control environments in government companies.

The closest approximation in the private sector to this ANAO internal control report is acknowledgement by the major professional bodies of accountants and auditors that auditors may be requested to prepare special purpose reports on the effectiveness of control procedures. On behalf of those bodies, the Auditing and Assurance Standards Board of the Australian Accounting Research Foundation has issued guidance to auditors engaged to report to either an entity's management either at the governing body or operational level, or to a third party such as a regulator or to another auditor. The aim of such special purpose work is to report on whether control procedures for a specified area or activity are effective. The standard states that it does not deal with engagements to:[18]

- report publicly; or
- report on an entity's entire internal control structure, control environment and/or information system.

---

[17] ANAO (1997), *Audits of the Financial Statements of Commonwealth Entities for 1996–97. Summary of Results and Outcomes*, Report No.22 1997–98, ANAO, Canberra.

[18] AARF (2002), *AUS 810. Special Purpose Reports on the Effectiveness of Control Procedures*, AARF, Melbourne, S02.

Recent corporate law reforms in Australia have not altered these requirements.[19] Therefore, there is no requirement of auditors of private sector companies to report publicly on internal control environments, similar to the requirements and practices of the Auditor-General.

In contrast, corporate law reforms in the United States have increased the responsibilities of private sector auditors to report on internal controls. S404 of the *Sarbanes-Oxley Act 2002* requires the management of firms to assess the effectiveness of the internal control structure and procedures for financial reporting. The auditor must attest to and report publicly on these management assertions.[20]

Effects of administrative law on auditing

Legislation governing the performance of government entities is of fundamental importance to the efficiency and effectiveness of the public sector. The relevant Australian legislation is the *Financial Management and Accountability Act 1997*, and the *Commonwealth Authorities and Companies Act* of the same year. We will describe their requirements of agency management because the ANAO audits agencies' compliance with them. The reader will remember from Chapter 1 that the JCPA recommended repeal of the *Audit Act 1901* and introduction of new laws for audit and financial management. The Committee's recommendation was the origin of the legislation discussed below. In the same period and also as mentioned in Chapter 1, the House Standing Committee review of the financial management improvement program helped create an environment for change.

The *Financial Management and Accountability Act 1997* applies largely to departments of state.[21] The Act defines the responsibilities of departmental management for the collection and custody of public moneys, accounting, appropriations and payments, borrowing and investment, control and management of public property, and for reporting and audit. Chief executive officers of government departments are expected to have fraud control plans, audit committees and to prepare financial statements for audit. Importantly, they are expected to promote efficient, effective and ethical use of public resources.

The *Commonwealth Authorities and Companies Act 1997* applies by definition to government authorities and companies. The Act specifies what is

---

[19] Parliament of the Commonwealth of Australia (2004), *Corporate Law Economic Reform Program (Audit Reform and Corporate Disclosure) Act 1994. No.103, 2004*, <http://scaleplus.law.gov.au/html/comact/browse/TOCN.htm>

[20] Sarbanes-Oxley Act of 2002, S404, FindLaw, <www.findlaw.com>

[21] Parliament of the Commonwealth of Australia (2000), *Financial Management and Accountability Act 1997. Act No.154 of 1997 as amended*, Attorney-General's Department, Canberra, <http://scaleplus.law.gov.au>

required of management of these organisations.[22] Requirements include those in regard to reporting obligations, banking and investment, the conduct of officers, and the Act defines the civil and criminal consequences of contravening civil penalty provisions.

Common features of the two Acts are the focus on requirements of agencies to prepare information about their performance, comply with specified accounting standards, prepare and publish financial statements, submit to external audits, and to have strong internal controls, such as is evident through audit committees and in internal audit units. Existence of clearly defined legislative requirements of all government entities, which also affirm the importance of external auditors, is a foundation for public sector auditing. Legislative definitions of the responsibilities of entities' management provide the public sector auditor with normative criteria for assessing the adequacy of those entities' financial and performance management. In other words, the complementary nature of financial management and auditing laws simplifies public sector auditing and gives it a solid base.

International harmonisation

Australia planned to adopt standards issued by the International Accounting Standards Board for reporting periods beginning on or after 1 January 2005. Harmonising national and international standards is a major change. To assist government agencies, the Audit Office issued model accounts, with suggested approaches for agencies on financial disclosure.[23] This is an example of how an Audit Office can provide advice, consistent with its audit role, while maintaining its authority to review agencies' adherence to financial reporting standards.

Another example of the ANAO's involvement with accounting standards setters is in its response to the Australian Accounting Standards Board's initiative to harmonise two sets of financial reporting requirements.[24] These are Government Finance Statistics (GFS) and Generally Accepted Accounting Principles (GAAP). The first set is issued by the International Monetary Fund, and the second is contained in pronouncements of the Australian Accounting Standards Board. The ANAO has advised the relevant Australian Government central agency, the Department of Finance and Administration, on technical issues in this initiative. At

---

[22] Parliament of the Commonwealth of Australia (1997), *Commonwealth Authorities and Companies Act 1997, No.153, 1997*, Attorney-General's Department, Canberra, <http://scaleplus.law.gov.au>

[23] ANAO (2004), *Comparison Between Pre-2005 Australian Standards and Australian Equivalents to International Financial Reporting Standards*, ANAO, Canberra.

[24] ANAO (2004), Report No.58.

the same time, there is convergence of auditing standards with those issued by the International Auditing and Assurance Board.[25]

Conclusions

The answer to the question that this chapter addressed is the Auditor-General's own standards. In answering it, we have seen how private sector practice is the source of the standards. Even though there is no difference between the two sectors' standards for financial statement and performance audits, the Auditor-General has developed his own guidance for the Audit Office's financial and performance auditors.

Shared standards are bases for consistent approaches between financial and performance auditors. Notwithstanding, we have seen how the two sets of auditors can differ on their definition of what is material. The difficulty for the ANAO is to communicate to government agencies the logic in two sets of auditors occasionally differing in assessments of management behaviour. Different interpretations of what is so important that it affects audit opinions occur because of the different purposes of the two kinds of audits. A financial statement auditor gives an opinion on whether the financial report is free of material misstatement. A performance auditor gives an opinion on whether, in all material respects, an entity's activities are effectively, efficiently and economically managed. Co-existence of the two kinds of audits means that the two groups of auditors must communicate about their work, and also that there is a natural tension between interpretations of what is sufficiently important to include in audit opinions. There were no reported instances of agencies being confused where financial and performance auditors reached different conclusions about an agency's management. Therefore, the ANAO appears to have succeeded, first, in understanding why there can be differences and managing them, and, second, in gaining agency acceptance of them.

There are many similarities in the legal requirements of private and public sector auditors. A primary similarity is in promotion of the credibility of the audit opinion through maintaining the auditor's independence. Yet there are differences in what private and public auditors are expected to do. The principal differences are, first, expectations of the Auditor-General to conduct performance audits of agencies, when it is rare to see performance audit reports of private sector companies; and, second, the Auditor-General's custom of publishing findings on agencies' financial controls. A benefit of these two major differences between auditing in the public and private sector is that Parliament, representing taxpayers and citizens, is better informed about the adequacy of agency management than are

---

[25] Australian Accounting Research Foundation (13 January 2003), *Auditing and Assurance Standards Board (AuASB) Policy on Harmonisation and Convergence with International Standards on Auditing (ISAs)*, AARF, Melbourne, <http://www.aarf.asn.au>

shareholders of private sector companies. A caveat is that the ANAO ceased informing Parliament about the adequacy of internal controls in government companies in the late 1990s when new audit legislation was introduced. There are no similar requirements of auditors of private companies to report to shareholders on internal controls, even after recent reforms to corporations legislation.

We have seen the interaction between general administrative law for government agencies and audit practice. The Government's expectations of improved agency efficiency are in legislation. These legislative requirements of government agencies have focused audits and provided both the Government and Parliament with information on implementation of administrative reforms.

Regulators and standard setters are reforming and harmonising accounting and auditing standards internationally. The ANAO has been active in leading and interpreting the effects of these changes for itself and for government agencies.

This discussion of what standards the Auditor-General applies has concluded that public sector audit – and accounting – are proceeding in the same direction and at the same speed as in the private sector but with significant exceptions for audit.

Chapter 4

Money for Audits

The beginnings of reform of public sector audit law in Australia were in an Auditor-General's dissatisfaction with how a government agency determined the audit budget. The Public Accounts Committee became curious, and investigated whether he had good reason for dissatisfaction. As we know, the Committee's work led to a report on the Audit Office and proposals for reform. Given this history, it is worthwhile examining the Australian model of public sector audit to see how it is funded. This examination will also reveal whether current mechanisms for determining the Auditor-General's budget provide sufficient resources for the mandate, and maintain independence from government. The chapter commences by examining what the law states about audit finance. It asks how much money does the Audit Office spend on audits, before drawing conclusions.

What the law states about audit finance

This part of the chapter describes the legal provisions for the Auditor-General's budget, which are contrasted with those for comparable countries, and for audit fees.

The Auditor-General's budget

The *Auditor-General Act 1997* requires the Minister for Finance, who is responsible for compiling the Government's annual budget, to work with the Auditor-General in preparing and considering the Auditor-General's annual budget. The legislation is firm on how the Minister for Finance cannot cancel or amend the Audit Office's budget unless the Auditor-General gives approval. This step is a limit on the Government's ability to curtail the Auditor-General's resources, which otherwise would have been an option if the Auditor-General criticised the Government's administration.

The law requires the Auditor-General to submit the Office's draft annual budget to the Joint Committee of Public Accounts and Audit for consideration. The Committee is responsible for reporting its views on the draft budget to both Houses of Parliament and to the responsible Minister. These requirements ensure some openness in the process of determining the Audit Office's annual budget, since Parliamentary consideration of the budget is public. The open nature of the process to set the Audit Office's budget allows persons outside Parliament to understand the budget bid and to come to their own views on whether the Parliament, with the Government, provides sufficient moneys for audit. The sufficiency of audit finance is important because of the Auditor-General's and the Audit Office's role in working to ensure the accountability of the Government to Parliament. The Audit Committee of Parliament reported to Parliament that the Auditor-General advised of sufficient resources for 2004–2005.[1]

Since the Joint Committee of Public Accounts' major 1989 report on the Audit Office, the Committee has published two other significant reports on public sector audit. The first of these did not comment extensively on the Office's finances, arguing briefly that Parliament should have a closer involvement in determining the Office's appropriations and priorities, with limited discussion of mechanisms for doing this.[2] The second report gave much more attention to this matter. In advising the Committee during its work on this second report, the Auditor-General affirmed that the Audit Office's appropriation should be included in a separate schedule to the Budget Papers solely for the Office, distinct from appropriations for departments and services. The Committee accepted this advice, considering that the appropriation for the Audit Office should be visibly separate from both departmental and even from Parliamentary appropriations, to reinforce the perception of independence and to facilitate comparison of the Audit Office's appropriation with the recommendation of the Audit Committee of Parliament.[3]

The Government did not accept the Committee's recommendation. This is evident by how the Government's mechanism for submitting the Audit Office's draft budget to the Audit Committee of Parliament for consideration is through budgetary documentation for the Prime Minister and Cabinet Portfolio. This documentation includes draft budgets for the Department of Prime Minister and Cabinet, four other government agencies, and the budget for the Office of the Governor-General.[4] This mechanism, that includes the budget for the Prime

---

[1] Department of Parliamentary Services (2004), *Hansard, House of Representatives, Tuesday, 11 May 2004*, pp.28163–28164, <www.aph.gov.au>

[2] Parliament of the Commonwealth of Australia, Joint Committee of Public Accounts (1994), *Report 331. An Advisory Report on the Financial Management and Accountability Bill 1994, the Commonwealth Authorities and Companies Bill 1994 and the Auditor-General's Bill 1994, and on a Proposal to Establish an Audit Committee of Parliament*, AGPS, Canberra, p.85, <http://www.aph.gov.au/house/committee/jpaa/index.htm>

[3] Parliament of the Commonwealth of Australia, Joint Committee of Public Accounts (1996), *Report 346. Guarding the Independence of the Auditor-General*, AGPS, Canberra, p. 67.

[4] The four other government agencies are the Australian Public Service Commission, the Office of National Assessment which advises the Prime Minister and Cabinet on national security, the Office of the Commonwealth Ombudsman, and the Office of the Inspector-General of Intelligence and Security. These last two officers have some independence from government but they are not Parliamentary posts like that of the Auditor-General: Department of Prime Minister and Cabinet, (2004). The *Ombudsman Act 1976* gives the

Minister's Department with the budget for the Office of the Auditor-General, is inconsistent with the Auditor-General's status as an independent officer of the Parliament. That is because it does not provide a clear separation of the budgetary needs of the Government from the budgetary needs of the Parliament.

The *Auditor-General Act 1997* is silent on procedures for forming and communicating the Auditor-General's budget to the Audit Committee of Parliament. Thus, the above procedures do not infringe any legal provision. The procedures are consistent with practices of successive Governments.

New Zealand, the United Kingdom and Canada

Funding procedures for the New Zealand Auditor-General contrast with those in Australia. The New Zealand Auditor-General submits a draft annual plan – containing proposed funding and any capital requirements based on a three-year business plan – to a Parliamentary Committee. The latter is chaired by the Speaker of the House with members from all significant political parties. The Committee does not always have a government majority. The Treasury comments and advises the Committee on the business plan and proposed finances, with the Committee free to accept or reject the Treasury's advice. The Committee then recommends to the House the level of annual appropriation for the Auditor-General. The Auditor-General completes and publishes the annual plan based on the amount of funding appropriated.[5] This arrangement provides a clearer separation of the Auditor-General's and the government's funding than in the Australian model.

Ombudsman the authority to investigate action relating to a matter of administration, (S5). A sign of the Ombudsman's independence is in how that Officer has the legal authority to report matters to Parliament at the Officer's discretion. S18 of the Act states that:

> 'Where the Ombudsman has ... furnished information to the Prime Minister in relation to a report concerning an investigation by him, the Ombudsman may also forward to the President of the Senate and the Speaker of the House of Representatives ... copies of a report prepared by him.'

Attorney-General's Department, (2004), *Ombudsman's Act 1976*, Canberra, <http://scaleplus.law.gov.au>

The *Inspector-General of Intelligence Act 1986* states that the objects of the Act are to assist Ministers in the oversight and review compliance with the law by Australian intelligence or security agencies (S4). Before making a recommendation to the Governor-General for the appointment of an Inspector-General, the Prime Minister must consult with the Leader of the Opposition in the House of Representatives (S6). The functions of the Inspector-General are at the request of the responsible Minister, or of the Inspector-General's own motion .to inquire into any matter that relates to (S8).

Attorney-General's Department (2004), *Inspector-General of Intelligence and Security Act 1986*, Canberra.

[5] Buchanan, Robert (April 2004), *The Independence of the Supreme Audit Institutions of New Zealand and other Pacific and Asian States*, Paper prepared for the 17th UN/INTOSAI

In the United Kingdom, the Comptroller and Auditor-General estimates the annual budget of the National Audit Office and submits those estimates to Parliament for consideration. The estimates are considered by a specially established Parliamentary Commission, called the Public Accounts Commission, comprised of senior Parliamentarians; for instance, it is chaired by the Leader of the House of Commons. The Commission's role is defined by the *National Audit Act 1983.* A principal duty is to examine the National Audit Office's budget estimates, and to report from time to time.[6] Commission members question the Auditor-General about the audit budget and, for instance, the relationship between government expenditure and the quality of auditing that arises as a consequence. The Commission approves the National Audit Office's budget estimates. This process opens to public view the Auditor-General's audit priorities and why the Audit Office needs more resources.[7] Also evidence of the Commission's desire to open to the public its scrutiny on behalf of the Parliament of the National Audit Office are its statements about its work.[8]

Of interest is how the Auditor-General of Canada has expressed her concern about the financing of her Office. In 2003, she wrote in her Performance Report to Parliament that:[9]

> The appropriate level of funding for the Office must be determined in an objective manner that is not influenced by those we audit. The existing process for arriving at our funding level is not sufficiently independent and impartial to ensure that our budget is appropriate for meeting Parliament's expectations.
>
> We are discussing alternative funding mechanisms with the Treasury Board Secretariat for determining future years' funding of the Office's requirements. At present, like almost all federal departments and agencies, we

---

Seminar, Symposium on the Independence of Supreme Audit Institutions, <www.oag.govt.nz>

6 United Kingdom Parliament (2 October 2004), *Public Accounts Commission*, <http://parliament.uk/parliamentary_committees/public_accounts_commission.cfm>

7 The Public Accounts Commission 24 February 2004 hearing queried the Comptroller and Auditor-General about his budget requirements. In conclusion, the Chairman asked:

> 'Can I ask the Commission if they now agree to approve the NAO's estimates?
> Members of the Commission: Agreed.
> Chairman: There you are; well, you have got your money.
> Auditor-General: Thank you very much, Chairman.'

United Kingdom Parliament (24 February 2004), *Public Accounts Commission*, <http://www.parliament.uk/documents/upload/TPACtscript24024.pdf>

8 The Commission listed recent activities as including National Audit Office Supply Estimates for 2003–04, National Audit Office Corporate Plan covering 2003–04 to 2005–06, and developments in financial audit. United Kingdom Parliament (2 October 2004), *Public Accounts Commission.*

9 Office of the Auditor-General of Canada (2003), *Performance Report for the period ending March 31, 2003*, Office of the Auditor-General of Canada, Ottawa, <http://www.tbs-sct.gc.ca/rma/dpr/02-03/OAG-BVG/OAG-BVG03D01_e.asp>

> negotiate our budget with representatives of the Treasury Board Secretariat. So far this has not caused a problem, but as a matter of principle, we believe that this situation should be corrected so there is no possibility of influence, real or perceived. Such a process should establish a balance between the independence of the Auditor-General and the rightful challenge to our expenditure of public funds.

Clearly, the financing of Audit Offices remains an issue.

Audit fees

Another source of funds is audit fees. The legislation provides for Federal Government authorities, companies and their subsidiaries to pay fees to the Auditor-General for financial statement audits. The Audit Committee of Parliament must consider fees that the Auditor-General sets. Also, the Auditor-General must include details of the basis for audit fees in the Audit Office's annual report.

Publication of the basis for fees is another example of the openness of processes for determining the sufficiency of audit resources. Their publication also allows comparison of the Auditor-General's costs with equivalent financial statement services in the private sector. By making possible comparisons of the costs of financial statement audits, the legislation encourages the Audit Office to function efficiently. The 1997–98 financial year was the first under the new audit legislation. In that year, fee revenue was almost 34 per cent of the budget.[10] For 2002–2003, the Audit Office received $11.2 million from audit fees,[11] which were 21 per cent of the total budget of $53.3 million.[12] For 2004–2005, projected fee revenue was $10.9 million or 18 per percent of the total budget of $60 million.[13] These data show that fee revenue has fallen as a percentage of total revenue since introduction of new audit legislation in 1997. A major reason for this fall is because the ANAO audits fewer commercially oriented government entities than before. This is due to the Government's sale of many of its businesses.

The Audit Office considers itself almost wholly budget funded by Parliament. The reason is that agencies pay fees for the costs of their financial statement audits to the Audit Office, which then forwards the revenue to a government fund.[14] Notwithstanding, the Audit Office reports the net outlays by the Government for its services as the Office's appropriation approved by Parliament less the revenue the Government receives from auditees' fees.[15]

---

[10] ANAO (1998), *Annual Report 1997–98*, ANAO, Canberra, p.38.

[11] ANAO (2003), *Annual Report 2002–2003*, p.87.

[12] These figures exclude revenue from leasing office space to another organisation.

[13] Department of Prime Minister and Cabinet (2004), pp.71, 88.

[14] This is the Consolidated Revenue Fund. Department of Prime Minister and Cabinet (2004), p.71.

[15] ANAO (2003), *Annual Report 2002–2003*, p.87. ANAO (2004), *Annual Report 2003–2004*, The Auditor-General, ANAO, Canberra, p.101.

In 1994 the Joint Committee of Public Accounts considered the issue of audit fees in preparation for new audit legislation enacted a few years later in 1997. The Committee identified practical difficulties with the Auditor-General's preference for Parliament to pay audit fees consistent with the user-pays principle. Parliament authorised the executive to spend money, but did not have money itself. For Parliament to pay audit fees, it would have to authorise the executive to give money to Parliament to give back to the Audit Office. The Committee considered this approach impractical, and proposed that the matter be reconsidered when an Audit Committee of Parliament was formed.[16]

Of note is that agencies audited by Auditors-General in the Australian states and territories also pay fees for some audit services, notably for financial statement audits. In some locations, these fees cover a proportion of audit costs, and in others they provide for all costs. In some cases, the Audit Office transferred fees income to a government account. In this way, the relevant central government agency that receives audit fees, such as a state Ministry of Finance or Treasury, acts like a broker between the Audit Office and audited agencies. Fees as proportions of total revenue varied considerably between states and territories. For instance, in 2002–2003, the smallest proportion of revenue was eight per cent, and the highest was 85 per cent. Audit fees as percentages of total revenue averaged 72 per cent.[17]

In general, agencies did not pay for performance audits, with the Australian Parliament or state and territory legislatures paying for these through annual budgetary allocation to Audit Offices. The reason for agencies not paying fees appears to be legislators' views that performance audits were more clearly for Parliament than financial statement audits, and were additional requirements of agencies compared to requirements in the private sector. While it is true that government agencies can be performance audited and the results reported publicly, with private firms not being subject to these audits, this is an insufficient reason for Parliament paying directly only for performance audits and not for all financial statement audits.

In order to understand the significance of government agencies paying an Audit Office for its work – even when an Audit Office transfers those payments

---

[16] Parliament of the Commonwealth of Australia, Joint Committee of Public Accounts (1994), *Report 331*, p. 62.

[17] Audit Office of New South Wales (2003), *Annual Report 2002–2003*, Audit Office of New South Wales, Sydney. Auditor-General Australian Capital Territory (2003). Auditor-General Victoria (2003). Auditor-General's Department South Australia (2003), *Annual Report on the Operations of the Auditor-General's Department for the Year Ending 30 June 2003*, Auditor-General's Department South Australia, Adelaide. Northern Territory Auditor-General's Office (2003), *Annual Report 2002–2003*, Northern Territory Auditor-General's Office, Darwin. Office of the Auditor-General for Western Australia (2003). Parliament of Tasmania (2003), *Auditor-General. Annual Report 2002–2003. September 2003*, Government Printer, Tasmania. Queensland Audit Office (2003). This figure is an unweighted average for the five state and two territory Audit Offices that reported data.

immediately on receipt to a government account – it is necessary to place these payments within the context of private sector practice. In the latter in Australia as described earlier, the *Corporations Act 2001* requires that annual general meetings of company shareholders appoint external auditors. The directors of the company recommend the appointment to the annual general meeting, with shareholders approving or not of the recommendation. Audit fees are negotiated between the company's directors and the external auditor, and disclosed in the annual financial statements on which the external auditor has given an opinion.

As indicated above, government companies and allied entities are liable to pay fees for audits of their financial statements, and these fees are disclosed in companies' financial statements. This public disclosure provides Parliamentary, media and citizen readers of the financial statements with basic information about the effort required to audit the statements. It is basic information because a well-informed reader can compare the cost of auditing the government company with the cost of auditing an equivalent private company. In turn, this permits some basic assessment of the efficiency of the audit effort in relation to the adequacy of statements prepared for audit. By itself, information about audit fees is only a starting point for forming a view on either item, and the information can be misleading. However, such information is a reasonable basis for a reader to ask questions about the adequacy of the company's financial statement presented for audit and the external auditor's efficiency. Therefore, there are sound reasons for government companies reporting the auditor's costs. The question is whether the company should pay those costs.

The Government requires its departments and allied entities to include audit costs in their financial statements. Therefore, Parliamentary and other readers have financial data to compare the costs of auditing other departments and similar entities. As with government companies, those readers and users of financial statement reports can draw some preliminary conclusions about departments' preparation of their statements and the external auditor's efficiency. But similar to government companies, this data on audit costs is insufficient to draw conclusions about either item, with its main use as a pointer towards other questions about financial reporting and auditing. As we know, the Parliament pays for all the costs of auditing Federal Government departments since it is the principal client. Therefore, the current system of paying for and reporting on the costs of auditing government departments acknowledges the identity of the principal audit client, while providing public information on audit costs to promote the preparation of adequate and complete financial statements and to promote their efficient audit.

For government companies it is less even. That is because the Parliament does not pay for those audits although it is the principal audit client. However, the requirement of public disclosure of audit costs is a tool for the efficient preparation and auditing of those companies' statements.

How much money does the Australian National Audit Office spend on audits?

For 2004–2005, the Auditor-General expected to spend $21.5 million on performance audit reports, and $38.4 million on financial statement audit reports in a total budget of $60 million.[18] Thirty-seven percent of resources were allocated to performance audits and 63 percent to financial statement audits. The Audit Office anticipated that it would produce 47 performance audit reports, 260 financial statement audit opinions, and 20 other products and services. They included better practice guides and seminars for agencies on model financial statements. These figures should be compared with those that the Audit Office provided to the Public Accounts Committee for its review. The Committee reported that in 1987–88 the Audit Office spent six per cent of its resources on efficiency audits, with the remainder on regularity audits.[19] Clearly, the Audit Office has increased greatly its expenditure on performance audits.

In 2002–2003, the Australian state and territory Audit Offices spent varying proportions of their resources on performance audits. These proportions varied from 4 to 37 per cent, with these Audit Offices using an average of approximately 17 per cent of their resources on these audits.[20] In a number of cases, it was difficult to find information about how much state and territory Audit Offices spent on performance audits. Some reported the numbers of staff, and others reported the numbers of reports. As later chapters demonstrate, INTOSAI identifies regularity and performance audits as the two main kinds of audits. The difficulty in finding publicly available state and territory Audit Office expenditure data on performance audits pointed to how some did not believe it necessary to report readily understood and comparable data on these audits. In general, state and territory Audit Offices devoted a considerably smaller proportion of their expenditure on performance audits than did the Australian National Audit Office. The major explanatory factor was legislature reluctance to provide more resources for this activity.

An effect was that state and territory Audit Offices had clear limits over the information they generated and provided to their governments and legislatures

[18] These figures included estimated expenditure on business support process and protective security audits, which are conducted under performance audit clauses of the legislation. Department of Prime Minister and Cabinet (2004), pp.80–82, 88.

[19] This excludes estimated expenditure on project audits. Joint Committee of Public Accounts (1989), *Report No. 296*, p.138.

[20] Since Audit Offices reported expenditure on performance audits in different ways, exact comparisons of expenditure were not possible in some cases. Therefore, the figures reported here should be interpreted as the most accurate estimates possible from publicly available data. Audit Office of New South Wales (2003); Auditor-General Australian Capital Territory (2003); Auditor-General Victoria (2003); Auditor-General's Department South Australia (2003); Northern Territory Auditor-General's Office (2003); Office of the Auditor-General for Western Australia (2003); Parliament of Tasmania (2003); Queensland Audit Office (2003).

on government agencies' efficient, economical and effective use of funds. In relative terms, the Australian Parliament was better informed about these characteristics of public sector agencies than were members of state and territory legislatures and their citizens. The greater attention of the national Audit Office to performance audits compared with its state and territory counterparts meant that the former was better resourced and equipped to provide its legislators with both an assurance of sound public sector management and ideas for improvement. Overall, the Australian model of public sector auditing was characterised by uneven use of performance audit to improve public sector management in ways consistent with the generally accepted roles of Auditors-General. There was a consensus amongst legislators and Auditors-General that the latter's dominant role, at least in terms of resources, was in regularity and principally in financial statement auditing. The strong and unanimous attention to regularity or financial statement auditing would be reassuring to citizens and taxpayers. However, most legislatures' acceptance of allocation of relatively small proportions of resources to performance audits suggested that, in some jurisdictions, public sector auditing remained similar to auditing in the private sector, where shareholders saw few performance audit reports from external auditors of companies listed on stock exchanges.

The Australian Auditor-General was required annually to conduct financial statement audits of all Australian Government agencies. He had limited discretion over the size of this expenditure to produce credible audit opinions – with the number of financial statements to be reviewed and audit methodology being the main determinants of costs. In comparison, he had much more discretion over how much money to spend on performance audits compared to state and territory peers. Although he increased significantly the proportion of ANAO resources for performance audits, he had the authority to spend no money on this activity if he so wished. That is, the legislation required financial statement audits but it did not require performance audits.

Consistent with Australia's mixed economy, the Auditor-General employs large numbers of auditors on contract from the private sector. Staff were employed mostly on financial statement audits.

1997–98 was the first year of the *Auditor-General Act 1997*. In that financial year, the Australian Government's combined expenditure and revenue was $270 billion.[21] Parliament provided the Audit Office with $45 million[22] for its reviews of these moneys. For 2004–2005, the Federal Government estimated its combined expenditure and revenue as $385.5 billion.[23] Parliament appropriated

---

[21] Parliament of the Commonwealth of Australia (1997), *Budget Strategy and Outlook 1997–98, 1997–98 Budget Paper No.1*, AGPS, Canberra, pp.1–3.

[22] ANAO (1998), *Annual Report*, p.38.

[23] Parliament of the Commonwealth of Australia (2004), *Budget Strategy and Outlook 2004–2005. Circulated by the Honourable Peter Costello MP, Treasurer of the Commonwealth of Australia, and Senator the Honourable Nick Minchin, Minister for Finance and Administration, For the Information of Honourable Members on the Occasion*

$58.6 million for the Audit Office for that year.[24] A ratio of expenditure on external audit in comparison to total government expenditure and revenue is a crude measure of the sufficiency of audit resources. Despite this limitation, it is evident that the costs of external audit are small, compared both with the moneys and management on which auditors give opinions, and in comparison to the benefits to the public sector of the ANAO's assurance role.

Conclusions

The ANAO's financial arrangements differ in two ways from those proposed by the Public Accounts Committee in its 1989 review.

First, the Committee proposed that the Audit Office's draft budget be included with those of Parliamentary departments. This proposal was to sharpen the distinction between the Government's draft budget for Executive Government agencies and the draft budget for the workings of Parliament. Since the Auditor-General was to be an officer of the Parliament, albeit an independent officer, inclusion of his budget proposals with those for other arms of Parliament was intended to reinforce in a clear and public way that the Auditor-General's client was Parliament. The Government did not adopt this proposal. Rather, as shown above, it included the Audit Office's draft budget in legislation for government agencies.

Current practices for the Government to include the Auditor-General's draft budget with the draft budget for the Department of Prime Minister and Cabinet suggested governmental influence over the audit budget. This was balanced by how the Auditor-General and the Minister for Finance, representing the Government, must agree on the Audit Office's appropriation. A balance to government influence over the audit budget was in the Audit Committee's authority to request the Auditor-General to submit the draft annual audit budget, so that the Committee in a bipartisan way could report on its adequacy.

Second, in its key 1989 report, the Committee stated firmly its conclusion that the Auditor-General's role was to serve Parliament. Yet while doing this, he would also assist agencies through analyses and reporting. The Committee upheld the user pays principle with Parliament being the principal user. Therefore, it was correct for Parliament to pay for the Auditor-General's services. In other words, the Committee argued that agencies' payment of fees to the Auditor-General was not an application of the user pays principle; rather, it was based on a misunderstanding of the principle of user pays. In the Committee's view, for agencies to pay the Auditor-General for audits risked creating the impression that they were principal or equal clients even though they were part of government. The

---

of the Budget 2004–2005. Budget Budget Paper No.1, Parliament of the Commonwealth of Australia, Canberra, pp. 5–2, 6–3, <www.budget.gov.au>

[24] Department of Prime Minister and Cabinet (2004), p.68.

Auditor-General's task of forming audit opinions independently of government was complicated when there was the possibility of at least some audited agencies expecting to be the Auditor-General's primary clients.

The Government did not share the Committee's view. Instead, it upheld that payment by commercially oriented government entities for financial statement audits placed those entities on the same footing as private companies. Therefore, according to the Government, it was desirable and necessary for government authorities, companies and subsidiaries to pay the Auditor-General, with the latter transferring those receipts to a government account. This arrangement had the potential to cloud the identity of the audit's principal client, although there was no publicly recorded evidence of this occurring and no research data. As explained earlier, agencies' payment of audit fees was inconsistent with the Public Accounts Committee's 1989 recommendation that the user pays principle led to Parliament paying for all audits. The Committee's 1994 position was that there were practical problems with the Auditor-General's preference for Parliament to pay audit fees, and that the Audit Committee of Parliament should reconsider the matter.

In 1997–98, which was the first year of new audit legislation, the ANAO's fee revenue was 34 per cent of resources. This percentage declined by 2004–2005 to 18 per cent of total funding, despite a significantly larger audit budget.

In 1987–88, the Audit Office set aside six per cent of its resources for efficiency or performance audit, and 94 per cent of resources for regularity audits. The Audit Office increased significantly its resources for performance audits, so that by 2004–2005, it expected to allocate 37 per cent of its resources to performance audits and 63 per cent to regularity – largely financial statement – audits. In general, Audit Offices in the states and territories allocated significantly smaller percentages of their resources to performance audits than did the ANAO, indicating legislatures' views that Audit Offices' primary role was in regularity including financial statement auditing.

In three comparable countries, budgetary mechanisms for funding the Audit Office differed. In summary, the Auditor-General advised Parliament that there were sufficient resources for the audit mandate. Implementation of the *Auditor-General Act 1997* provided greater scope for an Auditor-General to advise Parliament on the sufficiency of audit resources, but with the Government remaining influential over budget estimates. Consequently, despite the new legislation of the *Auditor-General Act 1997* affirming the office holder's independence from Parliament and the Government, current funding provisions suggested some ambiguity in the arrangements.

Chapter 5

The Special Case of Performance Audits

This chapter examines the place of performance audits in the Australian model. Performance audits are a special case because often their findings and recommendations are more accessible to Parliamentarians and the general public than those of financial statement audits and they lead to more Parliamentary interest than the latter.

The chapter revisits two definitions of performance audit, and introduces new ones. This revisit is because of curious answers to the question of whether there is a consensus on the meaning of performance audit. It examines the relationship between performance audit and evaluation, and introduces different approaches to annual audit planning. It examines what it means to be a national audit office when it has limited access to state and territory government expenditure and performance data on their use of Federal Government funds. Finally, it asks what does the ANAO communicate publicly to Parliament and the Government about its performance audit findings.

What are performance audits?

The Australian Accounting Research Foundation defines performance audit in these terms:[1]

> Performance auditing means an audit of all or part of an entity's or entities' activities to assess economy and/or efficiency and/or effectiveness. It includes any audit directed to:
> a. the adequacy of an internal control structure or specific internal controls, including those intended to safeguard assets and to ensure due regard for economy, efficiency and effectiveness;
> b. the extent to which resources have been managed economically and efficiently; and
> c. the extent to which activities have been effective.

The *Auditor-General Act 1997* has a more succinct definition.[2]

[1] AARF (2002), AUS 806. Performance Auditing.
[2] *Auditor-General Act 1997*, Part 2, S5.

> Performance audit, in relation to a person or body, means a review or examination of any aspect of the operations of the person or body.

The two definitions are consistent, although the legislative version is wider.

The states and territories have varying definitions. One state audit law emphasised the auditor's role in identifying the efficiency and economy of an agency's resource use, but excluded the auditor from identifying the effectiveness of the agency's resource use.[3] Within that jurisdiction, each government agency demonstrated its effective use of resources, but in an unaudited way, to the state government and legislature.

Two Audit Offices defined performance audits as reviews of performance management systems. The objective of such an audit included determining whether the performance management systems of the agency enabled it to assess whether its objectives were being achieved economically, efficiently and effectively.[4]

Legislation for the two largest state Audit Offices and for one territory Office defined a performance audit as determining whether the authority was carrying out its activities effectively and doing so economically, efficiently and in compliance with all relevant laws.[5] An example of a wide definition is one that described performance auditing as encompassing the range of audit and review activities from annual attest work on financial statements and performance indicators through to the preparation of direct reports on performance examinations. The latter was work performed in examining the accountability, efficiency and effectiveness of public sector activities.[6] Two states had this wider definition.

We can deduce these elements from this survey of definitions of performance audit:

- Australian Auditing Standards were considerations for the Australian Parliament and for state and territory legislatures. Nevertheless, with the exception of the smallest territory, each Parliament or legislature formed its own definition. The different audit laws in each jurisdiction were the legal basis for Audit Offices varying their definitions of performance audit from that in the standards. Of note is that the relevant standard stated

---

3 Auditor-General's Department South Australia (2003), p.11.

4 Queensland Audit Office (2003), p. 22. Northern Territory of Australia, (2002), *Audit Act*, Northern Territory Government, Darwin, S15.

5 New South Wales Consolidated Acts (1983), *Public Finance and Audit Act 1983*, S38A. Victorian Legislation and Parliamentary Documents (1994), *Version No.043. Audit Act 1994. Act No.2/1994*, S15. The Australian Capital Territory *Auditor-General Act 1996* incorporates the Australian Accounting Research Foundation AUS 806 definition, Auditor-General Australian Capital Territory (2003), p.3.

6 Office of the Auditor-General for Western Australia (2003), p.80. Parliament of Tasmania (2003), p.19.

that the principles and essential procedures were to be determined in the context of the legislative mandate;[7]
- three of the eight states and territories had narrower definitions than Australian Auditing Standards. One excluded reviews of management and agency effectiveness, and two focused on systems rather than on management. A caveat is that the definitions' wordings provided the option of reviewing management as well;
- the ANAO and two state Audit Offices defined performance audit more widely than Australian Accounting Standards.

Implications

In general, Audit Offices that defined a performance audit to exclude management and agency effectiveness, or that defined audit as a review of management systems, allocated less than ten per cent of their resources to performance audits. This was a smaller percentage than Offices with wider definitions. The reasons for state and territory legislatures adopting narrow definitions of performance audits are not clear.

The consensus was that performance audit included reviews of efficiency and economy, with some applying these concepts to management systems and others to whether an agency's management could demonstrate them, and beyond that to whether an agency was operating efficiently and economically. Audit Offices differed on whether performance audit included reviews of a program's, management's or an agency's effectiveness.

Audit Offices with similar definitions had firmer bases for cooperation than where definitions differed. That is because there were fewer legal obstacles than otherwise. A potential area for cooperation is the training of performance auditors. In 2002–2003, Audit Offices did not report publicly on whether they cooperated in training performance auditors. A number of Offices gave attention to their training of staff from Audit Offices in other countries. Later, we will describe the limited cooperation of Audit Offices in other aspects of performance auditing.

The auditor as evaluator

Evaluation is a type of review with many similarities to audit. A useful definition of evaluation is of a review that assesses whether an activity has succeeded or failed. Applied to the public sector in this study, an evaluation is a review of whether a government intervention has succeeded or failed. Federal audit legislation may provide some opportunity for evaluations to be conducted by the Auditor-General. That is because an initial reading of the relevant performance audit section of the Act (quoted above) does not prohibit the Auditor-General

---

[7] AARF (2002), *AUS 806 Performance Auditing*, S10.

asking whether a body's or an agency's administration of a government initiative succeeded or failed.[8] At the federal level from time to time, the Audit Office has commented on agencies' evaluation plans and practices. However, the Audit Office has not in general commissioned evaluations of whether an agency has achieved government objectives.

The Office has confined itself to evaluations of the administrative effectiveness of an agency's operations. In other words, its performance audits customarily ask whether an agency or program is well-managed. To inquire into whether a program has succeeded or failed would mean delving into program effectiveness rather than administrative effectiveness. There is a grey area wherein these two types of effectiveness overlap or are indistinguishable. The Joint Committee of Public Accounts and Audit has not publicly commented on whether performance audits have evaluated government programs and initiatives.

To return to audit law for the Australian states, in New South Wales, which is the largest state, the legislation makes clear what are not the purposes of audit. The legislation affirms that the Auditor-General is not entitled to question the merits of policy objectives of the Government, including:[9]

> (a) any policy directive of the Government contained in a record of a policy decision of Cabinet, and
> (b) a policy direction of a Minister, and
> (c) a policy statement in any Budget Paper or other document evidencing a policy direction of the Cabinet or a Minister.

Similarly, in 1996 when introducing the new federal legislation, the Minister for Finance clarified that performance audit functions did not extend to examining or reporting on the appropriateness of government policy.[10]

Clearly, the prospect of an Auditor-General commenting on whether a program succeeded or failed was outside what the state or Federal Government expected.

More widely at the federal level, there is strong audit legislation but there is no equivalent for evaluation. In other words, no Federal Government has established an officer or authority with the independence and resources to determine whether government initiatives succeeded or failed. This is in contrast, for instance, to the United States where the General Accountability Office can audit and evaluate the success of government initiatives.[11] Individual Australian Government agencies commission evaluations, and sometimes Ministers sponsor

---

[8] Legal advice would be necessary to confirm this view.

[9] New South Wales Consolidated Acts (1983), *Public Finance and Audit Act 1983*, S27B.

[10] Parliament of the Commonwealth of Australia, House of Representatives (1996), *Auditor-General Bill 1996. Explanatory Memorandum (Circulated by authority of the Minister for Finance, the Honourable John Fahey, MP)*, S25, <http://scaleplus.law.gov.au>

[11] General Accountability Office (2004), *Strategic Plan 2004–2009*, GAO, Washington, <http://www.gao.gov>

them. These activities, while potentially useful, are dependent on government and have many characteristics of internal evaluations or of internal audits since they are commissioned by management. They are not independent of government – with the advantages that flow from independence. Occasionally, Parliamentary committees attempt to assess the success of a government program. Restrictions on the authority of Parliamentary committees to access government data, documents and personnel limit their capacity. Notwithstanding, these committees are independent of government.

To summarise, acknowledging legislative constraints, Audit Offices in Australia have been reluctant to evaluate government programs, although performance audits and program evaluations overlap.

What do performance audits plan to look at?

The ANAO has explained how it plans its annual program of performance audits around the following factors:[12]

- business risks in major agencies;
- financial materiality;
- program significance;
- audit impact, which is likely gain from the audit;
- visibility of the program as reflected in its national importance or political sensitivity; and
- extent of recent audit coverage and internal and external review of the program.

A result of this planning is that it conducts performance audits in each government portfolio. Table 5.1 illustrates for 2004–2005 the numbers of performance audits planned for each portfolio in comparison with the Australian Government's appropriations for portfolios.

This comparison of the numbers of audits in each portfolio with each portfolio's budget does not include planned audit expenditure in each portfolio. Yet it is useful since it illustrates the absence of a linear relationship between the size of a portfolio's budget and the audit effort. It is logical that planning the numbers of audits for each portfolio reflects all factors influencing the selection of audit topics, where one factor is portfolio budget. Another way of saying this is to affirm that materiality in audit planning includes more than financial materiality. This topic was discussed more extensively in Chapter 3.

In any year for any SAI, the amount of resources for performance auditing will be a small fraction of government revenue and expenditure that could be reviewed. In 2004–2005, for example, the ANAO had a budget of $21.5 million for

[12] ANAO (2004), *Audit Work Program 2004–2005, July 2004*, ANAO, Canberra, p.6.

performance auditing,[13] when the sum of government revenue and expenditure was $385.5 billion.[14] This ratio of audit resources to potential audit topics, when expressed in financial terms, simplifies and complicates annual planning. It simplifies it because it is probable that most audits of very large sums or any large programs will identify issues for agency management. It complicates it because there are many factors that planners must consider if they are to have maximum impact with such relatively few resources. Here, maximum impact means maximising the validity and number of audit assurances to Parliament and agencies, and improving public administration.

Table 5.1 Australian Government Budgets for Portfolio Agencies and Numbers of Scheduled Performance Audits, 2004–2005

Portfolios	**2004–2005 Budget $ billion**	**Numbers of Performance Audits** (a)
Agriculture, Fisheries and Forestry	3.1	7
Attorney-General's (b)	3.2	7
Communications, Information Technology and the Arts	2.3	5
Defence	19.1	15
Veterans' Affairs (d)	10.7	4
Education, Science and Training	19.3	5
Employment and Workplace Relations	2.3	5
Environment and Heritage	1.1	1
Family and Community Services	71.5	14
Finance and Administration	6.4	5
Foreign Affairs and Trade	3.8	6
Health and Ageing	37.2	13
Immigration and Multicultural and Indigenous Affairs	2.9	10
Industry, Tourism and Resources	1.8	2
Prime Minister and Cabinet	0.2	0
Transport and Regional Services	4.2	3
Treasury (c)	16.5	17

(a) These figures include continuing and potential audits, and those cross-portfolio audits identified with each portfolio.

[13] Department of Prime Minister and Cabinet (2004), p.80.

[14] Parliament of the Commonwealth of Australia (2004), *Budget Paper No.1*, pp.5–2, 6–3.

(b) This portfolio includes the Australian Customs Service, which is a major revenue agency. The Australian Government's estimate of total indirect taxation in 2004–2005 was $27.5 billion. The Australian Customs Service had responsibility for raising most of this revenue.
(c) This portfolio includes the Australian Taxation Office, which is the most important revenue agency. The Australian Government's estimate of total income taxation in 2004–2005 was $150.1 billion. The Australian Taxation Office had responsibility for raising most of this revenue.[15]
(d) Veterans' Affairs is included here since it is part of the Defence Portfolio.

An alternative way to design a performance audit program would be to identify the portfolio with the greatest risk of management failure and to commission all performance audits within it. This would result, for instance, in the SAI, which in this case is the ANAO, conducting performance audits only within the Defence portfolio. The latter has a history of uneven management of large and expensive equipment development and acquisition programs.[16] Neither the ANAO nor any state or territory Audit Office planned on this basis.

Another foundation for a performance audit program is to focus on the most financially material portfolio or portfolios. On the revenue and expenditure sides of government respectfully, the most financially material portfolios would be Treasury, because of its inclusion of the Australian Taxation Office, and the Department of Family and Community Services, including major agencies that deliver its services. That Department's budget is almost twice that of the next largest expenditure agency, and the most significant part of the Australian Government's total expenditure. Again, neither the ANAO nor any state or territory Audit Office allocated all performance audit resources to the most material portfolios.

The fourth basis for annual planning would be to identify common management problems across all government agencies, and to audit only them. Examples of topics are agency leasing of offices, use of the Internet to deliver government programs and services, and management of intellectual property. Chapter 15 describes how ANAO has increased its cross-portfolio performance audits. In 1997–98, these were 19 per cent of all tabled performance audit reports, and 25 per cent in 2003–2004. For the ANAO to allocate all performance audit resources to cross-portfolio reviews would remove its capacity to address serious management issues in particular agencies. The Audit Office did not describe how it decided what percentage of resources was assigned to cross-portfolio work.

A fifth basis for annual planning and deciding what performance audits should look at is to plan around themes. Each 12 months, the ANAO identifies themes to focus either its audits or its reporting against them. For 2004–2005, new broad themes were:[17]

---

[15] Parliament of the Commonwealth of Australia (2004), *Budget Paper No. 1*, pp. 5–6.
[16] ANAO (2004), Report No.58 2003–2004.
[17] ANAO (2004), *Audit Work Program 2004–05*, p.6.

- security;
- economic management;
- ageing population;
- growing demand for better quality of life;
- growing interconnectivity and changing service delivery through information technology and telecommunications; and
- evolving governance structures, including higher community expectations for strong management and appropriate governance.

Auditing federal funding of other levels of government

Every year, the Federal Government makes payments to other levels of government for particular purposes, consistent with the Australian Constitution. These payments are called specific purpose payments to state, territory and local government.[18] Payments are for purposes, such as for state, territory and local governments to provide health, education, housing and public order services. For 2004–2005, the Australian Government budgeted $24.3 billion in these payments to the states.[19] These payments represented almost 13 per cent of total Australian Government expenditure in 2004–2005. There were over 90 specific purpose programs for which the Australian Government sought an appropriation in 2004–2005.

The ANAO reviews Australian Government agencies' payments systems for these purposes in its financial statement audits. Where these payments are materially important, audit opinions will include opinions on the latter. Otherwise, financial statement auditors operating under the Auditor-General's standards will not review them. In 2004–2005, the ANAO planned to conduct performance audits of three specific purpose programs.[20] Programs it planned to audit had budgets of

---

[18] Section 96 of the Australian Constitution states that:

> 'During a period of ten years after the establishment of the Commonwealth and thereafter until the Parliament otherwise provides, the Parliament may grant financial assistance to any State on such terms and conditions as the Parliament thinks fit.'

Attorney-General's Department (2004), *Australia. The Constitution – as in force on 1 June 2003,* Attorney-General's Department, Canberra, <http://scaleplus.law.gov.au/docs/Constitution.pdf>

[19] Parliament of the Commonwealth of Australia (2004), *Federal Financial Relations 2004–05. Circulated by the Honourable Peter Costello MP, Treasurer of the Commonwealth of Australia, and Senator the Honourable Nick Minchin, Minister for Finance and Administration, for the Information of Honourable Members on the Occasion of the Budget 2004–05, Budget Paper No. 3*, Department of the Treasury, Canberra, pp.22–23.

[20] Performance audits planned of specific purpose payments to the states and territories and their budgets were as follows: the National Action Plan for Salinity and Water Quality, $147

$2.26 billion of the $24.3 billion in Commonwealth specific purpose payments scheduled for that year. The ANAO applied the criteria described earlier in this chapter when deciding how many specific purpose programs and of what value it would audit in 2004–2005. Notwithstanding the Office's application of its own criteria, the number and value of specific purpose programs included in the annual work program were small.

The Auditor-General's audits of these programs focus on the roles and responsibilities of those Australian Government agencies that pay moneys. Generally, the Office's audits assess whether the relevant agency had sufficient information to confirm that its payments to other levels of government were used for the purposes intended, and that those purposes were achieved. A recent example is a performance audit of Commonwealth Government payments to state and territory governments for public hospitals.[21] These payments were almost $32 billion over the five years until 2003, making it the largest specific purpose program. The audit objective was to assess whether the Department of Health had performance information necessary to administer the Australian Government's agreements with state and territory governments. The audit opinion was that the Department had some, but not all, of the performance information it needed to adequately administer the very large sums the Australian Government provided to state and territory governments for public hospitals.

The auditors had access to financial and performance information available to the Australian Government agency that paid the states and territories and from which the information came. The ANAO did not have the legal authority to audit state and territory government agencies. Therefore, as in all the ANAO's audits of programs of this kind, the audit opinion was based on assumptions about the accuracy and completeness of state and territory data.

State and territory Auditors-General have the legal authority to audit local entities that receive Commonwealth specific purpose payments. From time to time, they audit these entities and report to their legislatures. The *Auditor-General Act 1997* provided the Commonwealth Auditor-General with the legal authority to conduct joint audits with state Auditors-General of Commonwealth and state activities. When introducing the legislation, the Minister for Finance stated that the Auditor-General must consider that it is in the Commonwealth's interests to use this legal authority.[22]

If state and territory audits coincided with ANAO audits, then taxpayers and residents in those localities were better informed about the uses of those

---

million; Commonwealth/State/Territory Disability Agreements, $570 million; Commonwealth road funding, $1.544b. ANAO (2004), *Audit Work Program 2004–2005.*

[21] ANAO (2002), *Performance Information in the Australian Health Care Agreements, Department of Health and Ageing*, Report No. 21 2002–2003, ANAO, Canberra.

[22] Parliament of the Commonwealth of Australia, House of Representatives (1996), *Auditor-General Bill 1996, Explanatory Memorandum*, S36–37, Attorney-General's Department, Canberra, <http://scaleplus.law.gov.au>

moneys and the soundness of their management. A review of reports tabled by national, state and territory Auditors-General found few examples of cooperation in audits of specific purpose payments to the states and territories. The only example of successful cooperation in performance audit planning and execution in the 1994–2004 period surveyed for this study was of an ANAO and a separate state Audit Office review of a federally funded urban development program.[23] The two performance audits were conducted under the separate federal and state audit legislation, and reported separately to the Australian Parliament and to the state legislature. When read together, the two audit reports provided a more comprehensive account of the relevant Australian Government program than was possible by reading either the ANAO or state Audit Office report.

In light of the large sums involved in Australian Government transfer payments to the states and territories, approaches to auditing these moneys were fragmented and incomplete. This was surprising given the potential benefits to all levels of administration from cooperation in planning, especially in light of the limited resources available for performance auditing and the importance of the services funded through these programs.

What does the ANAO communicate publicly to Parliament and the Government about its performance audit findings?

Each year, the ANAO reports against each theme to Parliament about what it has found in public administration. Parliamentary attention to this reporting will be discussed in the next chapter. The reports are brief and limited accounts of what was found by the several audits in the previous 12 months linked to each theme.[24] They can be contrasted with the US General Accountability Office, GAO, reporting to the US Congress against its themes. For instance, in mid-2004, the GAO reported publicly and extensively against several themes, including homeland security, airport security, terrorism, Operation Iraqi Freedom and its aftermath, the nation's growing fiscal imbalance, GAO's best practice work, major management challenges and program risks by agency, and outsourcing.[25] Most of this material summarised and drew together findings from a number of major audits. This approach simplified for Members of Congress, researchers and the public the task of understanding what GAO found.

Before commenting on the ANAO's reporting on its performance audit themes in more detail, it is obvious that there is a striking contrast between the

---

[23] Victorian Auditor-General's Office (1996), *Building Better Cities. A Joint Government Approach to Urban Development, Special Report No. 45, November 1996,* Victorian Government Printer, Melbourne; and ANAO (1996), *Building Better Cities. Department of Transport and Regional Development*, Report No. 9 1996–97, ANAO, Canberra.

[24] ANAO (2003), *Annual Report*, pp.18–21.

[25] GAO, <www.gao.gov>

ANAO's analyses of its financial statement and internal control findings and its analyses of performance audit findings. With the former, the ANAO publishes two omnibus or summary reports annually. The first is a comprehensive account of the major internal control weaknesses of government agencies.[26] This first report is published at the end of the financial year for which agencies prepared financial statements and for which the ANAO derives financial statement audit opinions. The internal controls report is a result of the ANAO's analyses of control strengths and weaknesses in government agencies. The timing of its publication – at the end of the financial year which is the focus of the hundreds of financial statement audits – gives its results an immediacy and, where these are serious, an urgency. It is too late for any Parliamentary action to remedy any serious issues for the financial year just ended. However, publication of the results so soon after the financial year is a focus for Parliamentary, governmental, public and media attention.

The ANAO's second omnibus or summary report is shortly after it completes its financial statement audits, and the Auditor-General has given his opinions on these. As with the internal controls report, there is an immediacy about this publication.[27] Similarly, it is too late for Parliament or the Government to require agencies with critical findings to improve their financial reporting for the year for which they had just prepared financial statements for audit. However, because of bipartisan Parliamentary acceptance of unqualified financial statement audit opinions as marks of sound management, the great majority of agencies are anxious to receive unqualified audit opinions and avoid Parliamentary and governmental attention.

In comparison with the United States General Accountability Office and with its own approach to drawing conclusions from its hundreds of financial statement audits, the ANAO has adopted a minimalist approach to communicating to Parliament and beyond the significance for the public sector as a whole of approximately 50 performance audit reports completed annually. There is a short mention in the Office's annual report, and a summary of the results of each individual performance audit published every six or twelve months. This summary repeats the audit opinions of each performance audit report tabled in the period beforehand. Each audit report is justified and clear on its findings and recommendations whatever the portfolio or issues it addresses. Also, since agencies are expected to respond to audit opinions and recommendations, individual audits can have substantial effects. An example of this was a review of the tendering process of four major information technology tenders, with the report

[26] The most recent report on internal controls was ANAO (2005), Report No. 56 2004–2005.
[27] The two reports for 2002–2003 were: ANAO (2003), *Control Structures as part of the Audit of Financial Statements of Major Commonwealth Entities for the Year Ending 30 June 2003,* Report No. 61 2002–2003; and *Audits of the Financial Statements of Australian Government Entities for the Period Ended 30 June 2003*, Report No. 22 2003–2004, ANAO, Canberra.

contributing to substantial change in the Government's approach to purchasing information technology services.[28]

However, other or additional patterns of public sector performance are detectable when findings of similar audits are re-analysed as sets of reviews. Examples of similar audits are agency purchasing of goods and services, payments, including grants, to other levels of government for services, reviews of performance information, agency use of information technology including the Internet, and audits of federal regulatory agencies. ANAO identification, from sets of similar audits, of patterns of findings about sound and unsound management and control would supplement the content of individual audit reports. This identification would communicate the condition of sector-wide management in these domains. It would also encourage the engagement of central agencies in addressing underlying issues across the public sector. Because this is not done, readers of individual audit reports are left to draw their own conclusions about national patterns of public administration. They can do this by reading various reports and series of reports. In practice, specialist public administration scholars and researchers are the most likely to read sets or series of performance audit reports in this way for underlying themes. By definition, there are very few of these specialists. The conclusion is that the gap – created by the ANAO's restricted analyses of its own findings for sets or series of performance audits – is not readily filled. This limited ANAO analysis reduces the potential impact of its work.

Conclusions

Performance auditing is a special case because of what the Australian model illustrates about the purposes of these audits and Audit Offices' communication of their results. We have seen that the majority of Audit Offices accept the Australian Accounting Research Foundation's definition of performance auditing in Australian Auditing Standards, but with some adjustments or changes to reflect work and priorities of their jurisdictions. Three state or territory Audit Offices applied a narrower definition of performance auditing than suggested by Australian Auditing Standards. The majority of state and territory Audit Offices and the ANAO defined performance audit at least as generously as the Australian Accounting Research Foundation's Australian Auditing Standards. In particular, the ANAO and two state Audit Offices extended the Standards' definition. All Audit Offices implemented performance auditing to avoid commenting on whether government initiatives succeeded or failed. In other words, Auditors-General interpreted their legislation as barring commentaries on the success or failure of programs. Notwithstanding, some Offices asked whether agencies had the

[28] ANAO (2000), *Implementation of Whole-of-Government Information Technology Infrastructure Consolidation and Outsourcing Initiative. Cross Agency*, Report No. 9 2000–2001, ANAO, Canberra.

information necessary to determine whether programs achieved what they were required to do. Overall, partly at least because of legislative barriers, Auditors-General baulked at using performance audits to evaluate programs, or were using them cautiously to move in the direction of program evaluations. Therefore, in general, performance audits were used to assess the efficiency and economy of agencies' operations, but not their effectiveness. There was no independent agency at any level of Australian government that evaluated the success or failure of government programs. This pointed to a significant gap in the completeness of information available to Parliament and taxpayers about the performance of government agencies.

In the Australian model of public sector auditing, the ANAO considered several factors in annual audit planning. One of these factors was financial materiality, or the amount of money involved in a program's expenditure or revenue. The importance of other factors in annual planning resulted in some portfolios with large expenditures and revenue receiving proportionately less audits than smaller portfolios. In annual planning, there was an unclear and unarticulated relationship between the themes behind the selection of topics and other selection criteria.

There was limited cooperation between Audit Offices in the conduct and reporting of audits. In other words, there was very limited ANAO use of the legal authority to conduct joint audits with state and territory Auditors-General of activities funded by the Australian Government. A consequence was that Parliamentarians and government officials had only partial views of the administration of payments provided by the Australian Government to state, territory and local governments for specific purposes such as health, education, housing and transport. While acknowledging potential problems in cooperation between independent Audit Offices, a result was that incomplete national pictures were available of the management of programs with national objectives.

The ANAO gave more emphasis to communicating in a consolidated and comprehensive way the findings of its financial statement audits than it did to communicating the results of its large number of performance audits. That was because the major findings of large numbers of internal control and financial statement audits were identified and communicated in two principal reports released at the most fitting times. In contrast, the ANAO had not committed the same resources to identifying the major findings of performance audits each year for the Australian government sector as a whole and to communicating those to Parliament and the public. Therefore, Parliamentary, administrator, media and public use of performance audit reports was more problematic than use of results of financial statement audits.

Finally, at the national level, legislation required the Auditor-General to conduct financial statement audits, while the conduct of performance audits was optional. This balance of requirements suggested that Parliament and Government were more at ease with financial statement than with performance audits. It also hinted that Parliament doubted the strength of the contribution that performance audits made to improving the efficiency, economy, effectiveness and accountability of government operations, and it pointed to government caution on the use of performance audits.

Chapter 6

What Happens to Audit Opinions?

This chapter examines the fate of financial statement and performance audit opinions. Although federal law is silent on the purposes of audit, we have seen how the ANAO affirmed that it audits to provide an assurance to Parliament about good management in agencies, and to contribute to improving management where necessary. To achieve either or both of these goals requires an interested and informed readership of audit opinions. The readership of primary importance is Parliament since this is the Office's primary client. Clearly though as well, agency management is important.

This chapter describes agencies' and Parliament's responses to audit opinions. Responses are addressed in this order since Parliament is partly reliant on agencies' reactions.

How do agencies and the Parliament respond to ANAO financial statement audit opinions?

Agencies' responses

In financial statement audits, draft findings about internal controls are communicated to agency management towards the end of audits. Those findings can contain recommendations for action. The process of financial statement auditing necessitates agency management responding in writing to these draft findings and recommendations. Management is not required to agree with draft findings and recommendations, but it is expected to respond to them. Communication between the auditor and auditee resolves whether draft findings are upheld or changed. At this stage, the auditee may provide further information or perspectives that influence them, knowing that the auditor will include an opinion on the financial statements in the auditee's annual report. Since the opinion will be about whether the auditor agrees with senior management's affirmation of the truth and fairness of the statements, agreement is in management's interests. Therefore, prior to the audit's commencement, there is a strong reason for management to ensure the adequacy of internal controls and financial reporting.

These factors increase the likelihood of management taking action on any deficiencies found by the financial statement auditor before, during, and after the audit's completion. Yet the relationship between the auditor and auditee is insufficient to avoid internal controls and reporting problems continuing and reappearing. ANAO's analyses of significant findings on major entities have demonstrated this. The analyses, which are included in the annual report on internal controls tabled at the end of each financial year, compare numbers of significant findings with those in the previous year.[1] The analyses show much consistency of internal control weaknesses from year to year for the government sector as a whole. The process described here contributes to agencies focusing on draft and final financial statement audit opinions, and addressing issues that arise from them.

Parliamentary responses

The ANAO rates financial control weaknesses into three groups. The most important includes those matters that pose significant business or financial risks to the entity and which must be addressed as matters of urgency. With the 2003–2004 accounts, there were two agencies in this group with severe findings; these were the Department of Defence and the Australian Taxation Office.[2] The next group of control weaknesses included any which posed moderate or financial risks to the entity or matters referred to management in the past which were not addressed satisfactorily. Twenty-one of the 24 agencies that the ANAO included in the report on 2003–2004 internal controls had moderate control weaknesses.

The annual reports of all Australian Government entities are tabled in Parliament. Since these contain entities' financial statements and the Auditor-General's opinions, all Members of Parliament and Senators have the opportunity to comment on them. In the 2003–2004 financial year, there were 35 questions asked in Parliament about ANAO reports,[3] with only one about a financial statement audit.[4] Members and Senators referred to ANAO audits in debates on 19 bills.[5] There were no debates in either House of Parliament about matters raised by the ANAO in its audits of agencies' financial statements. There was more interest shown in Parliamentary committees.

The House of Representatives has committees for every portfolio. A committee task is to review the annual reports of portfolio agencies which contain financial statements and the auditor's opinions on them. Few committees reported

---

1 ANAO (2004), Report No.58, p.226.

2 ANAO (2004), Report No.58, pp.96–97, 226.

3 Department of Parliamentary Services (2004), *Parlinfo Web*, <http://paralinfoweb.aph.gov.au>

4 Department of Parliamentary Services (2003), *Hansard, House of Representatives*, 7 October 2003, p. 20729.

5 There were references to ANAO audits in debates on seven bills in the House of Representatives, and references in debates on 16 bills in the Senate. Taking account of those bills debated in both Chambers, ANAO work was mentioned in debates on 19 bills or sets of bills. Department of Parliamentary Services (2004), *Parlinfo Web*.

on this task. Consistent with its interest in earlier years,[6] the Joint Committee on Foreign Affairs, Defence and Trade was one committee that reviewed the annual report of a relevant portfolio agency, which was the Department of Defence.[7] The Committee referred to the ANAO's performance audits. Notwithstanding the auditor's heavily qualified opinion on the financial statements in successive years, the Committee did not comment on them in its 2003 review of the Department's annual report for 2001–2002.[8] In general, then, House of Representatives and joint committees were not reviewing and commenting on financial statement and related issues.

The Senate has references committees to consider each portfolio's budget estimates. The latter include draft financial statements for all agencies seeking a budget. References committees do not focus on those statements, and they do not customarily pursue the previous year's audit findings. Therefore, overall, neither of the two main sets of Parliamentary committees with the mandate to address financial statement issues does so in any significant way.

As explained earlier, the Joint Committee of Public Accounts and Audit is the ANAO's first point of contact with Parliament. All ANAO reports are considered for review by the JCPAA. Since 2000, the JCPAA has conducted two inquiries into matters reported by the Auditor-General in the nine six-monthly reports tabled summarising the results of the hundreds of financial statement audits.[9] There were no reviews by this Committee into seven of these omnibus

---

6 In the period reviewed, the Joint Committee on Foreign Affairs, Defence and Trade stated that:

'On 28 August 2000, a decision was made by the Joint Standing Committee to examine a range of issues arising out of the Annual Reports of the Department of Defence. Among these was a specific reference to the conduct of military justice.'

The Committee's work led to an 11 April 2001 report, *Completed Inquiry: Rough Justice? An Investigation into Allegations of Brutality in the Army's Parachute Battalion.* Again in recent times, the Committee's first review of a Department of Defence annual report was on 8 May 2002; Parliament of the Commonwealth of Australia (8 May 2002), *Official Committee Hansard. Joint Standing Committee on Foreign Affairs, Defence and Trade, (Defence Subcommittee). Reference: Review of Defence Report 2000–2001.*

Results of two other inquiries of the Committee into the Department of Defence's annual reports were; *Review of the Defence Annual Report 2001–2002*, 13 October 2003; and *Review of the Defence Annual Report 2002–2003*, 11 August 2004. None of these Committee reports addressed the Department of Defence's accounts in the manner described in this chapter.

7 Joint committees have Members and Senators as representatives from both Houses of Parliament.

8 Joint Standing Committee on Foreign Affairs, Defence and Trade (2003), *Review of the Defence Annual Report 2001–2002*, Parliament of the Commonwealth of Australia, Canberra,
<http://www.aph.gov.au/house/committee/jfadt/defence_report2001-2002/report.htm>

9 The first ANAO major report on financial statement audits reviewed by the Joint Committee in recent years was a review of the ANAO's report on control structures for the

reports on financial statement audits. When the Committee did review financial statement audit opinions of government agencies, it was often critical.[10] A surprise was how the Committee conducted more reviews of performance audit reports, which audits are optional under audit law, than reviews of financial statement audits, which are mandatory for the Auditor-General. That is, from 2000, the Joint Committee of Public Accounts and Audit spent more time reviewing the results of performance audits than it assigned to financial statement and control audits to review public accounts. However, the Committee has used other means to attend to the public accounts. For instance, it reported on proposed changes to financial framework legislation, and it published a separate report on accrual budget documentation.[11]

There has been little analysis and commentary on Parliamentarians' low level of interest in financial statements and related audit opinions. Amongst the possible reasons for this is that it is not necessary for committees to address financial statement and internal control weaknesses since most agencies comply with reporting requirements. This view is valid since for 2002–2003, the Auditor-General qualified only four financial statement reports.[12] However, since 21 of the 24 agencies had moderate controls weaknesses in 2003–2004, there were opportunities for committees to inquire into and report on the adequacy of those agencies' actions to improve their financial management.

A second reason for low levels of Parliamentary interest in financial statements and related audit opinions was that few Parliamentarians are

---

period ending 30 June 1999, and included in the ANAO's Report No. 10 of 1999–2000. The Joint Committee reported on it in Joint Committee of Public Accounts and Audit (2000), *Review of Auditor-General's Reports 1999–2000, Report 376.* The second ANAO major report on financial statement audits that the Joint Committee reviewed in recent times was the ANAO's report on the financial statements of Commonwealth entities for 2001–2002, Report No.25 of 2002–2003. The Joint Committee reported on it in Joint Committee of Public Accounts and Audit (2003), *Review of Auditor-General's Reports 2002–2003: First, Second and Third Quarters, Report 396*, Parliament of the Commonwealth of Australia, Canberra.

[10] An example was the Committee's criticism of the Department of Defence in Joint Committee of Public Accounts and Audit (2003), *Report 396*, p. 73. The Committee noted:

> 'that Defence assets and operating expenses constitute a substantial part of the Commonwealth's assets and outlays. Ongoing problems with Defence's ability to account for its assets is of concern to the Committee. While reported fraud is said to be statistically low, continued poor accounting and controls provides the opportunity for fraud to occur and remain undetected.'

[11] Joint Committee of Public Accounts and Audit (August 2003), *Report 395. Inquiry into the Draft Financial Framework Legislation Amendment Bill*, Parliament of the Commonwealth of Australia, Canberra; Joint Committee of Public Accounts and Audit (June 2002), *Report 388. Review of the Accrual Budget Documentation*, Parliament of the Commonwealth of Australia, Canberra.

[12] ANAO (2003), Report No.22 2003–2004, p.36.

accountants, and the latter are more likely to understand a set of financial statements than other persons. In the 2004 Parliament, two of the 226 Members and Senators were accountants.[13] Therefore, there is validity in this explanation. Since the percentage of Parliamentarians who are accountants is unlikely to increase significantly, there is little prospect of more Parliamentary interest in the foreseeable future if attention to financial statements, controls and reports is left only to elected accountants. Assuming that all Parliamentarians are interested in sound financial reporting and control of the $385.5 billion of government expenditure and revenue, potentially there are Parliamentarians who are not accountants and who are interested in the results of these audits.

How do agencies and the Parliament respond to ANAO performance audit opinions?

Agencies' responses

Agencies are informed of the results of performance audits when the ANAO provides provisional opinions and draft recommendations for comment. These are discussed, the auditee provides written responses to the ANAO, and the Auditor-General finalises the audit opinion and any recommendations in reports tabled in Parliament. Agencies are expected to indicate in the reports whether they agree or disagree with audit opinions and recommendations. There is no requirement of agency management to agree to either. When they agree with an ANAO's recommendation, they are expected to state how and when they will implement it. Where they disagree, they are expected to give the reasons why.

Each chief executive officer is required to manage the agency in an efficient, ethical, economical and effective manner.[14] Therefore, where the performance audit's findings are consistent with the chief executive officer's assessments, the agency is likely to address any administrative difficulties found during the audit. Conversely, circumstances for implementation of recommendations are less favourable when the chief executive officer and the auditor disagree on the existence of administrative problems and when they disagree on solutions. In order to present a reasonable public image, it would be tempting for chief executive officers in disagreement with the auditor's analysis to minimise public airing of the disagreement. Subsequently, after the audit report's tabling, the chief executive officer's attention can turn elsewhere. A less critical explanation of why audit recommendations are not implemented or are

---

[13] One Member and one Senator identified accountancy as their previous occupation prior to election to Parliament. Parliament of the Commonwealth of Australia, Parliamentary Library (2004), *Parliamentary Handbook of the Commonwealth of Australia,* <http://www.aph.gov.au/library/handbook/index.htm>

[14] *Financial Management and Accountability Act 1997*, S44.

implemented slowly or partially is in new or altered government priorities or policies that take senior management attention away from issues uncovered in the audit.

From time to time, the ANAO revisits the site of earlier work and conducts later audits, called follow-up audits. Because these report to Parliament on agency implementation of recommendations of the earlier audits, they are further opportunities for Parliamentarians to address performance audit issues.

Performance audit reports are provided to relevant Ministers by the ANAO. Therefore, if they are interested in the topic, Ministers can inquire of their senior management about matters raised in audit reports. Frequently, Ministers view administrative issues as the province of administrative and managerial staff, and neither express interest nor become involved. They are likely to address administrative issues if matters raised in audit reports receive Parliamentary, media or public attention. Beyond the Minister responsible for each agency, there is no mechanism in the Australian model that involves government attention to performance audit findings.

However, there is a mechanism at the Parliamentary level. That is because the Government must prepare a written response to any Joint Committee of Public Accounts and Audit report on matters raised in the Auditor-General's reports. Government responses are often confined to responding to the Committee's recommendations. Similar to interaction with individual agencies, there is no requirement of Government to agree with the Committee's analyses and conclusions in responses to the Committee's reports.

Parliamentary attention

Since each performance audit report is about a separate topic, their public release to Parliamentarians has the potential to focus attention. This section explores the degree of attention received by performance audit reports.

As explained in an earlier chapter, legislation requires all ANAO performance audit reports to be tabled in both Houses of Parliament.[15] The Joint Committee of Public Accounts and Audit is the first to consider ANAO reports once tabled, deciding into which ANAO performance audit reports tabled in the previous three months it should inquire. In 2002–2003, the Committee conducted hearings into 11 of the 63 reports tabled in that year.[16] In addition, the Committee reported the results of its inquiry into issues raised by an ANAO report from the previous year, and it commenced an inquiry into matters raised by another ANAO report from the previous year. The Committee's reviews and inquiries involve the agencies in the ANAO's audits, with their representatives invited to attend Committee hearings and to respond to its queries. Overall, the Audit Committee

---

[15] *Auditor-General Act 1997*, S15.

[16] ANAO (2003), *Annual Report 2002–2003*, pp.30–32.

devotes much of its time and resources to reviewing administrative matters which the ANAO identifies.

In 2002–2003, a Senate committee inquired into matters raised by the ANAO in another of its reports from that year. This resulted in 12 of the 63 reports tabled in 2002–2003 being the subject of committee inquiries: 11 were inquiries of one committee, and another committee reviewed one report. From time to time, the ANAO also conducts audits at the request of Parliament. For instance, the ANAO reported that during 2002–2003, it commenced an audit at the request of a Parliamentary committee, and it tabled two reports requested in earlier years by either a committee or a Minister. In the same year, the ANAO briefed two other committees and a Minister.[17]

In 2004, there were 18 House of Representatives, 19 Senate and 12 joint committees or a total of 49 Parliamentary committees.[18] Not all of these were relevant to public administration issues addressed by the ANAO, with some, for instance, concerned only with the workings of Parliament. Two House Committees referred to ANAO work in 2003–2004.[19] The great majority of committees did not review ANAO work in that year. An example is the House of Representatives Family and Community Affairs Committee, whose terms of reference enabled it to review the work of portfolios with a combined budget of $108 billion, which was most of the Government's budget appropriations in 2004–2005. The Committee did not review any ANAO financial statement or performance audit report tabled between 2000 and 2004.[20]

Six Joint Committees, with representatives from both Houses, and 26 Senate Committees referred to or used ANAO work in 2003–2004.[21]

Notwithstanding these references, the ANAO's service to Parliament is concentrated on the Audit Committee of Parliament, with irregular or no contact with the majority of committees.

---

[17] ANAO (2003), *Annual Report 2002–2003*, pp.32–33.

[18] Parliament of the Commonwealth of Australia (2004), *Committees*, <http://www.aph.gov.au/committee/committees_type.htm>

[19] These were the Standing Committee on Economics, Finance and Public Administration, and the Standing Committee on Transport and Regional Services. Department of Parliamentary Services (2004), *Parlinfo Web.*

[20] Parliament of the Commonwealth of Australia, House of Representatives (2004), *Standing Committee on Family and Community Affairs*, <http://www.aph.gov.au/house/committee/fca/reports.htm>

[21] Of interest was that ANAO audits were referred to by nine Senate references committees, 13 Senate estimates committees dealing with budgetary matters, and four Senate legislation committees. Further research is necessary on the extent of Parliamentary committee use of ANAO opinions and recommendations. Such information would assist in construction of a longitudinal database to identify trends in Parliamentary usage of ANAO audits. Department of Parliamentary Services (2004), *Parlinfo Web.*

There is no research data to explain why the majority of House of Representatives committees show limited interest in what the ANAO finds in performance audits. Some speculation is warranted such as:

- members of most committees believed that the existence of the Audit Office was sufficient to ensure sound agency management;
- members did not consider that it was a committee role to inquire into unsound management identified in performance audits;
- members believed that it was the Audit Committee's task to inquire into administrative and control matters, and not the duty of their committee;
- members were uninformed and lacked understanding of the public sector, for instance, in appreciating the two-way relationship between policy and administration;
- committees had higher priorities. For instance, they focused on policy development rather than policy administration;
- committees were unaware of the majority of reports relevant to their committee work. The ANAO's practices of not issuing media releases and little direct contact with the media may result in other material, documentation and issues receiving greater committee attention. Audit Offices in the United Kingdom, Canada and New Zealand issue news and media releases about their work and reports.[22] A comparative study would be necessary to determine the effects of these media releases on Parliamentary interest in audit opinions;
- committees had insufficient resources; and
- committees' business models favoured long-running inquiries not shorter reviews of audit reports with ANAO and agency representatives.

The data quoted here on committee use of ANAO audits can be interpreted in two ways. The first interpretation is that the ANAO's selection of performance audit topics is accurate and consistent with committees' views – which is why House of Representatives committees find little reason to comment or show interest in audits, compared to the greater interest shown by Senate committees. In other words, committee inattention is a vote of confidence in the public sector auditor, with interest likely to rise only if there is a most serious set of audit findings or if there is some mismanagement of the Audit Office itself. The second interpretation is how the committees' minimal interest reflects unformed and unarticulated views that the Audit Office's selection of topics and results does not help members in their work.

[22] <http://www.nao.org.uk> Press Notices; <http://www.oag-bvg.gc.ca> Media Room; <http://www.oag.govt.nz> Latest News.

What are the implications of limited levels of Parliamentary interest in audit opinions?

A first implication is that it is easier for the ANAO to confirm that it provides an assurance to Parliament about sound management than it is for the ANAO to confirm that it is contributing to improving public administration. This conclusion can be drawn because, in the absence of research into Parliamentary understanding of audit opinions and with little criticism of the Audit Office, it can be assumed that limited Parliamentary interest outside the committee specialising in audit matters is because Parliamentarians read audit opinions mostly as providing assurances. Therefore, no Parliamentary responses are necessary. The caveat is that, from time to time, all Parliamentarians receive complaints from constituents about the delivery of government services. Therefore, limited Parliamentary interest in audits that identify major administrative failings is inconsistent with other responses of Parliamentarians to their constituents.

It is probable that strong Parliamentary interest and responses to audit opinions, such as through Parliamentary questions and committee inquiries, is more likely to increase the pressure on government agencies to reform than when there is no Parliamentary interest. Therefore, while acknowledging measurement difficulties associated with determining whether audit opinions contribute to improved public administration, the limited Parliamentary use of audit opinions is a concern. That is because it flags a less favourable environment for public sector reform than otherwise.

What then does the Audit Office do to determine whether it contributes to improved public administration? Its annual report stated that improving public administration was a responsibility shared by all government organisations, making it difficult to measure precisely the ANAO's contribution. In 2003–2004, the contribution to improved public administration was largely gauged by the impact on Parliament and agencies being audited.[23] Its impact on Parliament was assessed as reviews by the Joint Committee of Public Accounts and Audit, audits arising from a Parliamentary request, other work at the request of Parliament, such as a review of an audit report by another committee, two briefings of other committees on two audits and a briefing of a Minister. Contributions to public sector entities were measured by entities' acceptance and implementation of audit recommendations, entities' acceptance of a high proportion of recommendations, independently conducted surveys of management in recently audited agencies, and identification of potential financial benefits of performance audits. There were surveys of individual Members and Senators to gauge their knowledge of ANAO, but little information was available on the success of measures to promote the Audit Office's work to committees. The ANAO did not identify which of its reports and opinions were used in Parliamentary debates, nor patterns in their use by each House of Parliament.

[23] ANAO (2003), *Annual Report 2002–2003*, p.29.

There was no indication of whether the level of Parliamentary usage of financial and performance audit opinions was considered sufficient in light of the matters raised in audits, or whether it was insufficient in view of reappearance of similar audit findings from year to year. Rather, the Audit Office adopted a neutral stance towards Parliamentary interest in audit findings about public sector management. A neutral position on this matter was logical in light of the Auditor-General's independence from Parliament. An alternative view was that to increase the effect of regularity and performance audits on the speed and direction of public sector reform required more Parliamentary committees to address matters raised in audit reports. An effect of this alternative view would be adoption of measures to increase committee attention and use of audit reports.

These means could include encouragement of House of Representatives committees to note internal control weaknesses in agencies for which they had responsibility, annual consultation with committees about which topics were most relevant to committees' work, developing strong relationships with committees for the largest portfolios or portfolio agencies and with committees addressing matters in agencies with notable management problems, advising on the conduct of inquiries into matters raised in audit reports, and staff secondments where committees wished to address audit concerns but had inadequate resources. The terms of reference for some committees were more favourable than others in attending to public sector reform, with such committees being clearer foci for ANAO communication. Form, content and presentation of audit reports also affected the size and composition of any readership. Therefore, an objective of increasing Parliamentary attention to audit matters would involve fresh looks at audit publications. These means to increase committee attention would need a realistic appreciation of the large number of matters that Parliamentary committees addressed, resulting in attention to audit matters remaining a concern of a minority of members. However, an ANAO goal of a modest increase in the attention of committee members to audit opinions would strengthen conditions for public sector reform.[24]

Of relevance is the approach taken by the Office of the Auditor-General of Canada. The Office adopted an indicator of Parliamentary committee engagement in hearings on briefings on issues the Office reported. It reported that

---

[24] As a State Auditor-General has cautioned, realism about increased Parliamentary and other interest in financial statements is essential. The Tasmanian Auditor-General stated that:

> 'It would be idealistic to assume that annual reports and their financial statements are ever going to achieve a mass readership. But as in the stock market where it only takes a handful of analysts to influence prices, so too advances in public administration can come from only a relatively few interested readers who have access to timely and relevant information. Those involved in the process of preparing the annual reports should bear this in mind and eschew cynicism.'

Parliament of Tasmania (2003), p.2.

54 per cent of Parliamentarians indicated that they were knowledgeable about the actual findings and recommendations of the Office. In 2002–2003, Audit Office staff participated in 52 Parliamentary committee hearings and briefings. The Office of the Auditor-General of Canada had targets for Parliamentary use of the Office's reports, and it reported trend data. For instance, it reported its expectation that about 60 per cent of 2002–2003 value-for-money audits would be the subject of Parliamentary committee hearings, with only 41 per cent of reports actually being reviewed by a Committee. The Office also explained why its target was not achieved.[25]

The Parliamentary context for attention to audit

The Australian public sector changed markedly from 1994. Some changes stimulated Parliamentary interest in public sector reform, and others placed some obstacles before it. These changes were subjects of public sector audit, and the environment within which Parliament and the Government reflected on audit opinions. Changes included:[26]

- a more diverse public sector; for instance, in greater reliance on the private sector to deliver services, increased contracting of government services to the private sector, and blurring of boundaries and differences between the two sectors;
- increased complexity of government; for instance, government regulation of more activities and industries, as was evident by new approaches to regulation of gene technology and aged care;
- rapid organisational change;
- greater responsibility of chief executive officers for management and related affairs of their agencies, alongside greater use of limited tenure contracts for their employment and for employment of other senior management; and
- introduction of new financial management and reporting requirements of agencies. These included accrual budgeting and reporting, and reliance on agencies' communicating their roles as achievement of outputs and outcomes. Introduction of requirements of agencies to specify their outputs and outcomes coincided with the Government ending requirements for program evaluation, with very few evaluations published.

---

[25] Office of the Auditor-General of Canada (2003).

[26] Two addresses that canvassed these changes were: Shergold, Peter (23 June 2004), *Once was Camelot in Canberra? Reflections on Public Service Leadership*, Sir Roland Wilson Lecture 2004, Canberra; and Shergold, Peter (3 July 2003), *Administrative Law and Public Service,* Australian Institute of Administrative Law Opening Address, <www.pmc.gov.au>

The effects of these changes on Parliamentary committees have included:[27]

- drawing attention to the difficulty of tracking budget appropriations due, first, to agencies' reliance on outputs and outcomes statements that changed and reduced agency reporting on their programs, and, second, to the high level of aggregation of financial data in outputs and outcomes statements, complicating understanding of how agencies used their budgets;
- limited committee capacity to review the implementation and success of government services contracted to private sector firms. Despite large increases in government purchases from private firms over the last decade, there were very few examples of committees inviting company principals or personnel to appear before them when reviewing government operations.

It is contentious whether the above changes in public administration and their effects on committees strengthened or diminished committees' ability to understand agencies' use of public finance and to hold agencies accountable for their expenditures. Any discussion of what happens to audit opinions on public administration and public finance, and about whether the ANAO can determine by how much it has improved public administration, must take account of the contentious nature of this other information on public finance and administration used by Parliamentary committees.

Conclusions

This chapter has shown how government agencies treat financial statement and performance audit opinions seriously. Their treatment is motivated by a shared belief in better administration, and by the deterrent role of audit opinions tabled publicly in Parliament.

There was one Parliamentary question about ANAO financial statement audits in 2003–2004. There was more attention in both Houses to performance audits, with Parliamentarians referring to these in debates on 19 bills or draft legislation. The main mechanism for Parliamentary consideration of ANAO reports is the committee system. The Joint Committee of Public Accounts and Audit

---

[27] Examples of Parliamentary committee perspectives on budget information include the following reports: Parliament of the Commonwealth of Australia, Senate Finance and Public Administration Legislation Committee (2000), *The Format of the Portfolio Budget Statements. Third Report*, Canberra, November 2000; and Parliament of the Commonwealth of Australia, Joint Committee of Public Accounts and Audit (2002), *Report 388. Review of the Accrual Budget Documentation*, Canberra, June 2002. <www.aph.gov.au>

concentrated on addressing matters raised in audit opinions and reports. It did so by conducting brief and longer inquiries, depending on the topic. The Joint Committee gave more time to performance audit opinions than to financial statement opinions on the public accounts. Other committees gave almost no attention to financial statement audit opinions, but focused on performance audit opinions. Senate and joint committees used ANAO audit opinions significantly more than House committees, most of which did not use ANAO work.

The ANAO did not have comprehensive longitudinal measures of Parliamentary use of its work, with the few data that the ANAO reported on those measures informing audit planning modestly. The ANAO had regular contact with the Joint Committee of Public Accounts and Audit, and irregular or no contact with the majority of other committees. Therefore in practice, the legislative definition of the public sector auditor's principal client was the Audit Committee of Parliament. This was logical, expected and consistent with public sector law. However, the latter did not bar liaison and work with other parts of the Parliament. An effect of irregular or no contact with other committees was that their authority was little used to reinforce the content of audit opinions.

The ANAO rarely issued media releases. There were no research data on the effects of this practice on Parliamentarians' knowledge and awareness of ANAO audit opinions and work. There were different views on whether changes to the public sector in the last decade increased the capacity of Parliamentary committees to hold the Government to account. ANAO service to the Parliament and its committees must be interpreted against these different views.

Chapter 7

The Australian Model of Public Sector Audit Summarised

As stated at the beginning, this introduction to the Australian model of public sector auditing focused on characteristics potentially relevant to legislators and public sector auditors in developing countries with emerging markets. These characteristics are summarised below.

New law

The Office of the Auditor-General was established in 1901, the year Australia became independent from Great Britain. The Audit Act of that year was the fourth Act of the first Australian Parliament. Therefore, an obvious characteristic of the Australian model is early and continuous legislative recognition of the importance of the public sector auditor. For most of the Audit Office's first century, there was a consistency about the Auditor-General's role and relationship with Government and the Parliament. Consistency was because of the Audit Office's exclusive engagement with regularity audits. The Auditor-General's role evolved slowly with new approaches to accounting, financial reporting and auditing. A significant change occurred in 1979 with the *Audit Act 1901* amended to permit efficiency audits.[1] From then, there was Parliamentary and governmental legislative recognition that it was insufficient for public sector managers to comply with laws affecting their agencies. It was necessary as well that they manage public resources efficiently.

Parliamentary concern at disagreement between the Auditor-General and the Department of Finance on the adequacy of audit resources led to a Parliamentary inquiry into the Office of the Auditor-General. Concern was because the Department of Finance was both one of the most important agencies that the Auditor-General examined, and an important advisor to the Government on resources the Auditor-General should receive. In 1989, the Joint Committee of Public Accounts released the results of its inquiry. It reported that there was uncertainty about whether the Auditor-General was an officer of the Parliament or a servant of the executive. It also found that procedures for settling the Auditor-

[1] Parliament of the Commonwealth of Australia (1989), *Audit Act 1901*, Attorney-General's Department, Canberra, S48A.

General's resources were flawed. That was because the executive, which was the auditee, determined the level of resources it would make available to the Auditor-General to audit it. The Committee found other major anomalies and inconsistencies, of which one of the most notable was that both Parliament and the executive had neglected the critical role of the Auditor-General in maintaining modern and successful public administration. Accordingly, the Committee recommended repeal of the audit legislation and introduction of new financial management and audit laws. It also concluded that the Auditor-General was independent of both the Parliament and the Government, and that his principal role was to serve Parliament rather than the Government. Therefore, it recommended that new law make him an officer of the Parliament. To emphasise the importance of this role, the Committee also recommended that Parliament establish an Audit Committee to be the principal means to communicate with the Auditor-General. The Committee made a large number of other recommendations to the Parliament, the Government and the Auditor-General to refresh and modernise the Office of the Auditor-General. The majority of these recommendations were accepted. Perhaps the most important was new audit legislation introduced in 1997, which made the most significant and extensive reforms of the Office of the Auditor-General in almost a century. In addition, the new financial management and accountability legislation – introduced simultaneously with the new audit legislation and also as a result of the Joint Committee's work – were amongst the most significant reforms of the Australian Government sector. Their introduction showed the importance of reform of both audit and administrative law. This theme is discussed further in Part II of this book.

The Australian model of public sector audit was characterised by stability and slow evolution of the role of the auditor. Then, after 96 years, there was rapid change, with general acceptance that the Auditor-General's principal task was to serve Parliament but in an independent way. Changes in the wider public sector occurred at the same time as changes in the Audit Office.

What does the Auditor-General do?

The *Auditor-General Act 1997* gave the Auditor-General the authority to conduct financial statement and performance audits, and to determine audit standards for the Office. In the mid-1990s, the Australian Government introduced the requirement that agencies should prepare financial statements for audit. The form and content of these statements were modelled on those in the private sector. The Auditor-General's previous interpretation of regularity audits as compliance reviews developed into interpretations of regularity work as financial statement audits. Most of the Auditor-General's resources were used on financial statement audits.

Efficiency audits that were introduced in 1979 broadened to become performance audits. These were defined in the 1997 legislation as reviews or examinations of any aspects of the operations of a person or body. This generous definition increased the capacity of ANAO to inquire and report on matters the Auditor-General considered of interest and benefit to the Commonwealth. Responding to the opportunities created by the new definition of performance audits, the Office increased the proportion of its expenditure on performance audits from a few percentage points to 37 per cent in 2004–2005.

The law did not define the purposes of public sector audit. In the absence of a legislated purpose, the Audit Office defined its preferred outcomes as independent assurance to Parliament on public sector reporting, administration, control and accountability; and improvement in public administration. The Audit Committee accepted these non-legislated purposes of public sector audit. The absence of legally defined purposes of audit made more difficult the Audit Committee's and Parliament's task of assessing the impact of financial statement and performance audits. That was because, although the legislation led to an assessment of the Office's performance against compliance with auditing standards determined by the Auditor-General, it did not require an answer to the question of whether auditing improves public administration. Were the Audit Committee of Parliament to attempt to determine whether the Audit Office improved public administration, the Committee would need to establish its own definition of improvements. The Audit Committee moved in this direction through its commission of an Independent Auditor to assess whether the Audit Office's performance audits give value-for-money to the Parliament. In 2004, the Independent Auditor reported to the Committee and to Parliament that the Audit Office's performance audits did do so.[2]

---

2 The Independent Auditor concluded as follows:

> 'My review indicates that the ANAO's over riding objective through the conduct of a performance audit is to endeavour at all times to improve public administration and accountability. The (Office) seeks to achieve this in a cooperative fashion with the bodies being audited and welcomes suggestions and comments at any time. The ANAO facilitates this interaction through regular meetings during audits, post-audit surveys for a significant cross-section of performance audits undertaken and consultation on audit programs.
>
> The question of whether the ANAO provides "value for money" is a circuitous one. The Auditor-General is independent and must make his own assessment of whatever work he considers it necessary to undertake. However, he does seek counsel from the JCPAA in the determination of the audit program for performance audits. The JCPAA in turn takes a lead role in co-ordinating parliamentary input into the program. Therefore, although it is the Auditor-General who makes the final decisions, the JCPAA has input into the program and is in a position to express its views about whether the services being delivered by the ANAO are appropriate and constitute "value for money".
>
> My observation is that the ANAO does provide "value for money" when assessed against these criteria. However, the way that services are currently being delivered is not necessarily the only way that "value for money" can be achieved

Audit standards

Legislation gave the Auditor-General the authority to determine audit standards for the public sector. In practice, this has meant applying standards devised primarily for the private sector without change.

There were no differences in the application of those standards from their use in the private sector. However, there were significant differences between what the law required the public sector auditor and the private sector auditor to report. Those differences were to table in Parliament for government departments and similar entities the results of, first, performance audits, and, second, the results of audits of key financial systems and controls. These two reporting requirements resulted in managerial accountability in parts of the Australian public sector being stronger than in the private sector. Unlike in Australia, corporate law reform in the United States in light of a number of major business failures required company auditors to provide their opinions to shareholders on the adequacy of companies' internal controls. In that way, these new requirements of company auditors in the United States were closer to current public sector audit law in Australia for government departments and similar entities than they were to requirements of company auditors under Australian corporate law, even after recent corporate law reforms in Australia.

Assessments of internal control matters in companies solely or majority owned by the Australian Government were provided to Parliament until new law in 1997. From then, Ministers but not Parliamentarians were informed of the content of internal control reports on government companies. Advocates of this new

---

and indeed the JCPAA is in a position to question and challenge the delivery as it sees fit. For example, over recent years, most performance audits have been performed by teams of two or three people, commonly over a period of eleven months. An alternative approach might be to amend the annual audit program so that in addition to these small scale performance audits, the Auditor-General might undertake a small number of larger projects focused on issues of major concern.

There currently is a framework for dialogue between the Auditor-General and the JCPAA. Recommendations 1 and 5 of my report suggest that the JCPAA might consider providing the Auditor-General with more specific guidance about what it considers to be the major themes facing the Parliament. The Auditor-General would then be in a position to assess his program against those themes with a view to determining whether in specific years his program might take into account specific targeted reviews using larger teams.

While my review identified some areas where minor performance opportunities exist, overall arrangements within the (Office) are, in my opinion, designed to increase accountability, improve effectiveness and increase efficiencies.'

Report by the Independent Auditor of the Australian National Audit Office on the Results of a Performance Audit of 'Value for Money' Provided by the Australian National Audit Office, (June 2004), Canberra, ANAO, <www.anao.gov.au>

practice argued that market forces were sufficient to ensure sound management in government companies, and that there was no need to inform all shareholders of the adequacy of internal controls. The advantage of this new practice of management of government companies was that there was the same level of disclosure of management practices for government companies as for private companies. The disadvantages were:

- managerial accountability in government companies is less than in departments of state, although both were established by government; and,
- Parliament and minority shareholders in government companies had less information than the majority shareholder on matters that could affect share prices in the short and long term.

The introduction of new financial management laws at the same time as new audit law provided a firm foundation for audit. That was because audit could determine compliance of agency management against well-defined legislated requirements. Developments in the Auditor-General's role were to some extent consistent with changes in the broader public sector. To the forefront of those changes was the expectation of successive governments that government agencies would function better if they adopted certain private sector approaches to financial management, reporting and organisation.

Resources

The Auditor-General and the relevant central agency of government negotiated the Audit Office's annual budget. The Government submitted these budget estimates to the Parliament for approval along with those of government agencies. This mechanism overlapped finance for government with finance for the independent Audit Office, and did not distinguish between these functions as clearly as mechanisms in at least one comparable country. The Auditor-General had the legal authority to advise the Audit Committee of Parliament on the adequacy of the Government's proposed budget for his work. So far, the Auditor-General has advised that there were sufficient funds for audit.

All Australian Audit Offices charged fees for financial statement audits. The proportion of total income from fees varied between Offices. In some cases, audited agencies paid fees to central finance agencies rather than directly to the auditor, and other Offices transferred fees immediately on receipt to a government account or fund. Notwithstanding, payment of these fees either to the auditor or to a central government agency was a misapplication of the user pays principle, since legislatures and not auditees were the prime users of audit opinions.

In no jurisdiction did audited agencies pay the auditor for performance audits. In general, the ANAO spent a higher proportion of its budget on performance audits than Audit Offices in the states and territories. In some jurisdictions, expenditure on performance audits was small. This reflected legislators' and governments' views that Audit Offices' principal role was to advise on compliance with legislation, and not to advise at the same time on the efficiency and effectiveness of agency management.

Performance audits

Australian, state and territory legislation defined performance audits in different ways. All Auditors-General interpreted their legislation as prohibiting the conduct of program evaluations. There was no law equivalent to audit legislation at the national, state or territory level establishing a legal base for independent program evaluations. The effect was that Parliamentarians had more credible information from audit about agency management than from evaluations about whether programs succeeded or failed in their objectives.

There was little cooperation between Audit Offices in the planning and conduct of audits of the same programs. Therefore, legislators and officials commonly did not receive national pictures of programs with national objectives, minimising the contribution of audits to improving administration of programs funded by the Australian Government and delivered by other levels of government.

Readers of each performance audit report would find opinions and recommendations about auditee management. However, Parliamentarians would not find extensive accounts of major trends and patterns in public administration – identified in performance audits – because of their limited identification by the Audit Office. This contrasted with reporting on financial statement audits, where the Audit Office communicated to Parliament the major findings of each year's work.

The Audit Office explained that its annual performance audit planning was based on several factors, of which financial materiality was one element. Its planning also took account of themes in public administration. There was no explanation of how the relationship between planning factors and themes led to the selection of major topics in each portfolio.

The effects of audits

In most cases, agencies' senior management responded to draft audit opinions and recommendations so that there was discussion and negotiation with the auditor. Also in most cases, senior management gave attention to implementing recommendations. Notwithstanding, financial statement audits found similar control weaknesses from year to year.

The Joint Committee of Public Accounts and Audit allocated significant resources to inquiring into matters raised in audit reports. More Senate and joint committees than House committees were interested in audit matters. Almost all committee attention was on performance audits and not on financial statement and controls audit opinions. Most Parliamentarians showed little interest in audit matters. Other than through the Joint Committee of Public Accounts and Audit, their relatively low level of interest was simultaneously a sign of Parliamentary confidence in the Audit Office, and also an indication that the Audit Office was not relevant to most Parliamentarians and committees.[3]

This ambiguous level of interest complicated assessments of how much the Audit Office contributed to improving public administration. It will be remembered that the Audit Office was not required to improve public administration, but had adopted this as a goal. The public sector changed much in the last decade. This change was accompanied by different views on whether the Parliament and its committees were better or less able to hold government agencies to account for use of public moneys. Overall, any assessment of the Audit Office's impact on public administration must take account of these other factors and forces for change. Since this assessment is a research task, it could be pursued by researchers or evaluators outside the Audit Office. Assessment is future work, and it will lead to conclusions on whether the public sector auditor is a minor or major contributor to maintenance of confidence in public administration and to public sector reform.

---

[3] An impassioned account of the relationship between governments and Auditors-General in Australia, including at state government level, is: Funnell, W. (2001), *Government by Fiat. The Retreat from Responsibility*, UNSW Press, Sydney.

PART II

WHAT IS A SUPREME AUDIT INSTITUTION (SAI)?

What is a Supreme Audit Institution (SAI)?

In this study, a Supreme Audit Institution (SAI) is defined as the authority that audits public sector entities at the national level.[1] The functions of SAIs are explored through answering a number of questions. These are:

- Why and how can a legislature use audit?
- What are the purposes of public sector audit?
- Should public sector audit be at the front?
- Who should pay for audits?
- What are the different kinds of audits?
- How do audits lead to change? Living with two masters – the client and the auditee.

The Part I discussion of the Australian model of public sector auditing led to these questions. Part I provided answers for Australia, within its Parliamentary expression or system of accountability. These questions are now posed more generally to explore other answers and solutions to the problem of defining the public sector auditor's role.

The simplicity of the definition of a Supreme Audit Institution rests on top of complex matters that affect the public interest. Some of these matters are political. Therefore, it might seem strange to assert that they can be addressed only when the SAI maintains political neutrality. Since their resolution occurs within each nation's polity, economy and culture, it is not possible to be prescriptive about them. It will be seen that, while their resolution and manifestation are determined by the political, economic and cultural environments in which they are addressed, the issues and concepts in turn affect their environment. Fundamentally, it will be argued here that the characteristics of an SAI are determined most strongly by the legislature and government. The SAI works with them, responding to their concerns and meeting their expectations where they can be met, but also it lives with them. The challenge of living with and between them makes the existence and success of an SAI like a dance where it cannot abandon its partner, or in this case, its partners. The art of public sector auditing is for the SAI to dance

---

[1] The National Audit Office in the United Kingdom has published an account of the role of each state audit office (SAI) in the European Union and the European Court of Auditors. National Audit Office (2002), *State Audit in the European Union*, NAO, London.

with its two partners simultaneously rather than to struggle with them. The challenge is also about confronting issues at the heart of democracies.

The first issue is about who controls audit. Responses lead to the latter's constitutional and legal bases. We consider the SAI's relationship with the legislature and executive, especially in terms of the selection of audit topics and determination of what will be reported and how. The purposes of public sector audit are introduced. An SAI may have the legal authority to conduct any audit it wishes, and the legal right to report its findings. But if it has insufficient resources, then its legal independence is shallow. Consequently, we introduce the notion of the sufficiency of audit resources.

A legislature must be aware of the existence of different kinds of audits when drafting audit law. That way, it can be sure that it asks the SAI to conduct the kinds or types of audits that it wants. Finally, we examine the role of audits in fostering change and modernisation in the public sector, noting those factors that contribute to such change.

Public and political perceptions of audit are powerful. The reform process is about understanding those perceptions, and investigating whether any of them include audit as necessary for good government. The latter is marked, amongst other characteristics, by taxpayers' moneys being well-spent, stable and effective public services, and by a culture that discourages corruption.

Chapter 8

Why and How Can a Legislature Use Audit?

Independence of the legislature, government and judiciary assists in ensuring and maintaining a balance of powers between these arms of the state. Together, an independent legislature, government and judiciary provide complementary controls over the power of the state.

Audit independence

There is wide agreement internationally on the necessity of public sector auditing being independent from government. This independence creates confidence within the legislature in the work of the audit office or SAI. A legal basis is essential to maintain this independence. In 1977, following a major conference of INTOSAI in Peru, INTOSAI issued a declaration, known as the Lima Declaration of Guidelines on Auditing Precepts.[1] The Secretary-General of INTOSAI re-issued the Lima Declaration in 1998, stating that:

> The chief aim of the Lima Declaration is to call for independent government auditing. A Supreme Audit Institution which cannot live up to this demand does not come up to standard. It is not surprising, therefore, that the issue of the independence of Supreme Audit Institutions continues to be a theme repeatedly discussed within the INTOSAI community. However, the demands of the Lima Declaration are not satisfied by an SAI just achieving independence; this independence is also required to be anchored in the legislation. For this, however, well-functioning institutions of legal security must exist, and these are only to be found in a democracy based on the rule of law.

While there is broad agreement on the importance of an SAI's independence, there are degrees of legislative control. For instance, an SAI can be controlled by a legislature, an SAI can be equidistant from the legislature and government, or an SAI can be controlled by government with the legislature showing little influence. These scenarios show that SAIs can have different degrees

---

[1] INTOSAI (1988), *The Lima Declaration of Guidelines on Auditing Precepts*, INTOSAI, Vienna, Austria, <www.intosai.org/2_LIMADe.html>

of accountability to the legislature, and different ways in which their accountability is evident.[2] The three scenarios are shown in Figure 8.1.

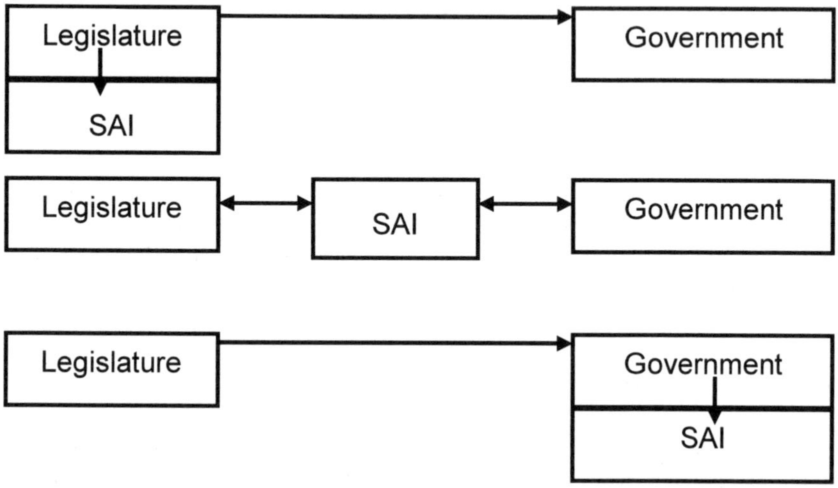

Figure 8.1 Three SAI Scenarios with the Legislature and Government

The legislature and the SAI

Why would a legislature want control over audit topics and over audit reporting? Answers to this question are as revealing about the purposes of public sector audit as are answers to the question of why a legislature would not want such authority. Public sector audit is always about relations between the legislature and government. Sometimes it is only about this relationship. The role of public sector audit is political in the end. That is because, simultaneously, it is about the legislature's control over public moneys and their use, while it is about the government's exercise of authority over the same items. The insights provided by public sector audit weaken or strengthen government. In particular, they can weaken or strengthen legislative and popular perceptions of executive competence and power. A legislature may want control over audit topics and reporting because public sector audit has the capacity to determine whether a government is following the same policies as those of the elected legislature. A government may

[2] A comprehensive analysis of accountability in government is in Mulgrave, R. (2003), *Holding Power to Account. Accountability in Modern Democracies*, Palgrave Macmillan, Hampshire, UK.

claim that it is doing so, while public sector audit's ability to identify what is happening with public moneys reveals whether that is the case. An SAI's determination of whether a government is following different policies from those set by the legislature will always interest a legislature.

The legislature's relationship with an SAI can be separated into:

- selection of audit topics;
- determination of what will be reported and how; and
- decisions on the sufficiency of audit resources.

The first two of these matters are considered here, and decisions on the sufficiency of audit resources broached in a later chapter. Where a legislature controls an SAI, it can direct the SAI to conduct audits of specific topics that it chooses. This means that legislators can determine what functions of government will be scrutinised. Such authority is attractive to elected representatives, and once it is used, audit becomes a political tool.

A legislature may also control the SAI's reporting of its findings. In this situation, elected representatives can direct the SAI to include or exclude certain material from reports. The head of the SAI would be directly accountable to the legislature. The disadvantage would be that he or she could not exercise professional judgement about what should be reported and how it should be reported. A legislature that controls audit reporting has an even more potent tool than a legislature that only selects topics for audit.

A legislature will permit the head of the SAI to exercise professional judgement over the SAI's reports when the legislature has confidence in the person. Later we will explore appointments to such positions.

A legislature must decide whether it wants to control both, one or neither of these dimensions of the SAI's work. Its decisions will depend on national circumstances. That can be seen from differences between national legislatures on their authority over the SAI. For instance, the United States Congress refers certain matters for audit to the General Accountability Office (GAO), which is the SAI in the United States. However, the US SAI maintains discretion over reporting of audit findings. In Australia from time to time, the Parliament requests the ANAO to conduct certain audits. The head of the ANAO, who is the Auditor-General of Australia as we saw earlier, maintains the legal right to conduct those audits or to place resources elsewhere.

One option is for the legislature to forgo any authority over decisions on what should be audited and reported. The legislature could advise or recommend to the SAI what should be audited and reported, with the SAI free to accept or to reject the legislature's advice or recommendation. Authority would rest with the SAI. This situation favours the SAI using its judgement on audit topics and reporting. Some legislators would be reluctant to surrender such authority over an SAI. Possible reasons for this reluctance are doubt about the SAI's capacity, questions about the government's influence over the SAI, and uncertainty over whether the SAI has the same priorities as them.

An equidistant SAI

The SAI becomes equidistant from both the legislature and government, not being captured by either, where:

- the legislature has advisory or recommendatory powers over the SAI;
- the latter can select audits and choose what and how it reports; and
- where these powers have a legal basis.

The SAI becomes a form of 'third force', influenced by both the legislature and by government while being separate from them. Then, both the legislature and government will be careful in their communication with the SAI. That is because neither would control it. Both would want to use the SAI's work, but for different purposes.[3]

The government and the SAI

Public sector audit is a legislative control over government because the legislature can use a public sector audit office to assess the government's compliance with laws, and to assess how well the government manages public moneys and programs. In order for a public sector audit office to assess a government's legislative compliance and management performance, it needs independence from government. The alternative would lead to the government instructing it what to do. Then, rather than the legislature using public sector audit to determine what the government is doing, the government would control audit. Over time, this power and authority would restrict information that the legislature would have about public programs and services because the government would influence and even control selection of audit topics, conduct of audits, and the content of audit reports.

Once a nation's legislature has decided what authority it wants over the SAI's selection of audit topics and reporting, its decision can be written in law. Awareness that there are different answers to the questions of what authority and for what purposes will enliven debate about these issues. A range of answers to the

---

[3] The Philippine Commission on Audit is an example of an SAI that is separate from government and the legislature. According to Tendero, 'The Commission of Audit is now as separate and independent as the Supreme Court, the Congress and the Executive Office.' Tendero, Avelino P. (2000), *Theory and Practice of Public Administration in the Philippines*, Fiscal Administration Foundation, Inc., Manila, Philippines, p. 257.

question of whether the legislature should control the selection of audits and audit reporting points to differences between legislatures in various countries on the purposes of public sector auditing.

Auditing the SAI

Legislative assemblies require all state agencies to manage their resources well. This requirement extends to SAIs. In order to assure itself that the SAI is well managed, some legislators appoint a reviewer of the SAI's approach to its work. This reviewer when appointed by the legislature is an auditor of the SAI. He or she is an independent auditor, reporting to the legislature on the SAI's compliance with official regulations and on the adequacy of its management. Such independence of the SAI's management builds confidence amongst legislators in the SAI's capacity. The legislature may need a separate law in order to appoint an auditor or reviewer of the SAI's management. Publication of the report of this independent auditor or reviewer demonstrates that the SAI provides information to a wide audience on its performance and stewardship of resources. Therein, the SAI acts as a role model for government entities.

Conclusions

The Chapter described how an SAI can be controlled by a legislature or by a government, or the SAI can be equidistant and independent from both. These idealised representations of SAI-legislature-executive government relationships exist. Perhaps the most common is where executive government either is a powerful influence or controller of the SAI.

To summarise, a legislature with authority over public sector audit has a means of keeping executive government accountable for implementation of legislation. A legislature can use public sector audit for this end once it is aware of where lies authority for selection of audit topics, and the authority for deciding what will be reported and how. A government that decides which matters will be audited, and how the results of audits are reported, would have reduced accountability to the legislature for its actions in spending taxpayers' moneys.

Chapter 9

What Are the Purposes of Public Sector Audit?

The Lima Declaration of Guidelines on Auditing Precepts affirms that:[1]

> The concept and establishment of audit is inherent in public financial administration as the management of public funds represents a trust. Audit is not an end in itself but an indispensable part of a regulatory system whose aim is to reveal deviations from accepted standards and violations of the principles of legality, efficiency, effectiveness and economy of financial management early enough to make it possible to take corrective action in individual cases, to make those accountable accept responsibility, to obtain compensation, or to take steps to prevent – or at least render more difficult – such breaches.

Using the Lima Declaration as a starting point, this chapter discusses the purposes of audit by examining a number of issues as shown below.

- Identifying deviations and violations.
- Who should set administrative standards?
- Identifying efficient, effective and economical management, and its opposite.
- Audit as affirmation.
- Audit to change public administration.
- Audit as advice.
- Why is the SAI an adviser?
- Can the SAI audit its own advice?
- How the SAI can avoid a conflict of interest.
- Extending the role of audit.

---

[1] INTOSAI (1998), The Lima Declaration of Guidelines on Auditing Precepts, (reissued), <www.intosai.org>

Audit to identify deviations and violations

According to INTOSAI, public sector audit identifies deviations from accepted standards. In so doing, it points out those deviations can be corrected and public moneys managed better. In order for audit to succeed in its task, those accepted standards must be defined, preferably by those who have trusted others with management of public moneys. If those standards are not defined or are unclear, then the SAI will not be able to detect deviations. Or if it comes to a view on deviations from accepted standards, its view may not be accepted.

Let us consider an example. A government agency requires all staff who use photocopiers to complete a form with details of why they need to use the machines and how much use they make of them. The SAI conducts an audit within the agency, with the aim of determining whether the agency's business rules are implemented. The SAI finds that most agency staff do not complete the form. The audit finding is of non-compliance with official requirements, which is deviation from accepted standards. From similar audits, the SAI knows that this particular agency is one of a minority which requires written permission before staff can use photocopiers. In other words, there are various requirements within the public service on staff use of photocopiers. Accepted standards can be interpreted as those that the agency has devised. But the SAI can also conclude that there are no accepted standards governing photocopier use across government. Within the particular agency, there appears to be deviation from accepted standards, but from a wider perspective, there is no deviation because of the absence of consistent expectations of the need to seek permission before using photocopiers. This is a small example, introduced to highlight some of the complications associated with identifying deviance from standard practice. The problem of identifying deviance from accepted standards becomes more complicated with program design and program delivery to large numbers of people.

Who should set administrative standards?

There are various answers to the question of who should set standards for acceptable administrative practice. The legislature has a role through its ability to make laws on administrative practice. Public administration is a large and complex area and it is not feasible for a legislature to make laws for every administrative and financial eventuality. Laws made by the legislature determine general expectations. However, often they will require interpretation by particular agencies and programs. Government has a role in this interpretation because it has overall responsibility for use of public moneys and implementation of its programs. Consistent with this responsibility, government can promulgate standards of accounting and management for its agencies. Agencies also have a role, since they can interpret legislative and governmental requirements for their particular circumstances. Finally, the SAI has a role as well. That is because it can interpret legislative, governmental and agency requirements of acceptable administrative practice.

Therefore, at the level of the individual audit, both the agency and the SAI will interpret requirements of acceptable administration, and come to their own opinions on what are deviations from accepted standards. Both entities can arrive at the same conclusions on what is acceptable. It becomes more problematic where the agency and SAI differ on what is acceptable administration and what are deviations from accepted standards. A means to discuss those differences of opinion is through the SAI's provision of draft opinions and issues papers – with draft findings and possibly with draft recommendations – to the agency. Circulation of draft opinions and issues papers will be discussed in more detail later. Here they are introduced since SAI-agency discussion of their content assists both entities to find common ground and areas where differences are substantial. Following presentation of the draft opinion, findings and recommendations, those discussions between SAI and the agency under audit will result in the SAI coming to a final view on whether administrative behaviour deviates from accepted standards; and, if so, the extent of the deviation. If there is no deviation, then the SAI is able to assure the legislature, and also the government, on application of relevant standards. If there is deviation, then the SAI will be able to provide information on this, and also to gather information and ideas on how accepted standards can be implemented. In so doing, the SAI is fulfilling a second role of public sector audit, which is to improve public sector administration.

In the above audit, the SAI also finds that completion of the approval forms for use of the photocopier slows the work of staff, and that the agency does not use information in the forms, with completed forms filed unread and disposed in the following month. The SAI can report how it found that most staff did not comply with official requirements on use of photocopiers. If its report stopped with that information, then it would have accomplished one purpose of audit, which is to reveal deviations from accepted standards. The caveat, though, and as explained above, is that the SAI must still take into account administrative practices in comparable agencies.

Efficiency, effectiveness and economy

The added dimension for the SAI is that INTOSAI's definition of the purpose of audit also refers to efficiency, effectiveness and economy of financial management. Since completion of the photocopier use approval forms takes time and nothing is done with those forms, then the SAI can question whether the agency's requirement for staff to complete the form ensures efficient, effective and economical administration. While we would need more evidence before coming to a firm conclusion, the limited information that is available in the above example points to how the agency's requirement appeared to reduce the efficiency and economy of its staff's work. The audit opinion would refer to staff's disregard of the agency's requirement for completion of photocopier use forms, and it would refer to how the agency's requirement did not contribute to efficient and economical use of resources. Here, simultaneously, the audit opinion would be demonstrating the assurance and improvements to public administration functions of audits.

Audit can identify how efficiently, effectively and economically a government agency delivers its services. There are techniques that an SAI can use for this identification, which are discussed later.

Audit as affirmation

Public sector audit can provide an assurance that those trusted with public moneys are managing them consistently with the purposes of the trust. In performing this role, the SAI is expanding popular and political perceptions of audit beyond finding deviations and violations. It is expanding those perceptions to illustrate how public sector audit can find and affirm sound agency management, which is a hallmark of good government. This is the assurance role of audit.

Audit to change public administration

Public sector audit can affirm the satisfactory nature of current approaches to management, or it can lead to change. It can also do both, for instance, when it identifies sound management while describing how public sector management can improve further. Later we will explore how audit can lead to change.

It is highly important for audit legislation to state clearly the purposes of audit. An SAI which has a clear legal expression of the purposes of audit is well placed to achieve those purposes.

Here we argue that public sector audit is an agent of public sector modernisation and reform. It is not the sole agent, and, while its role is important, it is very much secondary to the role of government. The main way for an SAI to advance reform is through audit. This is self-evident. However, there is another way by which an SAI can pursue reform. It is through using insights from audit to advise government agencies on change.

Audit as advice

If the SAI is attracted to this course, it will have two roles – the first is audit and the other is as adviser or consultant. SAIs build expertise in many areas, such as financial analysis, financial controls, financial reporting, program design, resource allocation, performance measurement and performance reporting. Once both the SAIs and government agencies become aware of this, agencies can demand that their SAIs provide them with their knowledge. Existence of this demand points to momentum within the public sector for change, and thus the demand is a welcome sign. If there is no demand from agencies for access to knowledge of sound management held by an SAI, then:

- first, the latter may not have this knowledge, suggesting that it is at an early stage in its evolution;
- second, there is another source of such advice, such as a finance department or ministry that provides advice and guidance to government entities; or
- third, the desire for modernisation and reform is small within government.

Why is the SAI an adviser?

An SAI which is asked for advice from agencies on management matters would be advised to reflect on why the request has come to it. As pointed out, the SAI is not the only public sector entity concerned with reform. Reform is an issue for the public sector as a whole. If requests for advice come to it, the SAI can see whether there are other entities providing advice, and inquire after its nature. A government may not have established a centre or centres for advice on public sector reform. In that case, the role of adviser falls to the SAI by default. The SAI would be then in a dilemma. To accept the role of adviser provides government with a reason for not establishing a centre or centres of advice on reform. To refuse the role of adviser to agencies results in the latter receiving insufficient guidance on how, why and in what direction to change. What is the best way for the SAI to resolve this dilemma?

INTOSAI has provided guidance through its description of pre-audit, which in this context is broadly equivalent to the SAI's provision of advice outside of, including before, an audit. INTOSAI has defined pre-audit as follows:[2]

> Pre-audit represents a before the fact type of review of administrative or financial audit; post-audit is audit after the fact.

Effective pre-audit is indispensable for the sound management of public funds entrusted to the state. It may be carried out by a Supreme Audit Institution or by other audit institutions.

> Pre-audit by a Supreme Audit Institution has the advantage of being able to prevent damage before it occurs, but has the disadvantage of creating an excessive amount of work and of blurring responsibilities under public law.

---

[2] INTOSAI (1998), *The Lima Declaration of Guidelines on Auditing Precepts.*

> The legal situation and the conditions and requirements of each country determine whether a Supreme Audit Institution carries out pre-audit. Post-audit is an indispensable task of every Supreme Audit Institution regardless of whether or not it also carries out pre-audits.

The Court of Accounts of the State of Rio de Janeiro in Brazil provides an example of pre-audit. A Tribunal task is to analyse economic, financial, demographic and social data on each municipality in the State. The Tribunal affirms that these studies represent powerful instruments for the conception and formulation of government policies and programs.[3]

A broader SAI role as an adviser is in advising on new legislation. The Chamber of Accounts of the Russian Federation is an example of an SAI with this wider role. In 2003, the Deputy Chairman of the Chamber of Accounts described the latter's role in the following terms:[4]

> It is worth noting that the Chamber of Accounts takes the most active part in the process of public audit quality improvement of improving the legislation: we are members of all working groups in the Parliament working out draft law on public financial control and a single conception of state financial control in the Russian Federation.

Can the SAI audit its own advice?

One consideration is for the SAI to be aware of risks it faces by providing advice such as through engagement in pre-audit. Given the authoritative nature of the SAI's role, agencies would be inclined to act on SAI advice and to implement it. The SAI's primary role is audit, which is why it audits entities implementing its advice. A conflict of interest arises, since then the SAI would be auditing its own advice. In these circumstances, the SAI will be constrained in forming an audit opinion where it finds fault with its own proposals and suggestions to others. Self-critical organisations are to be encouraged. However, where an organisation continually or frequently criticises itself, then stakeholders become doubtful. The key stakeholder is the legislature. Always, a percentage of audit opinions will be critical. An SAI that provides advice outside its audits risks compromising its capacity to form critical audit opinions on the activities of agencies that have implemented its advice.[5]

---

3 *TCE RJ Noticia,* Ano 2, No. 19, Dezembro 2003, <www.tce.rj.br>

4 9th ASOSAI Assembly (October 2003), *Quality Improvement of Public Audit, National Report: the Chamber of Accounts of the Russian Federation*, Manila, Philippines, <www.asosai.org>

5 Some SAIs have or have had roles outside of audit. For instance, the Philippine Commission on Audit had a number of other functions, prior to the Commission's reform. These other functions were described by a Philippine author as follows:

INTOSAI provides further guidance on this matter as follows:[6]

> SAIs often carry out activities that by strict definition do not qualify as audits, but which contribute to better government. Examples of non-audit work may include (a) gathering data without conducting substantial analysis, (b) legal work, (c) an information mission of the elected Assembly as regards the examination of draft budgets, (d) an assistance mission for members of the elected Assemblies as regards investigations and consultations of SAIs' file, (e) administrative activities and (f) computer-processing functions. These non-audit activities provide valuable information to decision-makers and should be of consistently high quality.

The above discussion focused on advice given outside an audit. This is separate from advice during an audit or as an immediate result of one. Audit reports often contain recommendations to improve management and administration. Those audit recommendations are advice, but they are linked closely to the conduct of the audit and to the latter's findings. Since one purpose of audit is to improve public administration, it is logical for the SAI to advise the agency under audit through those audit recommendations. The risks of compromising the audit opinion are negligible when audit advice is given in this context.

- 'The preparation of the annual financial report of the government. This function was carried over when the Department of Budget and Management was only a liaison office in the Department of Finance.
- The verification of appropriations of national government agencies and control of fund releases. This is a cashiering function.
- Preparation of statements on revenues and expenditures of local government units and on their legal borrowing and net paying capacities for re-classification and other purposes. This also is a carry-over from the time when there was no Department of Interior and Local Government.
- The authority to examine accounts of public utilities. Public utilities are private enterprises allowed only limited profits.
- The keeping of the general accounts of government and the preservation of vouchers pertaining thereto are accounting and custodial functions not that of an external auditor. This will need a constitutional amendment.
- Authority to give prior direction for transfer of government funds from one office to another is not an audit function.
- The power to compromise claims belongs to the head of office, is not an audit function, and is better left to be post audited. Otherwise, who will audit the auditor who compromised the claim or liability?'

Tantuico Jr, Francisco S. (1994), *Performance and Accountability: Central Pillars of Democracy*, Fiscal Administration Foundation, City of Mandaluyong, Philippines.

[6] INTOSAI (2001), *Auditing Standards*, INTOSAI, Vienna, Austria.

How the SAI can avoid a conflict of interest

Risks exist when agencies not being audited approach the SAI and request information and insight. If the SAI wishes to respond to those requests, it must do so in a way that does not jeopardise its capacity to form audit opinions on the management and administration of those agencies which implement its advice. In some countries, the SAI has found a way through issuing general guides to better administrative and financial management practice. It is worthwhile noting the work of those SAIs, and studying how they manage to audit agencies at the same time as advising other agencies on good practice. An SAI that prepares guides to good practice must also be aware that development and circulation of guides can overlap with the functions of central government agencies established to provide administrative guidance to other entities.

INTOSAI has published a Code of Ethics which provides guidance on how to avoid conflicts of interest. The Code states that:[7]

> When auditors are permitted to provide advice or services other than audit to an audited entity, care should be taken that these services do not lead to a conflict of interest. In particular, auditors should ensure that such advice or services do not include management responsibilities or powers, which must remain firmly with the management of the audited entity.

Auditors should protect their independence and avoid any possible conflict of interest by refusing gifts or gratuities which could influence or be perceived as influencing their independence and integrity.

A further consideration is the need to provide resources to permit the SAI to perform all of its responsibilities, which may include general advisory as well as audit roles. The legislature or the SAI must then determine what proportion of its resources should be set aside to provide advice, in either written or oral forms. Tight budgetary limits on many SAIs restrict the great majority of their work to audit rather than to advisory roles. This resourcing matter is discussed in more detail later.

Extending the role of audit

In some countries, the role of audit is far wider than explored in the discussion above. For instance, the Chamber of Accounts of the Russian Federation exercises control over the execution of the federal budget, state extra-budgetary funds and federal property use.[8] The Chamber of Accounts upholds that a modern democratic

---

[7] INTOSAI (1998), *Code of Ethics*, Vienna, Austria.

[8] ASOSAI (October 2003), *National Report: The Chamber of Accounts of the Russian Federation.*

state requires strong financial controls, and public sector audit can play a prominent role in their creation and maintenance.

> Efficient state control over public funds administration is, first of all, the important factor confidence building of the society to state power, a means to consolidate the power in order to provide well-being of citizens as well as state power stability.

The role of the Chamber of Accounts in that country is influenced by the nature of executive control. For, as the Deputy Chairman of the Chamber of Accounts described:

> The difficulty of quality improvement of the public audit in Russia is connected to the fact that there is no modern internal control system within the executive power structure.

It is possible that the Chamber's role has expanded to fill a power vacuum.

The Court of Accounts in the State of Rio de Janeiro, Brazil is another example of an SAI with wide responsibilities. An example is in how the Court or Tribunal has the legal authority to confirm pension entitlements of retired persons. The Tribunal allocates considerable resources to this task.[9]

Earlier, this discussion affirmed the necessity of audit legislation clarifying the purposes of audit. The above reflections on the relationship between an SAI's audit and advisory roles suggest that the purposes of the SAI should also be clarified in audit legislation.

Conclusions

To summarise this part of the discussion, we have asked what are the purposes of audit. The answers are in providing assurances on compliance with the law, and in identifying how management of the public sector can improve. In order to determine whether there is compliance with the law, there must be clear guidance on standards for acceptable administration. We have shown how the SAI can improve public administration through its audits and through provision of advice outside of audits. There are risks in this second role which must be managed so that the SAI avoids conflicts of interest and maintains the integrity of its audit opinions and public confidence in them.

[9] Tribunal de Contas do Estado do Rio de Janeiro (March 2003), *Relatório de Atividades, Exercicio de 2002*, Rio de Janeiro, Brazil.

Chapter 10

Should Public Sector Audit Be at the Front?

We consider the question of public sector leadership in administrative and management reform in two areas of legislation as follows:

- Audit law in the public and private sectors.
- Audit and general administrative law governing the role and performance of public sector entities.

This chapter argues that the probability of reform of public sector audit law being successful is increased where reform takes account of the status of private sector audit law, and the status of administrative law for the public sector. This is represented in the following figure. An important question is what is the relationship between public sector audit law, public sector administrative law, and private sector audit law?

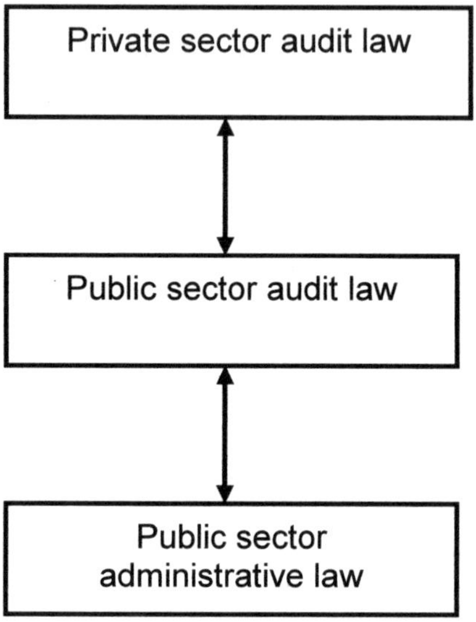

Figure 10.1 Public and Private Sector Audit Law, and Public Sector Administrative Law

Leadership in audit law

In a mixed economy wherein state owned enterprises function alongside privately owned entities, both kinds of enterprises will require audit services. A legislature must consider whether it has one law governing all audits in both sectors, or whether it has two sets of laws – one set for the public sector and one for the private sector.

In the former case, there is no question of one sector leading another, for instance, in its approach to using audit to ensure entities' accountability to their owners. However, in the second case, public sector audit can lead the private sector by showing how audit can be used to shape accountability. Alternatively, a legislature may choose a stronger definition of accountability for the private than the public sector. In that case, public sector audit will lag private sector law and practice.

The laws surrounding audit practice in the two sectors must be examined to determine which situation prevails. Legislators will benefit from results of this examination since it will provide information and knowledge for their work. Specifically, the results will assist them to determine what should be the relationship between public and private sector audit law. Therefore, a first step for the legislature in determining its preferred relationship between public and private sector audit law is to seek information about the two, so that similarities and differences of the two laws are understood. The SAI's personnel can take the initiative in promoting understanding of laws governing public and private sector audit. This promotion will require research and dissemination of results of that research.

There are risks for public sector audit if it is far in front of its private sector equivalent. The risks are in allegations that its expectations are unrealistic, since the values and organisations necessary to support the leadership position will not be sufficiently strong. A major risk is in application of a strong definition of the accountability of public sector managers to the owner of the entities, where the owner is the legislature or congress. There may not be popular or political support for this strong definition of accountability inherent in public sector audit law. Also, it may be impractical to apply a strong definition of the accountability of executive government to the legislature because of local circumstances. Then, a weaker definition of the accountability of executive government to the legislature would survive.

A controversial topic for determining whether the public sector is in front of the private sector in reform is the issue of circulation of the results of internal control audits. Release of the results informs stakeholders of the adequacy of management in any private company or public sector entity audited. Those stakeholders are private sector shareholders, and they are legislators and citizens in the public sector. Customarily in many jurisdictions, the results of internal control reports are not released to private sector shareholders. In the public sector, legislatures that do not have access to the SAI's internal control reports on government entities have information as limited as private sector shareholders. Their limited knowledge places the public sector on the same footing as the private sector in the use of audit to inform stakeholders and to further accountability. Yet were the SAI to provide the legislature and public with at least the most material findings from internal control reports, then public sector audit would be in a leadership position compared to the private sector.

Where public sector audit law leads private sector law, then the former is an agent of modernisation of the private sector. This may be an intended or unintended consequence of the answer of legislators to the question of whether public sector audit law should lead the private sector. The twist is that the private sector is most commonly held as a model for modernisation of the other sector. Surprisingly, then, depending on the position of legislators, the change agent can be the public sector where audit legislation is concerned.

The Chinese National Audit Office has highlighted the importance of trade and commerce in modernising the audit function and the economy. It has argued that China's membership of the World Trade Organization (WTO) has given impetus to forming a unified, normative and transparent legal framework in conducting audit.[1] The Chinese National Audit Office wrote that:

> for a long time, auditors have been puzzled about several bottle-necks like unconsolidated legal frameworks, legal regulations contradictory with each other and interference with audit law-enforcing of departmental document and notification. With China's accession to WTO, the above-mentioned puzzles could be solved step by step.

If public sector audit law lags its private sector equivalent in expectations of audit practice, then the legislature and the population will be ill-served. That is because of legal limits on the SAI's role restricting the authority of the legislature to call executive government to account.

Leadership through administrative law

Whose responsibility is it if a public sector entity does not perform well or collapses? How can the responsibility be encapsuled in law?

These questions are phrased to allow consideration of the relationship between public sector audit law and public sector administrative law, and to explore the consequences of one of these sets of laws being more developed than the other. The questions are important since, in any public sector, some government organisations will perform better than others, and some will collapse – not providing the services that they are funded to provide to citizens and to society. If all public sector entities are audited, then auditors become party to government organisations' service delivery failures, and they can be held at least partly responsible for them. Therefore, it is necessary to identify the reasons for service delivery or organisational failures.

A government has overall responsibility for delivery of its services to citizens and society. Once elected, it accepts that responsibility. The latter is allocated or delegated to government organisations, for instance, in health, education, transport, construction and defence. It is very clear that those government organisations for practical purposes are responsible for service delivery. If those health, education, transport, construction and defence services are provided according to the government's requirements, then those agencies have performed their role. If those services are not well delivered, those agencies remain responsible for whatever form and amount of services were provided. Service delivery includes stewardship of public moneys. In other words, the agencies are responsible for management of the finances allocated to them by government.

---

[1] CNAO, 'Applicable Model for Audit Testing', *Asian Journal of Government Audit 3*, ASOSAI, New Delhi, India, pp. 86–96.

The notion of agency responsibility for service delivery is self-evident. It is a starting point for considering whether auditors have any responsibility for these agencies' service delivery failures where those agencies are audited by the SAI.

Senior management within government agencies has primary responsibility for functions of their agencies. Sorting out the role of auditors in poor service delivery, malfunctioning or collapse of public sector entities is easier where the responsibilities of senior management are specified in public sector law. Specification of management responsibilities in the public sector clarifies for those managers, the legislature, government and the wider society what is expected of those who work in and for government. This is because all stakeholders benefit from clear expression of what senior managers in the public service are expected to do. Once those expectations are clear, then management can be held accountable for the quality of its service delivery, including being held accountable for use of public moneys. Unclear law reflects uncertainty about lines of responsibility and control within the public sector. An SAI or any other entity operating within this environment risks being held at least partially responsible for the service delivery failure or misuse of public moneys.

An example is where administrative law does not define clearly the aims and objectives of an agency's service delivery. A government entity regulates activities in that sector of the economy in which the agency provides services. There is a major service delivery failure with serious public interest consequences. The public wants to find out whether the service delivery agency was responsible for the problems, and whether there was regulatory failure. Unclear administrative law will result in the regulator's work being given more weight than warranted compared to circumstances where the responsibilities of the service delivery agency were defined unambiguously.

Legislation governing the performance of government entities is of fundamental importance to the efficiency and effectiveness of the public sector. The legislation should stipulate the roles of agencies, and define the role and responsibility of senior management for performance of the entities in which they work. Agency management and the agency's auditor, the SAI, both have responsibilities in regard to the performance of the agency. However, the SAI's responsibility is secondary to that of management. Since it is secondary, a starting point for public sector reform is the adequacy of current legislation surrounding the performance of government entities.

The Indonesian Parliament recognised this point when, in 2003, it approved the state financial act. The new law was meant to ensure transparency and accountability in managing state finance, curbing corruption and promoting best practice in financial management and public sector governance.[2] Subsequently, a new draft audit law was developed, which restated the mandate, function, position and responsibility of the Audit Board of Indonesia. The Brazilian Fiscal Responsibility Law of 2000 is another example of legislation to first reform

---

[2] ASOSAI (April 2004), *Asian Journal of Government Audit*, pp. 38–40.

the public sector. The Act establishes norms for agency management of public finance.[3]

Similar legislation is essential in those countries where it does not exist. As we have seen, public sector reform also involves a review of the adequacy of audit law. Reviews or formulation of the two sets of laws can occur at the same time. But if public sector audit law is enhanced before the adequacy of laws governing the performance of government entities is reviewed, then public sector law will function within an environment only partially defined and open to further change. The fluidity of legal expectations of government entities will maintain uncertainty about the role of the SAI, even though its law may have been reviewed and amended first. Ideally, therefore, reform of public sector audit law should occur simultaneously with reform of law on the performance of public sector entities.

In general terms, recent legislative reform in the United States has addressed simultaneously regulation of the performance of private sector companies and regulation of the work of auditors. The reform is represented by the *Sarbanes-Oxley Act 2002*. The Act's title suggests this dual movement as follows:[4]

> An Act to protect investors by improving the accuracy and reliability of corporate disclosures made pursuant to the securities law, and for other purposes.

Earlier we mentioned the views of the Chinese National Audit Office on the impact on public sector auditing of China's membership of the World Trade Organization. Its views extended to the World Trade Organization's effects on a nation's administrative law. The Chinese National Audit Office stated that:[5]

> WTO rules are characteristic of their function in regulating and restricting government's behaviour (some experts would like to take it for an international administrative law) as well as a legal binding force and compulsive and authoritative power prevailing over domestic law.

The Chinese National Audit Office also believed that China's membership of the World Trade Organization would influence the demand for and environment of certain types of audits.

> With China's accession to WTO, we are sure to witness a more regulated government and business behaviour, improved truthfulness and compliance of revenues and expenditures of public finance as well as the decrease of irregularities and misbehaviours, paving the way for a better audit context. Audit

---

[3] Tribunal de Contas do Estado do Rio de Janeiro (2000), *Lei Complementar 101 de 4 de Maio de 2000, Lei De Responsabilidade Fiscal*, Tribunal de Contas do Estado do Rio de Janeiro, Brazil.

[4] *Sarbanes-Oxley Act of 2002,* United States Congress, <www.findlaw.com>

[5] CNAO, *Asian Journal of Government Audit 3*, pp. 86–96.

> institutions can reset work priorities with less burden for the audit of truthfulness like error-checking and fraud prevention, but (with) more devotion to performance audit in order to urge the audited bodies to perform their duties, improve management and promote quality and effectiveness of economic management.

These views of the Chinese National Audit Office are recognition that introducing market-based reforms without an effective legal and regulatory (including accounting) structure frustrates rather than facilitates development.[6]

Six issues for administrative law

The following discussion gives six examples of how an SAI's performance is affected by administrative law as follows.

- Performance information
- Accounting standards
- Financial statements
- Audit committees
- Internal controls
- Internal audit

Performance information

A practical example is where audit law requires the SAI to form an opinion on the performance information of public sector bodies. This is a familiar task for many SAIs. In conducting it, the SAI will look for agencies' performance information, such as performance indicators, as starting points. If administrative law does not require agencies to prepare performance information at all or even to prepare it solely for external review, then the SAI's task will be difficult. There will be no performance information, including indicators, prepared by agencies and submitted to the SAI for the latter to form an opinion on the accuracy and completeness of the information and on the validity of indicators. Here, audit law would have outstripped general administrative law, creating problems for the SAI.

INTOSAI proposes that SAIs should recommend to the audited entities that measurable and clearly stated objectives be established and that performance targets be set for those objectives.[7]

---

[6] Hopper, T. and Hoque, Z. (ed.) (2004), *Accounting and Accountability in Emerging and Transition Economies*, Research in Accounting in Emerging Economies Supplement 2, Elsevier, Oxford, p. 3. The introduction to these readings gives an excellent account of this view.

Accounting standards

Accounting standards define the principles and practice of accounting. They are essential in the public sector since they guide agencies' internal controls and interpretation of financial data. Accounting standards and their application are the foundation for financial control and reporting.

INTOSAI recommends that appropriate authorities should ensure the promulgation of acceptable standards for financial reporting and disclosure relevant to the needs of government. SAIs should work with the accounting standards-setting organisations to help ensure that proper accounting standards are issued for the government.[8] Thus, it is clear that the SAI does not set standards. Rather, it is a responsibility of other bodies. These can be governmental or professional authorities, with which the SAI can work to facilitate development of accounting standards. But it remains the responsibility of those appropriate authorities to define and promulgate them. This arrangement removes the onus from the SAI in this critical area of public sector reform.

Those appropriate authorities must consider whether they develop the same accounting standards for the public as for the private sector. This is a fundamental question, responses to which reflect local realities. The question is noted but not explored here since it is outside the scope of this study.

Financial statements

Once appropriate authorities have defined and released accounting standards for the public sector, the relationship between general administrative and public sector law is seen clearly in regard to preparation of financial reports for audit. Government agencies which prepare reports on their expenditure and revenue open their activities to scrutiny by other parts of government, such as ministries, and they open themselves to scrutiny by audit. Financial statements prepared according to a country's accounting standards provide comprehensive information about assets and liabilities as well as about revenue and expenditure. Administrative law can require agencies to prepare financial statements for audit. This requirement would suggest that public sector reform was progressing. Once financial statements were available, then the SAI could form an opinion on their completeness and accuracy.

Financial statement analysis identifies the expected relationships within and between various elements of the financial statements, identifying any unexpected relationships and any unusual trends. The methods and techniques of financial analysis depend to a large degree on the nature, scope and objective of the audit, and on the knowledge and judgement of the auditor.[9]

---

[7] INTOSAI (2001), *Auditing Standards*.
[8] INTOSAI (2001), *Auditing Standards*, p.30.
[9] INTOSAI (2001), *Auditing Standards*, pp.58–59.

In the above example, administrative and audit law would move in tandem. Amendments to both sets of law would be necessary so that agencies prepared financial statements for audit, and so that the SAI audited them.

An unfortunate situation would be where the SAI was required to audit agencies' financial reports, when agencies were not required to prepare them. Again, this lack of congruence between administrative and audit law would cause strain within the public sector, and confusion about the SAI's capacity.

The reverse of this situation is conceivable. Administrative law could require agencies to prepare financial reports, including financial statements. However, these would be prepared for ministers and government and not for independent audit. In that case, administrative law would lead audit law. The absence of authority for the SAI to audit the financial reports, or the presence of the authority but the absence of a requirement, results in the SAI having a weak role in assisting the legislature to hold executive government accountable for its expenditure and revenue.

Audit committees

Audit committees are committees formed of senior management in a government agency. Where a government agency has a governing board, then the audit committee will be comprised of board members. Audit committees often have an independent member to provide an outside perspective on the matters placed before them. The functions of audit committees are to address matters raised by internal and external audit, to identify tasks for internal audit, in some cases to consider the financial statements prepared by the organisation for audit, and to ensure their robustness before they are submitted to the SAI for audit.

Public sector agencies with audit committees are likely to have stronger internal controls than those agencies without them. Therefore, general administrative law for the public sector can require public sector agencies to form audit committees.

The Australian Government's legislation for government bodies is an example of this. For ministerial departments and other agencies dependent on the Government's budget for funding, the legislation states that:[10]

> A Chief Executive must establish and maintain an audit committee for the Agency, with the functions and responsibilities required by the Finance Minister's Orders.

For government companies, the Government's requirements are more elaborate as follows:[11]

---

[10] *Financial Management and Accountability Act 1997*, S48, <www.dofa.gov.au/scripts/search.idq>

> The directors of a Commonwealth authority must establish and maintain an audit committee with functions that include:
> - helping the authority and its directors to comply with obligations under this Act; and
> - providing a forum for communication between the directors, the senior managers of the authority and the internal and external auditors of the authority.
>
> If the regulations state how the committee is to be constituted, it must be constituted in accordance with the regulations.

Internal controls

Management has internal controls to assist it in utilising resources. Resource control, consistent with the purposes of the agency and the programs and services it delivers, is essential for sound management. Only management can create internal controls, meaning that their creation is not the SAI's responsibility.

INTOSAI defines internal control as the whole system of financial and other controls, including the organisational structure, methods, procedures and internal audit, established by management within its corporate goals, to assist in conducting the business of the audited entity in a regular economic, efficient and effective manner; ensuring adherence to management policies; safeguarding assets and resources; securing the accuracy and completeness of accounting records; and producing timely and reliable financial and management information.[12]

It is a governmental and legislative responsibility to require all public sector agencies to have strong internal controls. This requirement is essential for an efficient and effective public sector. The work of the SAI includes assessment of the adequacy of those internal controls.

Internal audit

Management creates internal audit to provide it with information about aspects of financial and non-financial performance of the government agency. Information that internal audit offers is separate from information that line management provides to senior management. Internal audit is not involved in the daily tasks of government agencies, but is to one side of them. Its relationship to the agency's management is similar to the relationship of the SAI, the external auditor, to the legislature.

Internal audit is a powerful tool to inform management of matters, such as the adequacy of financial controls, the effectiveness of lower levels of management, and the accuracy of financial and non-financial reporting. A government agency that has a strong internal audit unit is more likely to have

---

[11] *Commonwealth Authorities and Companies Act 1997*, No. 153, 1997, S32, <www.dofa.gov.au/scripts/search.idq>

[12] INTOSAI (2001), *Auditing Standards*, p.71.

strong internal controls – increasing the agency's efficiency and economy and possibly its effectiveness – than an agency without internal audit. Internal audit has the same role as in the private sector, which is to assist management in its work. Private sector companies which have strong internal audit units are in the same situation as public sector bodies with them, since entities in both sectors benefit from internal audit's work.

An SAI which observes a strong internal audit unit within an entity is more likely to find a soundly functioning entity than where internal audit does not exist. In light of this, general administrative law for the public sector can require government agencies to establish internal audit units. An increasing number of countries are expecting private sector companies to have internal audit. Public sector audit and financial management legislation must keep pace with these developments, otherwise the level of financial management and control in the public sector will fall behind the private sector. South Africa provides an example of how expectations of relevant professionals are that companies have strong internal audit units. The Institute of Directors in Southern Africa 2002 report on corporate governance sets out the Institute's policies on this matter.[13] They are quoted here as examples that can be adapted for administrative reform in the public sector.

> Companies should have an effective internal audit function that has the respect and co-operation of both the board and management. Where the board, in its discretion, decides not to establish an internal audit function, full reasons must be disclosed in the company's annual report, with an explanation as to how assurance of effective internal controls, processes and systems will be obtained.
>
> Consistent with the Institute of Internal Auditors' definition of internal auditing in an internal audit charter approved by the board, the purpose, authority and responsibility of the internal audit activity should be formally defined…
>
> Internal audit should report at a level within the company that allows it to fully accomplish its responsibilities. The head of internal audit should report administratively to the chief executive officer, and should have ready and regular access to the chairperson of the company and the chairperson of the audit committee.
>
> Internal audit should report at all audit committee meetings.
>
> The appointment or dismissal of the head of the internal audit should be with the concurrence of the audit committee.
>
> If the external and internal audit functions are carried out by the same accounting firm, the audit committee and the board should satisfy themselves that there is adequate segregation between the two functions in order to ensure that their independence is not impaired.

---

[13] Institute of Directors in Southern Africa (2002), *Executive Summary of the King Report 2002*, Institute of Directors in Southern Africa, Parktown, South Africa, <www.iodsa.co.za>

This last point is controversial, since it accepts that internal and external audit can be conducted by the same entity. This is not permitted in some jurisdictions, such as the United States, where it is believed that an audit firm that served the two purposes would have a conflict of interest. Recent United States legislation states that external auditors are prohibited from providing internal audit services that relate to an external audit client's internal accounting controls, financial systems or financial statements.[14]

Bangladesh provides an example of an internal audit unit that has become part of external audit. Railways are vital for Bangladesh's economy and society. The Railway Audit Directorate was an internal audit organ of Bangladesh Railway, with its expenditures being charges against the budget of the railway department. A review of the Railway Audit Directorate found that there were inefficiencies in its work, since its offices were in ten locations across the country, creating inconsistencies and complicating the focus of scarce resources. Subsequently, from the 2003–2004 financial year, the railway audit budget was included in the budget for the Office of the Comptroller and Auditor-General, establishing its constitutional status as part of external audit.[15] Movement of an entire internal audit unit to external audit does not occur very often. Here it indicates the National Parliament has given priority to external audit. However, Bangladesh Railway will still need an internal audit unit as a key control. It will be interesting to see if and when a new railway internal audit unit emerges.

Earlier it was stated that the SAI's work includes assessment of the adequacy of internal controls. Since internal audit is a key internal control, the SAI will find itself reviewing its adequacy. The collapse of Enron in the United States and new corporate and audit-related legislation has led to greater attention there and in other countries to the relationship between external and internal audit. As indicated above, these must be separated to avoid a conflict of interest and to ensure the best service to their respective clients. An SAI that can rely on the work of internal audit will have less work than otherwise. The difficulty for the SAI is to determine when it can place such reliance.[16]

Conclusions

We return to the question of what role the legislature envisages for the SAI in assisting it to hold executive government to account. What we have seen is that general administrative law surrounding the role and performance of entities affects

---

14 *Business Credit* (February 2004), Volume 106, No. 2, 'The Sarbanes-Oxley Act of 2002: Understanding the Independent Auditor's Role in Building Public Trust.' <www.pwc.com>

15 Office of the Comptroller and Auditor-General of Bangladesh (2003), *Enhancing Management for Quality Audit*, Dhaka, Bangladesh.

16 This issue is addressed in NAO, *Co-operation Between Internal and External Auditors. A Good Practice Guide*, NAO, London.

the SAI's role. A well-defined set of requirements of entity management assists the SAI to do its work. Requirements considered here were for:

- agency preparation of performance information;
- appropriate authorities to set accounting standards;
- agency preparation of financial reports, preferably preparation of financial statements;
- agency creation of audit committees;
- agency establishment of strong internal controls; and
- agency formation of internal audit units.

Legislative consideration of and action on these dimensions of public sector reform will strengthen the capacity of public sector agencies. Within this environment, an SAI will have a sharper focus and be seen as one factor in the larger picture of enhancement of the public sector's capacity, rather than the source of most change. The selected dimensions of public sector reform highlighted above are illustrative of the direction and degree of change. It is not a complete list. Further analysis would be necessary to complete the picture of legislative change to enhance the public sector's capacity. That further analysis is outside the scope of this study.

If the requirements described above are absent from the public sector while legislation is amended to strengthen the SAI's capacity, then the SAI is at risk. That is because the limitation of legislative change to audit law – and exclusion of administrative law from amendment – fosters the perception that the SAI is the major agent of modernisation and reform. It is unlikely that this expectation can ever be fully met and, indeed, it is illusory. It is unrealistic for an SAI to be the major agent of modernisation and change since it controls neither agencies' management nor resources. The government controls those. A legislature that portrays the SAI as the major change agent is signalling that it does not believe that executive government is reforming or changing fast enough or changing in the direction preferred by elected representatives. Again, we have returned to the SAI's location between the legislature and executive government.

Chapter 11

Who Should Pay for Audits?

An SAI is strong when it has the legal authority to select its audits and the legal authority to report its findings. It will be even stronger where it has sufficient resources to conduct and to report those audits. But who should decide what are sufficient resources for the SAI? The question of who should pay for audits offers other insights into what is an SAI. This chapter explores this question by noting relevant issues as shown below.

- Should the government, the legislature or the SAI determine the sufficiency of the SAI's resources?
- Who pays for audits in the private sector?
- Disclosure of audit fees and costs.
- User pays in the public sector.

Should the government, the legislature or the SAI determine the sufficiency of the SAI's resources?

This question is represented in Figure 11.1.

If the government determines the sufficiency of resources for an SAI, then it would have strong influence over its capacity to audit. That is because the government would have the temptation to restrict or reduce resources were the SAI to criticise government activities. This is the same temptation for government as when the judiciary criticises government activity, and where government decides the resources available to the judiciary. When the government settles the sufficiency of the SAI's resources, the SAI is dependent on rather than independent of it. Audit law, then, must be written in knowledge of the importance of resources to the independence of the SAI.

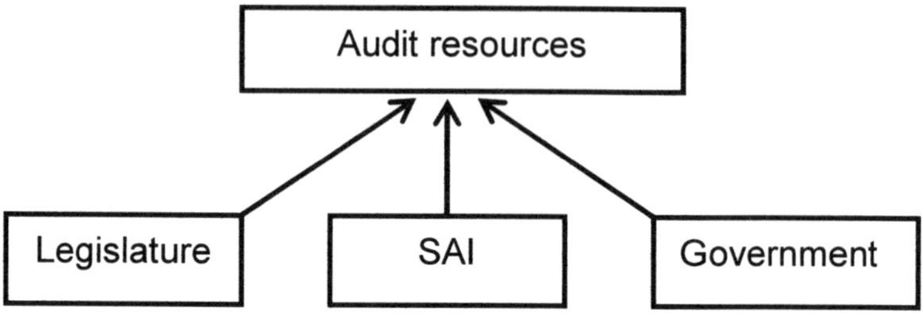

Figure 11.1 Paying for Audits

There is a firmer basis than government decision-making for decisions on the sufficiency of an SAI's resources. An SAI is an instrument of the legislature. Therefore, it is logical for the legislature to settle the resources matter.

All governments have stronger demands on their budgets than there are resources available to address them. That is why it is the responsibility of governments to determine budgetary priorities. A government can determine what budgetary resources it would make available to the SAI, consistent with its approach to fiscal discipline in the public sector. The government could use that information to advise the legislature on resources for the SAI. An advisory role for government on the SAI's resources does not impinge on the SAI's independence. The advisory role on budget priorities and fiscal restraint is consistent with a government's overall responsibilities for sound administration of public moneys.

Of interest is that it is possible for a legislature to determine the SAI's resource levels without seeking the government's advice. This legislature would not be as well informed as where it sought and was provided with that advice. It is noteworthy that the legislature does not have to limit itself to the government's views, since it can seek advice from elsewhere.

A measure of sound management is where public sector agencies operate within their budgets, setting priorities and achieving their goals. An SAI must have regard to this measure, and must seek to function within its budget An SAI, then, must develop its budget priorities. Knowing that the SAI has a budget policy, the legislature can invite it to advise on what resources it needs to fulfil its charter. An SAI can advise the legislature on its budgetary needs even if the legislature does not seek such advice. However, there would be difficulties in the relationship between the legislature and the SAI were the former not to seek the SAI's views on its resource requirements. It is possible that a legislature would give the SAI the authority for it to determine its own resources for public sector audit. This ideal situation would give the SAI the maximum independence and responsibility.

To return to the question of who should determine the resources necessary for public sector audit, the legislature must have the authority to make the decision. The government and the SAI can advise the legislature on this matter, although the legislature should be the arbiter.

Who pays for audits in the private sector?

Audit clients pay for audits in the private sector. The clients are shareholders in private or listed companies. In many countries, audit firms' fees are generally recorded in companies' financial statements. With knowledge of this, an argument is that public sector agencies subject to audit by the SAI should pay fees to the SAI.

To explore this argument and its implications for audit law, further examination is necessary of aspects of the work of private sector auditors. In many western countries in the private sector, an audit firm is appointed at an annual general meeting of shareholders. The firm's board of directors makes a recommendation to the annual general meeting on which audit firm should be appointed as the company auditor. In other words, the audit firm is appointed because of the board of directors' recommendation. Where this practice is determined by a country's law governing private sector corporations, the auditor's client is clear. However, in practice, it is more complicated.

Generally, private sector auditors have more contact with management at all levels in the companies they audit than with shareholders. Also, private sector auditors have more contact with boards of directors than with shareholders. This has led at times to private sector auditors believing that their primary clients were the board or management rather than shareholders.[1] In these cases, shareholders will not be as well informed about the financial affairs of companies as they will be where the auditors in practice accept shareholders as their primary clients. Auditors are aware that management and boards recommend the appointment of auditors.[2]

The collapse in recent years of a major accounting and auditing firm, Arthur Andersons, occurred at least partially because the firm appeared to accept

---

[1] The classic recent example of this in Australia is the collapse of a major general insurance company, HIH. The reasons for this collapse, including the role of auditors, are described in: Main, Andrew (2003), *Other People's Money. The Complete Story of the Extraordinary Collapse of HIH*, Harper Collins Publishers, Sydney.

[2] Two relevant research studies are: Kornish, L. and Levine, C. (2004), *Discipline with Common Agency: The Case of Audit and Nonaudit Services*, The Accounting Review, Vol.79, No.1, pp. 173–200; Houghton, K. and Jubb, C. (November 2003), *Auditor Selection: What Influences Decisions by Listed Companies?* Australian Accounting Review, Vol.13, No.3, pp. 67–72.

that its primary clients were senior management and the boards of the companies it audited, rather than shareholders. This was especially so in the audits of Enron and WorldCom in the United States.[3]

It is customary in many countries for the board of directors of a company to recommend an audit fee at the annual general meeting. The recommendation on who should be the auditor occurs at the same time as the recommendation on how much the auditor should be paid. This practice has strengths where it is determined by a country's laws governing private companies, and where audit firms distinguish correctly between their primary and secondary clients. However, it is open to risks if either of these conditions is not met.

Disclosure of audit fees and costs

As noted above, it is a common requirement for the fees paid by private companies to audit firms to be disclosed, such as in companies' annual reports. Public disclosure of fees permits readers of companies' reports to compare and contrast fees charged by audit firms for similar work. In other words, disclosure of audit fees informs the audit market. This market pressure is a discipline on audit firms to operate economically.

To apply this practice to the public sector would mean that audit fees would be disclosed in government agencies' reports, such as in annual reports. The position adopted here is that the agency should not pay audit fees, but the legislature should. Then, the term 'audit costs' is more fitting than 'audit fees'. The expectation that the legislature pays audit costs is compatible with releasing information about the costs of audits in individual agencies. That is because the SAI can estimate the costs of its audit in any particular agency, and provide that information to the legislature and to the agency, whereupon it can be released more widely. A vehicle for public release of audit costs is in a report, such as an annual report, of the government agency audited. Another possible vehicle is for the SAI to provide the legislature with data on the costs of all audits, and for that information to be published by either the legislature or the SAI. This public disclosure would open audit costs to legislative and public scrutiny, maintaining pressure on the SAI to work efficiently.

Audit costs are functions of the aims and conduct of audits, and of the management of the agencies being audited. For example, an SAI would spend more time coming to an audit opinion on the financial statements of an agency with poor controls and inadequate record keeping and financial systems, than it would

---

[3] Semple, J. (Fall 2002), *Accountants' Liability after Enron*, FDCC Quarterly, Vol.53, No.1, pp. 85–98: see also an interesting coverage of audit committee composition and shareholder actions in Raghunandan, K., and Rama, D (September 2003), *Audit Committee Composition and Shareholder Actions: Evidence from Voting on Auditor Ratification*, Auditing: A Journal of Practice and Theory, Vol.22, No.2, pp. 253–263.

in an agency with exemplary controls and systems. The additional time for the audit would translate into higher audit costs. Publication of those higher audit costs would permit informed readers to conclude that the audit was difficult. It would be a task for the auditor and for the agency's management to explain why audit costs were high. In other words, variations in the costs of public sector audits are subject matter for the SAI's reports to the legislature and to government agencies. High audit costs are proxy measures of inefficient agency management or inefficient auditing. That is why the costs of public sector audits should be disclosed.

In order for the SAI to disclose those costs, it must have financial management systems that permit it to estimate them. That is, a requirement on the SAI to estimate and publish its audit costs is a stimulus for the SAI to have financial management as sound as that which it expects in government agencies.

User pays in the public sector

In the public sector as in the private sector, there is a clear distinction between the auditor's primary and secondary clients. The primary client is the legislature, and the secondary client is the government, its staff and its agencies.

Because the legislature is the principal client, it is logical for it to pay audit fees or the costs of audits. Were a government agency to pay fees, there is a risk that the SAI would act, over time, as if it audited primarily for the agency rather than auditing for the legislature. In other words, the SAI would be confused over its clients. Then, a hazard is that the SAI would report more to the agency than to the legislature, acting to reduce the accountability of the government agency to the legislature.

Modernisation of the public sector in some countries has seen greater use of the user pays principle. In public sector audit, the user pays principle is applied fully where the legislature pays for public sector audits directly, such as through an annual budget appropriation. It is a mis-application of the user pays principle for agencies to transfer funds to the SAI to cover the costs of audits. The simplest way for the legislature to pay for audits is through the annual budget. Knowledge of this reinforces the importance of establishing a sound basis for the SAI's finances.

In mixed economies, government companies operate alongside privately owned businesses. Examples are in the telecommunications, transport and other infrastructure areas. Requiring government agencies to disclose their audit costs when audited by the SAI means that government companies are subject to the same disclosure requirements as private companies. That is so in countries where private sector firms must disclose their audit fees. However, company legislation in some countries may not require disclosure of audit costs. In those places, this practice of not disclosing public sector audit costs is related to the question of whether public sector audit law should be the same as in the private sector, or whether it should lead or follow private enterprise.

Conclusions

This chapter has answered the question of who should pay for audits by arguing that the legislature should have the authority to do so. However, the legislature can be advised by the government and by the SAI. An SAI that had the authority to determine its own resources would be maximising its independence. Only a small number of SAIs are in this situation. The chapter has described who pays for audits in the private sector, emphasised the importance of disclosure of audit costs, and noted risks in the public sector where audited agencies pay fees directly to the SAI.

Chapter 12

What Are the Different Kinds of Audits?

A legislature must take account of the different kinds of audits when revising audit law. The discussion below introduces the main kinds of audits. While most of this discussion is oriented towards the public sector, the definitions and perspectives can apply to the private sector with little change. The introduction proceeds through a number of questions as follows:

- What are the differences between regularity and performance audits?
- What are the differences between administrative and program effectiveness?
- How can audits assist in combating corruption?
- Who can commission audits?
- What are the differences between externally and internally commissioned audits?

What are the differences between regularity and performance audits?

INTOSAI states that regularity audits include:[1]

- attestation of financial accountability of accountable entities, involving examination and evaluation of financial records and expression of opinions on financial statements;
- attestation of financial accountability of the government administration as a whole;
- audit of financial systems and transactions including an evaluation of compliance with applicable statutes and regulations;
- audit of internal control and internal audit functions;
- audit of the probity and propriety of administrative decisions taken within the audited entity; and

---

[1] INTOSAI (1998), *Code of Ethics and Accounting Standards*, Auditing Standards Committee, p. 1.0.39.

- reporting of any other matters arising from or relating to the audit that the SAI considers should be disclosed.

Regularity auditing includes compliance auditing. It has preceded performance auditing in many countries, largely because governments have wanted to know whether taxpayers' funds were used for their intended purposes. For instance, if a country's legislature or government approved funding for construction of a bridge, a regularity audit can assist to determine whether the money was spent on bridge construction, a railway or construction of a hospital. Legislatures and governments will always have an interest in determining whether public moneys were spent as intended. Therefore, there will always be a demand for regularity audits.

Legislatures and governments set guidelines for financial control and expenditure. Financial audits concentrate on agencies' use of public funds in conformity with these official requirements, and on reporting of those funds. Thus, financial audits can determine whether an agency complies with requirements. Financial audits are often a form of regularity and compliance audits.

Financial statement audits are a particular kind of financial audit. In those countries where public sector agencies prepare financial statements for audits, the financial statement auditor will ask whether the agency's financial statements were prepared in accordance with the government's requirements. The financial statement auditor will also ask whether the financial statements offer a true and fair view of the agency's financial position or performance. Their ability to ask and answer such questions leads to government reliance on financial statement auditors to provide independent assessments of agencies' finances.

In some countries, government agencies do not prepare financial statements for audit. Then, there is no demand for financial statement auditors of government entities. In those places, the financial auditor is more likely to have a compliance role, forming an opinion on whether government funds are used by government entities in ways consistent with government requirements.

Notwithstanding the usefulness of regularity audits, legislatures and governments often ask additional questions that regularity audits cannot answer. That is because, although the government's money may have been spent on bridge construction as intended, rather than on housing or hospitals, it may not have been well spent. The latter would occur, for instance, if the bridge cost much more than planned, or if it were narrower than intended, reducing its usefulness.

Examples of additional questions that governments ask are:

- Was the bridge built for the lowest price?
- Was bridge construction well managed?
- Was the bridge built on time?
- Was construction consistent with industry standards?
- How well does the completed bridge provide for the transport needs of its users?

These are examples of questions that regularity audits would have difficulty in answering. They can be addressed in performance audits. Performance audits are distinguished from other kinds of audits by the questions they ask and issues they address. They complement rather than replace regularity, including financial statement, audits. Together, performance and regularity audits are powerful tools in public sector reform.

INTOSAI defines a performance audit as a review of the economy, efficiency and effectiveness with which the audited entity uses its resources in carrying out its responsibilities.[2] Performance audits are also known as:

- operational audits;
- efficiency audits; or
- value for money (VFM) audits.

INTOSAI describes how performance audits embrace:[3]

- audit of the economy of administrative activities in accordance with sound administrative principles and practices, and management policies;
- audit of the efficiency of utilisation of human, financial and other resources, including examination of information systems, performance measures and monitoring arrangements, and procedures followed by audited entities for remedying identified deficiencies; and
- audit of the effectiveness of performance in relation to achievement of the objectives of the audited entity, and audit of the actual impact of activities compared with the intended impact.

The great majority of governments have limited resources to meet their policies, whether these are domestically focused, such as in the provision of housing, education and health services, or externally focused, such as in maintenance of strong defence forces and foreign policies. Resource limitations require governments to operate economically and efficiently. Elected legislatures will also expect government to operate in this way. Performance audits are one tool to assist both the legislature and government in this task.

The following figure encapsulates the main features of regularity and performance auditing.

---

2 INTOSAI (1998), *Code of Ethics and Accounting Standards*, p.73.

3 INTOSAI (1998), *Code of Ethics and Accounting Standards*.

Regularity Audits	Performance Audits
• Compliance oriented • Focus on finance matters • Financial decisions, records and controls • Probity of administrative decisions	• Economy of operations • Efficiency of administration • Effectiveness of operations • Focus on management decisions • Value for money is a priority

Figure 12.1 Main Differences between Regularity and Performance Audits

The definition of performance audit also refers to the effectiveness of performance. Two kinds of effectiveness are involved. These are administrative and program effectiveness. Because these are frequently confused, we will clarify the distinction between these concepts.

What are the differences between administrative and program effectiveness?

Administrative effectiveness refers to how well a program is administered. It usually means that an administrator has a rational and clear way to implement a program. Characteristics of an administratively effective program or activity include well-defined goals or objectives, a resource allocation focusing on a program's most important goals, well-trained staff, guidelines, established lines of authority, and a clear definition of roles and responsibilities. These are not the only marks of an administratively effective program, but they are amongst the most important ones. You may care to add to this list.

A program can be administratively effective but it can fail. That could be because its goals were unattainable under all circumstances, or because, for instance, it had insufficient resources.

First Example

The former Community Employment Program is an example of an Australian program which was administratively effective but which did not achieve all of its goals. It was a well-resourced program created in the 1980s to address the problem of unemployment. Its total budget at that time was more than $1 billion. Probably, it was Australia's largest post-Second World War employment program, and it may still have that status. The program had three objectives as follows:

- to reduce cyclical unemployment;
- to reduce structural unemployment; and
- to provide benefits to the community largely through construction and maintenance projects judged, for instance, by local government to be socially useful.

A government agency evaluated the program. Its report concluded that the program provided large numbers of short-term jobs to combat cyclical unemployment, and that the construction and maintenance projects benefited the community. However, program participants were no more likely to find unsubsidised work after their time on the program than were those long-term unemployed who did not participate in the program. In other words, the program had not achieved its objective of alleviating structural unemployment, or unemployment occurring through structural change in the Australian economy.

The evaluation determined that the program was overburdened with objectives, and could not achieve each to the level desired by government. The program had given priority to combating cyclical unemployment through providing short-term jobs and priority to community projects. It had given far less priority to structural unemployment. There was an unresolved tension in the design of the program by government, which contributed to its success in addressing cyclical unemployment and to its small impact on structural unemployment. Notwithstanding, the program was well managed and was probably administratively effective.

The agency that evaluated the program was an organisation within a government department. It was a government organisation rather than an organisation independent of government. Shortly after the evaluating agency issued its draft evaluation report on the employment program, indicating that the latter was a partial not a complete success, the evaluating agency was abolished.

The notion of the independence or dependence of the audit, evaluation and review functions will be explored as we progress. These notions are important since they help us understand the role and functions of performance auditing in particular, and auditing in general.

Let us consider another example to highlight the difference between program and administrative effectiveness.

Second Example

Consider a small city where some residents have severe acute respiratory syndrome (SARS). The city's government is very concerned to slow and to stop the increase in the number of SARS cases. Consequently, the city government provides its chief health administrator with hundreds of millions of dollars to address the problem. With these funds, the administrator can take the following action:

- employ health specialists;
- purchase medicines;
- prepare isolation wards in hospitals;
- commence a public education campaign;
- purchase food for residents who are in quarantine and who cannot work; and
- seek and pay for the expert international assistance.

These measures will have an effect, slowing and containing the spread of SARS. Let us develop this scenario.

> **Third Example**
>
> The same small city has an outbreak of SARS. This time, the city government has fewer resources. It has only one million dollars for the health administrator to take measures to slow the spread of the illness.

In this case, the health administrator can implement only some of the measures to contain the illness. There would be insufficient resources to establish isolation wards in hospitals, and insufficient resources to purchase medicines. The effect of the health administrator's efforts would be less than were the administrator to have ample resources, and SARS continues to spread.

In the second example, a program evaluation would suggest that the health program was effective. In the third example, an evaluation would suggest that the health program was ineffective.

It would be problematic to determine whether management of the health program was effective. That is because the abundance of resources in the first instance, where the administrator accessed hundreds of millions of dollars, could disguise waste and inefficiency. For example, the administrator may have purchased the wrong kinds of many medicines, or many more hospital isolation wards than necessary may have been prepared, leading to the lack of space in hospitals to treat other serious illnesses. This would lead to higher morbidity rates from other causes, although SARS was contained. Medical care could have been concentrated in one part of the city, such as high income areas, when most patients were in less affluent areas. These are signs that the program was not well administered, although it was successful.

The health administrator with fewer resources would have made more difficult decisions about priorities. Those decisions could have been to place more emphasis on a public education campaign than on the importing of international experts, and more emphasis on suspected cases being restricted to their homes rather than all being sent to acute care hospitals. In other words, the program could have been well managed, although it may not have been as successful as in the first scenario.

An administrator may be employed in managing a program with limited chance of success. Notwithstanding poor program design or inadequate resources to implement a program, a professional administrator must manage a program as well as he or she can. This means that a program can be administratively effective but fail.

The converse also applies. That is because a program can be badly managed or administered and still succeed. A sign of a badly managed program can be excessive administrative costs, perhaps visible on the basis of a comparison with other programs or activities.

Administrative ineffectiveness and administrative inefficiency are linked. It is possible to make a theoretical distinction, but in practice it can be hard to distinguish between them. Administrative ineffectiveness may explain a program's ineffectiveness.

Performance audit and evaluation are related since they can review the same program or activity, albeit from different perspectives. They may be understood as being at different points in a spectrum of types of review. As we saw earlier, INTOSAI defines performance auditing to include program evaluation. However, many evaluators define evaluation to include performance auditing. Different views are possible on whether performance audit is part of evaluation, or whether evaluation is part of performance audit. To debate such distinctions leads us to compare and to contrast these two types of review, and to understand them in a fuller way. However, for our purposes, it is sufficient to acknowledge that they are different but related activities.

A program evaluation will conclude that a program succeeded or failed. Only the best evaluations will explain why there was success or failure. Performance audit, through its concentration on administrative machinery, can explain a good part of that success or failure. Therefore, both performance audit and evaluation can contribute to our understanding of sound public and private administration.

Consequently, it is possible to conduct a performance audit of a program, to conduct an evaluation of the same program, or to conduct simultaneously a performance audit and an evaluation. To pursue the two reviews at the same time is unusual and infrequent.

How can audits assist in combating corruption?

A major international problem is corruption in the public sector. Corruption can occur in the public sector in many ways to benefit individuals or groups, such as through theft, manipulation of tenders and decisions on tenders, inflated pricing, favoured costing, and fraud, including through use of the Internet. The Public sector can be subject to corrupt forces from outside. A public sector experiencing rapid change can find that key financial and other controls and a culture of integrity and service are threatened as change accelerates. This is a fertile environment for corruption.

As ASOSAI has emphasised:[4]

---

[4] ASOSAI (2003), *ASOSAI Guidelines for Dealing with Fraud and Corruption*, <http:www.asosai.org/fraud_guidelines/index.htm> These guidelines were developed initially for ASOSAI by the Board of Audit in Japan.

> The primary responsibility for establishing an environment that prevents valuable entity assets from being lost through fraud and corruption... clearly rests with the management. Further, since good management practices require the establishment of adequate control and checks, the responsibility to detect fraud and corruption is a natural corollary of the responsibility to establish an environment that prevents and deters fraud and corruption.

SAIs are renowned for their integrity and impartiality. Therefore, it is logical for legislators, government and the citizenry to turn to them for assistance in opposing corruption. Again, as ASOSAI has reminded us:

> This reaffirmation and unambiguous recognition of the primary role and responsibility of the management, however, does not relieve the auditor of his responsibility to provide a credible assurance within his SAI's audit mandate about the actions taken by management or those that may materially affect the picture that emerges from the audited financial reports. This responsibility covers situations where the financial reports or other auditable record may be materially misrepresented and the misrepresentation may or may not have taken place with the knowledge or involvement of the management. This responsibility of the auditor is the extension of his responsibility to provide assurance about the audited entity and its financial statements and his obligation to make the management (either in each entity individually or through reports to the legislature) aware of any weaknesses in the design or operation of the accounting and internal control systems which are reviewed by him in the discharge of his professional duties. Although auditors are not primarily responsible for preventing fraud and corruption, audit can be a significant influence in reducing fraud and corruption.

The question is what is the best way for an SAI to assist in this task? INTOSAI's Code of Ethics outlines how public sector auditors must work so as to merit the trust and confidence of their clients and auditees.[5] Their audit opinions are credible when stakeholders trust and have confidence in their work. The personnel of SAIs must also demonstrate personal integrity. Consequently, an SAI is an ally in combating corruption when staff manifest these personal characteristics. Beyond that, the Code of Ethics and INTOSAI's Auditing Standards do not provide a great deal of guidance on the role of SAIs in opposing corruption.

Auditors who combat corruption and misuse of power can be at risk. For instance, the Chairman of the Philippines Commission on Audit has spoken of how:[6]

---

[5] INTOSAI (1998), *Code of Ethics*, pp.11–12.

[6] Chairman Guillermo N. Carague, Commission on Audit (2 October 2003), *COA Directions During Critical Times in the Philippine Economy*, Conference of the Philippine Computer Society (PCS), and Philippine State Universities and Colleges Computer Education and System Society (PSUCCESS), AIM Conference Center, Manila, Philippines.

> In the years 1998 and 2001, we lost three of our dedicated young auditors who were gunned down by unknown killers, simply because they were brave enough to expose the anomalies committed by some people in power.

The Chairman of the Philippines Commission on Audit also spoke about the Commission's steps to reduce the exposure of its staff to allegations of corruption. Since 1995, the Commission has not permitted its staff to be involved in the pre-audit of financial transactions. Staff focused on post-audit reviews of transactions after they were completed. In addition, the Commission stopped the practice of some of its auditors receiving stipends, allowances and benefits from other government agencies.

Political and popular expectations can be that SAIs have a major role in anti-corruption activities. SAIs have a significant role when their regularity work tests compliance with legislative and other official provisions. A strong legal compliance audit program is of fundamental importance. The SAI's strategic audit planning should include a significant element of compliance testing, either by designing entire audits as compliance assignments, or through designing audits that address selected aspects of agencies' initiatives to limit and reduce corruption. Examples of audits to address selected agency initiatives are audits of the adequacy of an agency's planning, policies and measures to combat fraud. The ANAO has conducted a series of performance audits of fraud control arrangements in Australian Government agencies. The main objective of these audits was to assess whether agencies implemented fraud control arrangements in line with the Government's Fraud Control Policy, and whether these arrangements were operating effectively. As well as these audits, the ANAO also surveyed fraud control arrangements in government, which led to an overview report on agency arrangements to manage fraud in the national government.[7]

Another ANAO example is of a cross-portfolio or cross-ministry audit of Internet security. The audit led to improvements in Internet security and fraud control in those agencies whose practices were reviewed. The objective was to form an opinion on the adequacy of Commonwealth agencies' management of Internet security. In order to achieve this objective, the audit addressed:[8]

- Internet security risk assessments, policies and plans;
- agencies' Internet security management procedures, to determine whether these were consistent with relevant government guidelines and requirements, and with examples of industry better practice;

---

[7] ANAO (2003), *Survey of Fraud Control Arrangements in APS Agencies*, Audit Report No. 14 2003–2004, ANAO, Canberra.

[8] ANAO (2001), *Internet Security Within Commonwealth Agencies*, Audit Report No. 13 2001–2002, ANAO, Canberra.

- Internet site management, including virus protection and detection strategies, prevention and detection of unauthorised access and incident response arrangements; and
- test performances of selected sites.

An SAI can concentrate on high risk areas, which ASOSAI identified as including:[9]

- contracts of services and procurement;
- inventory management;
- sanctions and clearances;
- program management;
- revenue receipt;
- cash management;
- general expenditure; and
- other areas with public interfaces.

SAIs would identify which were the high risk areas in their domains.

An extreme example of an anti-corruption focus in an SAI's audit program is when all an SAI's activities test agencies' compliance with laws and official regulations. This would leave no room for the SAI to determine how well managed were government programs. The need for audits to form opinions on the level of agency management is evident from observing that a program may have such strong internal controls that fraud and corruption are highly unlikely. Yet the agency focuses so much energy on combating fraud and corruption that it has no regard to the need to manage efficiently and effectively. Well-designed performance audits can identify this imbalance. With knowledge that there are different kinds of audits for different purposes, the SAI, and/or the legislature, when planning strategically, must decide how much of the SAI's resources will be spent on anti-corruption activities, and how much on other SAI work. When they do so, they are practising the independence encouraged by the Lima Declaration introduced in Chapter 8.

Theft, fraud and other financial misdeeds can cost taxpayers a small or a large amount. A problem for the SAI in designing compliance audits is to decide which internal control weaknesses lead to the probability of small and large frauds. This is a decision about financial thresholds beyond which breakdowns in financial controls should be investigated.

The Asian Organisation of Supreme Audit Institutions, ASOSAI, offers guidance about such decisions. ASOSAI's Guidelines state that:[10]

---

9 ASOSAI (2003), *ASOSAI Guidelines for Dealing with Fraud and Corruption.*

10 ASOSAI *Guideline 1*, <www.asosai.org>

> While determining materiality levels for different audit areas, the SAI may take into account adjustments to the materiality level that may make audit more responsive to risk arising from fraud and corruption.

Audits most likely to find fraud and corruption are those planned to investigate these matters. Most audits are not planned for this purpose. Therefore, discovery or uncovering of fraud is likely to be a secondary effect of an audit created for other aims. This can be difficult for an SAI to communicate to those interested in audits and those wanting the SAI to do more to combat corruption. It is difficult because common perceptions of audit are that it has a major role in anti-corruption activities. It can have a major role, depending on its planning and on the objectives of each audit.

In some countries, the SAI is expected to have a major role in combating fraud. Vietnam and Brazil are examples of this. The Auditor-General of the State Audit of Vietnam has highlighted the four-part role of his office in preventing and mitigating corrupt practices.[11] He described how, first, SAIs' mandates are usually undertaken by auditors possessing high professional competence; second, SAIs' discharge functions of warning on the possibilities of corruption and so are capable of putting forward suitable measures for uprooting corrupt practices; third, although the SAIs of most countries do not have executive functions, they can affect executive bodies through their audit recommendations to have in place necessary behaviours to curb corrupt commitments; and, fourth, on the basis of audit results, the SAI can propose recommendations to the legislature, the executive and other state bodies on revising and supplementing relevant policies and statutory regulations.

The Brazilian SAI is a second example. The Brazilian Court of Accounts Strategic Plan for 2003–2007 affirms that a major strategic objective is to combat corruption, the diversion of public moneys, and fraud in the management of federal public resources.[12]

> The continuing combat of corruption and the waste of federal government resources constitute a primary preoccupation of the work of the Tribunal. The scandals follow one another, but the tolerance of the taxpayer with diversion of public money and waste is less on each occasion. Besides this, public resources are scarce and social demands are rising. Therefore, the development and implementation of mechanisms and forms of control capable of effectively combating and inhibiting the improper application of resources are fundamental, as much as making those involved responsible. For all of this, key questions are areas of risk, materiality and relevance; the importance of access to information in

---

[11] Do Binh Duong (April 2004), 'Corruption in Public Sector Investment Projects: Preventive Role of the Office of the State Audit of Vietnam, SAV'. *Asian Journal of Government Audit*, ASOSAI, pp. 43–48.

[12] Tribunal de Contas da União (2003), *Plano Estratégico 2003–2007*, Março de 2003, Tribunal de Contas da União, Brasilia.

> respect of public management; timely preventive action; a high level of integration of systems of external and internal control and the development of alliances with public agencies, the media and organized sectors of society, and greater dissemination of information about public expenditure. As well, it is indispensable for society to perceive the forces of the agencies of control in combating corruption and believe in the effectiveness of their work. The effective construction of this relationship can stimulate positive attitudes in the population, disposing it to involve itself actively in social control.

The Brazilian Court of Accounts Strategic Plan expands on the notion of social control of corruption, and the role of the Court.

> The exercise of social control depends, essentially, on the information available and the degrees of confidence of society in relation to the institutions of control. It is necessary that society has access to information and that it sees the strength of the agencies of control in combating corruption and in defending their interests. Without these elements, it is not possible to stimulate positive attitudes in the population, disposing it to involve itself actively in social control of corruption.
>
> It is necessary to adopt mechanisms that stimulate the participation of civil society and government organizations in action to prevent corruption and waste. The work of the Court of Accounts has a decisive role in this aspect of the relationship between the state and society, through the diffusion of information about the utilisation of public resources, of the results of the management of public resources, as well as of the benefits derived from the actions of control agencies. With this, it is possible to develop, in each citizen, a position of co-responsibility for control of public resources.

Another part of the role of an SAI in confronting corruption is in its supply of information to the police. Audit legislation can provide for an SAI to provide relevant information to the police. An example is the Australian *Auditor-General Act 1997* that permits the Auditor-General to disclose particular information to the police if the Auditor-General is of the opinion that the disclosure is in the public interest.[13] One method of promoting understanding of the best way to use audit is to highlight how police have a more prominent and accepted role in anti-corruption activities than the SAI. The latter can work with the police force, for instance, through communicating to the police that serious breakdowns in an entities' financial controls increased the likelihood of internal fraud and of the agency's exposure to externally sourced fraud. A memorandum of understanding between the SAI and the police can promote the work of both agencies, and describe their complementary roles. The Chairman of the Philippine Commission on Audit's comments are relevant in affirming that:[14]

---

[13] *Auditor-General Act 1997*, S36, <www.anao.gov.au>

[14] Chairman Guillermo N. Carague (2003).

> Other government agencies and officials in authority have to do their part, especially after the Commission on Audit has done its job of reporting anomalies.

Another approach for the SAI in pointing out that it is only one player active in anti-corruption activities is to emphasise that the agencies themselves have primary responsibility for these activities. Senior management are appointed to control agencies. Consequently, within agencies, primary responsibility for combating fraud and corruption resides with senior management. Beyond individual agencies, there are examples of specialist units established to combat fraud. The European Union, for instance, established in 1999 the European Anti-Fraud Office. Its mission is to protect the financial interests of the European Union, to fight fraud, corruption and any other illegal activity that has a financial consequence. The Office complements the work of the European Court of Auditors.[15]

An SAI may have the authority to identify fraud and corruption, which is different from the authority to prosecute those involved in them. In this regard, ASOSAI's guidelines are relevant.[16]

> When in the opinion of the auditor the financial statements include material fraudulent transactions, or such transactions have not been adequately disclosed, or the audit conducted by the auditor leads him to the conclusion that instance(s) of fraud and/or corruption have taken place and when the auditor has adequate evidence to support his conclusion, he should qualify the audit certificate and/or ensure that his findings are adequately included in his audit report. However, the term fraud or corruption may not be used in a conclusive sense unless such action is established in a court of law.

Earlier we mentioned how audits can test compliance with legislation and with official regulations. Countries differ in the numbers of laws that apply to the public sector. SAIs in countries with large numbers of laws perhaps are more likely to find non-compliance than SAIs in countries where there are few laws for the public sector. One way for a legislature to confront large numbers of findings of non-compliance is to enact more laws. More laws do not of themselves lead to greater compliance. In fact, a large number of laws can create confusion for entities attempting to implement legislation. Large numbers of laws can also lead to agencies realising that they cannot implement all legislation, so they select which they will apply. This scenario, which exists in at least one large developing country, illustrates how general legislation for the public sector can shape an SAI's priorities and confuse the meaning of public sector reform.

---

[15] NAO (2004), *Financial Management of the European Union. A Progress Report*, Report by the Comptroller and Auditor-General, HC 529 Session 2003–2004, 6 May 2004, NAO, London.

[16] ASOSAI, *Guideline 28*, <www.asosai.org>

Who can commission audits?

Audits can be commissioned by an external body or by an agency's management. In the public sector, SAIs, such as chambers of accounts, courts of accounts or audit offices, are the external bodies which are most commonly associated with performance audits.

Agency management is sometimes concerned about the agency's efficiency or administration, and commission a performance audit. This authority to commission an independent review is an important management tool. Since the term 'performance audit' is uncommon, management is more likely to label its initiative a review, a management review, or management consultancy. The function of these reviews is similar. Each can assist agency management and staff – provided they are well designed and implemented. Internal audit can also commission a performance audit. Internal audit is becoming more involved in performance audits, although in many cases the emphasis is likely to be more focused on compliance and 'waste watch', rather than on efficiency and effectiveness.

Agency management involves line management, senior management or a board of management. In an ideal world, each would desire the same result from a performance audit that they commissioned. In practice, they often desire different outcomes. We will explore a scenario to illustrate this point.

In this scenario, line management knows that the program for which it has responsibility is neither administratively efficient nor effective. It acts to improve efficiency and effectiveness. Action is only partially successful and inefficiencies remain. Line management is held responsible for the excess costs of the continuing inefficiencies and problematic administration. Line management may talk with senior management about those difficulties, or conceal them. Both responses are logical depending on the circumstances. Where line management conceals inefficiencies and ineffective administration, it will not commission a performance audit. If senior management is unaware of them, then administrative problems will continue. However, senior management's lack of knowledge points to inadequate performance data within the organisation, which is an internal accountability problem.

Senior management becomes aware of the administrative problems. It works with line management to remedy them. Action is successful, and the agency moves to address other challenges. However, if action is unsuccessful, senior management may commission a performance audit or review.

Let us continue with this scenario and see what it reveals about motivations for performance audit.

The agency may have a board of directors if it is in either the public or private sectors, or the agency may have a minister. In some situations when confronted with administrative problems which conventional action does not resolve, senior management will commission a performance audit or review. In other circumstances, it will not do so because the board or minister may assess poorly senior management's performance because of the existence in the first place of those administrative problems.

The board of directors has responsibilities defined in law. If it learns about administrative inefficiencies or ineffectiveness, it must exercise its responsibilities. Its action can include the commissioning of a performance audit or review. It can use the results of the review to address the administrative problems.

There are degrees of separation from an administrative task. For example, a line manager is one step removed from the clerk in the office: senior management is two steps removed, and so on. These degrees of separation approximate degrees of independence. However, since agency management maintains overall responsibility for implementation of the relevant government policy, management remains part of the system of internal accountability. A minister of a government agency is external to it. Therefore, the head of the government agency could be described as being accountable to the minister. For the chief of the agency, this may appear as external accountability. However, since the minister is part of government, taxpayers can describe the agency head's reporting arrangements to the minister as internal accountability, since it is within government.

The minister would be answerable to the head of the government. This relationship can be described as one of external accountability, since it is a relationship between what happens in the minister's portfolio and the rest of government. It is also a demonstration of internal accountability since, by definition, both the head of government and the minister are part of government.

These examples illustrate how an authority relationship can involve both internal and external accountability. Awareness of the dual nature of accountability is necessary to understand the role of audits.

What are the differences between externally and internally commissioned audits?

This matter is important since it highlights other essential characteristics of SAIs. The Australian Government's Energy Policy required all government agencies to conduct energy audits (or approved alternative energy use assessments) of all commercial buildings within the first year of occupancy, and at intervals not exceeding five years thereafter. All resulting cost-effective recommendations were required to be implemented.

The ANAO reviewed agencies' implementation of the Energy Policy in a report tabled in Parliament in June 1999.[17] The audit found that the mandatory nature of the requirement to implement all cost effective recommendations of energy audits raised the risk that energy audits would be less than objective.

---

[17] ANAO (1999), *Energy Efficiency in Commonwealth Operations. Department of Industry, Science and Resources, Australian Greenhouse Office*, Audit Report No. 47 1998–99, ANAO, Canberra.

Agencies determined the terms of reference for energy audits, and selected the auditors. Thus, these energy audits, which were performance audits since they were designed to improve efficiency, were internal audits. All management likes to maintain control of its programs and activities. The Energy Policy's requirement that management implement all cost-effective recommendations of energy audits reduced management's options. A temptation would be to ensure that the terms of reference, the selection of the specialist auditor, and the auditor's report were such to ensure that management kept control of its options. This is to say that the mandatory nature of the requirement for a performance audit and compulsory implementation of its recommendations, when management could choose critical elements of the review, may have reduced the amount of change from that possible with an externally sourced and conducted audit. There are no data available to describe the effects on energy use of this part of the Energy Policy.

The previous scenario and the above example illustrate how an agency's environment and reward structure influence whether an audit or review is commissioned, and how the agency's environment can influence an audit's terms of reference.

The results of most internally commissioned performance audits are not published, because there is no need for them to be published. They are reports to management, and it is the right of management to determine how to respond to them. Sometimes the results of internally commissioned performance audits are not released to staff. Again, it is the right of management to decide on an appropriate dissemination policy for all reports that they have commissioned. It is easy for management to ensure that a performance audit which it has commissioned reaches the conclusion which management wants. Further, it can be a logical strategy for management to ensure that a performance audit for which it pays comes to a conclusion that management desires: whether it is legitimate depends on the environment. One viewpoint is that a management decision not to release the results of an internally commissioned performance audit implies some form of conspiracy to hide unpleasant results. However, that may not be the reason for not releasing an internally commissioned report. Statistical data on this matter are hard to obtain.

We will be better armed to understand those audits and reviews which management commissions once we appreciate the similarities and differences between internally and externally commissioned audits and reviews. Knowledge that different kinds of reviews have different roles informs management of action which it can take. That knowledge also informs staff of why management may have commissioned an audit or review when there were other options. In addition, staff will be better informed about how to respond to the results of an internally commissioned audit or review, if management decides to release the results.

There are degrees of independence for internal reviews. Senior management can be more independent than line management from the implementation of a program or activity to be audited. The caution is that careful analysis of the organisation is necessary before reaching that conclusion. A board of directors can be more independent than senior or line management involved in a program's administration. This points to the need for information about the role and responsibilities of the commissioners of internally sourced audits or reviews.

An essential difference between audits commissioned externally and internally is that the former have more independence than an internally commissioned review. This is not a criticism of internally commissioned and sourced audits and reviews, since these latter are valuable. In fact, they should be encouraged and conducted more often because they can provide management with valuable information to continue with administrative reforms.

Few empirical data are available on methodological differences between internally and externally commissioned audits and reviews. A scanning of the literature suggests that there are few methodological differences, although research is necessary to establish this point. A caveat is that the external auditor is unlikely to have the authority to ensure that the agency implements any recommendations while, in comparison, the closer links of internal audit and management increase the probability of internal audit recommendations being addressed. Notwithstanding, the likely existence of few, if any, methodological differences between internal and external audits and reviews is good news for management. That is because management can fund these activities knowing that it can obtain the same result as if an external body, such as an SAI, conducted an audit. The significant difference is that management retains control of the methodology and therefore of the results, in comparison with an externally commissioned review where it controls neither.

Conclusions

This chapter identified further matters for any review of public sector audit, including of its legislation. These matters included:

- the desirability of legislation requiring the SAI to conduct regularity and performance audits;
- clarification of whether the SAI must evaluate government programs as well as conduct performance audits of them;
- identification of how the SAI can assist in combating corruption, and the limits to the SAI's capacity in this area;
- acknowledgement that both the SAI and agency management can commission audits; and
- recognition of the legitimacy of agency management controlling the use of audits, including audit reports, that it commissions.

Chapter 13

How Do Audits Lead to Change? Living with Two Masters – The Client and the Auditee

We introduced earlier how an often-discussed issue with audits is whether their prime objective should be to provide an assurance, generally through preparation of a written report, or to affect change and reform. Both objectives are challenging. In asking whether and how audits can change organisations, we develop another perspective on what is an SAI, which is the focus of Part II of this book.

The notion of how audits lead to change will be explored by highlighting the following issues:

- The importance of audit opinions.
- How audits conducted independently of the agency being audited provide credible audit opinions.
- The value of public sector wide audits.
- The utility of second or follow-up audits.
- The necessity of understanding the expectations of stakeholders in the audit.

Why are audit opinions important?

Auditors are employed to give audit opinions. An audit opinion is the auditor's conclusion about the agency or program being studied. It is where the auditor relies on the evidence collected during the audit to reach a logical and defensible view.

In black and white terms, an audit opinion provides an assurance of sound management of the program, activity or agency audited, or it provides the view that management is inefficient, ineffective and unaccountable. We will give examples of how many audit opinions provide both an assurance and a critical view. The issue of audit expectations will also be introduced. This will be done through comparison with the work of medical practitioners.

A medical doctor is paid to give his or her medical opinion on a patient's health. That opinion consists of an assessment of the patient's health, a diagnosis of any illness, and treatment to address any illness and to improve the patient's health. Similarly, an auditor is paid to give an audit opinion on aspects of the management of an agency, activity or program, whether these are in the public or private sectors. That audit opinion consists of an overall opinion on the adequacy of management, identification of any management problems, and advice to management on how to address those problems. We will return to this medical analogy later.

Assurance opinions

An opinion which provides assurance of sound management can be produced or written for both an external and an internal client. No change or reform is necessary if the report provides a positive opinion on a program's or agencies financial or other performance. That does not mean that the audit opinion will lead to no change in the agency, activity or program audited, but it decreases the likelihood of change.

In an audit report, the ANAO provided an assurance that an Australian Government entity was managing well its responsibilities for the National Aboriginal Health Strategy. That Strategy is largely a housing and related infrastructure program.[1] The audit opinion was that contracted program management arrangements implemented by the entity for the National Aboriginal Health Strategy were effective in delivering major housing and infrastructure projects to Indigenous communities. Notwithstanding, the entity was encouraged to improve the program's administration.

Critical audit opinions

Critical audit opinions occur where management shortcomings are found. An example is in an ANAO report on the management of performance information resulting from the national government's payments to state and territory governments for specific purposes.[2] The audit opinion noted agencies' efforts to improve the quality of performance information in payment agreements with the states and territories and in documented administrative arrangements. The critical component of the audit opinion was its conclusion that disappointing aspects were the limited inclusion and use of performance indicators, targets and milestones and program evaluation as management tools.

---

[1] ANAO (1999), National Aboriginal Health Strategy – Delivery of Housing and Infrastructure to Aboriginal and Torres Strait Islander Communities. Aboriginal and Torres Strait Islander Commission, Report No.39 1998–99, ANAO, Canberra.

[2] ANAO (1999), *The Management of Performance Information for Specific Purpose Payments – The State of Play*, Report No.31 1998–99, ANAO, Canberra.

What we see in the above two examples of audit opinions is a mixture of assurance that program administration was sound, with proposals to develop that administration. Such a mixed opinion is common in audit reports. It is similar to an opinion of a medical doctor on a patient's health.

A medical doctor can tell the patient that he or she is healthy, but has an illness. The latter could be as light as a cold, or as serious as a heart condition requiring surgery. A light cold and a heart condition are very different. It is easy for the doctor to diagnose the patient with the cold as a healthy individual but with a problem which can be remedied in a relatively short time, provided the person follows a particular course of action. It is more difficult for the doctor to affirm a patient's health when the patient has an operable heart condition.

The doctor must decide at what point a patient's morbidity leads to a medical opinion that the patient is unhealthy. There are limits to how far we can develop the analogy with an audit opinion, but the comparison remains worth pursuing.

There are different behavioural implications of a medical opinion which says that a patient is healthy but suffers from a particular medical condition, to a medical opinion which says that the patient is unhealthy. However, in the case of the patient with a cold, the behavioural implications may not be different. But the implications can be very different for the patient with the operable heart condition. That is because an opinion that the patient is healthy but suffers from just one problem could lead to different patient behaviour from an opinion that the patient was unhealthy. For instance, the patient may initiate different action from the two opinions.

We should also keep in mind that different medical doctors may come to different conclusions about the health status of the patient with the operable heart condition. Others, such as health insurance companies, may rely on the medical reports.

Auditors, too, must give opinions on whether an agency's, activity's or program's management is sound but with one or two problems, or whether management is unsound. As with medical doctors, auditors can reach different opinions. The judgement and the difficulty are in formulating and expressing the audit opinion.

Formulation and expression of the audit opinion take into account the purpose of the audit and the audit objective. Clearly, whatever the audit's objective, the auditors must understand the nature of what they are reviewing. It is essential that the auditors have data to support their audit opinion. Those data are their bases for forming strong, clear and defensible arguments to support the audit opinion.

What are the characteristics of independent audits?

The characteristics of independent externally commissioned audits, such as those conducted by SAIs, include:

- as indicated previously, little or no management control by the agency over how the audit is conducted, its personnel, its direction and its report;
- more formal and possibly more difficult relations between the auditor and the agency. This can involve agency suspicion about the motives for conducting the audit, and unease about release of findings. The nature of this relationship affects the selection of staff for audits and their training;
- if the results of the independent review will be published, then the external auditor must have a publicly defensible methodology and a publicly defensible audit opinion and audit findings. Certainly an internal auditor who conducts audits must also have a defensible methodology, but because it is internal, that methodology is less open to scrutiny than that of the external auditor. The importance of an external auditor being able to defend publicly his or her audit opinion also affects the selection of audit staff and their training. In addition, it leads to a tendency for external audit reports to be cautious, and sometimes – in order to reduce the risk of the audit opinion being undermined – to the audit opinion also being more conservative;
- the expectations of different stakeholders must be considered by the external auditor. Stakeholders include, not necessarily in order of importance, agency management and staff, an agency minister if there is one, agency business or individual clients, and the agency to which the external auditor is accountable. This is likely to be the legislature if the external auditor is an SAI. The most influential audits manage stakeholders' expectations well. This does not mean that audit leads to stakeholders having the same expectations.

Evaluation as much as audit is affected by the independence of those involved. For instance, management can and does exert the same amount of control over evaluations it commissions as it does over audits it sponsors. Therefore, in reading an evaluation report, it is important to know, first, whether the evaluation was commissioned by management and, second, its independence from management. Unlike in some other countries, in Australia there are very few evaluations of Federal government programs conducted independently of management, in the same way as there are independent performance audits, conducted by an audit office, of government programs. This was noted in Chapter 5. A relevant question is whether an SAI has the legal authority to evaluate the success or failure of government initiatives. The answer can highlight the responsibility of a government agency or agencies for this task, or it can lead to the realisation that it is not possible to identify who is responsible for program evaluation.

The value of public sector-wide audits

SAIs are unique where they are the only entities with legislated independence, powerful access rights, and with the capacity to identify trends and patterns in public sector activity. They can identify trends by accumulating and re-analysing the results of individual audits. They can also identify administrative patterns by forming audit objectives to include more than one agency in an audit. Then, the audit can compare and contrast management behaviour. Where agencies are in different portfolios, the SAI can still compare management. On an even broader scale, cross-portfolio audits can include several or all portfolios. There are numerous possibilities for cross-portfolio audits, such as audits of the processing of accounts, property management, information technology, use of the Internet to deliver services, employment conditions, tendering processes, asset sales, contract management, and service delivery.

The government may have information about these trends. In that case, the SAI's cross-portfolio audits will verify the government's information, and report it to the legislature and publicly where the government has not done this. In many cases in cross-portfolio audits, the SAI will gather information and data that the government will not have. This information can be hazardous for a government which will be reluctant to support such work. One reason for this is that data from cross-portfolio or service-wide studies can reveal whether the government is implementing legislation, and, if so, the degree of skill in its implementation, and whether it has interpreted the legislation consistent with the assembly's intent.

Credible information about what is happening in the wider public sector is critical to understanding the success of reform efforts. Information and explanation of trends found in cross-portfolio work are so important that cross-portfolio audits should be included in the SAI's strategic planning. Once an SAI has conducted a cross-portfolio audit on a matter of public and professional importance, it can schedule another audit with the same objective a year or so later. The results of the second and first audits can be compared to determine the degree of change in the administrative phenomena studied.

Second or follow-up audits

As described above, an audited agency is not necessarily compelled to implement audit recommendations. A possible exception covers findings and recommendations made by courts of account, which have judicial power. Where an agency has agreed to implement audit recommendations and where it is compelled to implement them by force of law, it is necessary to find out whether they have been implemented. That is because, once the SAI turned its attention away, no change occurred, resulting in underlying administrative problems continuing. It is the responsibility of executive government to implement audit recommendations. Agencies' audit committees have a role in monitoring implementation of audit findings. Sometimes as well, government has a central agency to which audited agencies report progress in implementation of the SAI's recommendations. It is just as likely that the government leaves it to individual agencies audited to address the SAI's recommendations, including whether to pursue or to ignore them.

An SAI can consider that it has completed its work once the audit report is finalised. But if it has a continuing interest in administrative reform, it can seek information from its former auditee on progress on implementing the SAI's earlier recommendations, or at least on what the agency is doing to try to remedy the underlying administrative problems that the SAI identified. The SAI can simply request this information from the auditee, analyse it and conclude that progress has or has not been made. But how will the SAI assure itself that this supplementary information provided by the government entity is accurate? It can do so through a second audit. This second audit would be restricted to visiting the former auditee, that becomes an auditee once more, and observing for itself what was done to address administrative problems. This second audit is a follow-up audit. Audits of this kind keep the pressure on agencies to continue to consider the SAI's recommendations as aids to administrative change. The SAI can determine its priority for second or follow-up audits in its annual planning.

Are audit expectations important?

Production of a report could be for an external or an internal audience. If the report is for an external audience, then any change or reform will be the responsibility of the audience that commissioned it. In that case, the auditors' responsibilities are met with the report's production. The goal may not be to affect change, but to have an audit report. Similarly with an internal audience, it can be the responsibility of senior management or a governing board to affect change.

The internal or external client or audience probably will have the legal or other authority to require any change which is required. In the case of chambers or courts of accounts, these may have the legal authority to take action on certain irregularities discovered in financial statements.[3] They may be authorised to reconcile the accounts prepared by the accountants, to impose fines on them, and in certain circumstances to cause their suspension or dismissal. It is very easy to see how change occurs in these situations.

Change can occur because of an audit opinion, including audit findings. It can also occur because of an audit report's recommendations. Many audit reports

---

[3] INTOSAI (1992 and 1995), *Accounting Standards*, INTOSAI, Vienna, Austria, p.65, <www.intosai.org>

lead to recommendations. Those reports which provide an assurance of good management may not include recommendations to improve administration because it is not necessary to do so. But for most audits, recommendations are the key to achieving change and reform. Therefore, their wording is very important.

Recommendations can point out a general direction for improved agency administration, or they can propose an immediate course of action. They can stimulate management of the audited body to reform, or they can lead to management resisting change. The art of the audit is to affect reform. If an audit recommendation is worded so that management feels offended or belittled, then it is unlikely that it will respond to the audit opinion and findings in the way the auditors hoped.

Countries have different practices in regard to accepting and implementing an SAI's recommendations. Usually, management of the Australian agency, activity or program being audited is not compelled to accept the auditor's recommendations. One explanation for an absence of a requirement to accept an auditor's recommendations is that the auditor may have made a mistake in the opinion and in the recommendation. While professional approaches to preparation of the audit opinion, recommendations and report reduce the risk of auditor error, they do not eliminate it. That is one reason why auditors should seek the auditee's comments on the draft report. It would be unwise for any auditee to agree to implement a recommendation which does not address key management issues or to agree to implement an impractical recommendation.

Most clients of audits require management of a body being audited to explain why it rejects an audit finding or recommendation. It is inadequate for management to say only that it does not agree with an audit opinion or recommendation. That is because a simple and direct management statement of 'I disagree' or 'No', can be more evocative of how the audit is perceived, rather than a management attempt to address any underlying issues. Management disagreement with an audit finding or recommendation has more legitimacy when management explains why it disagrees.

The auditor should work towards creating an environment, wherein if management disagrees with an audit recommendation because it has a better way to improve its administration, then it should be encouraged to say so. Some auditors go further: for instance, the view of an auditor from Bangladesh is that:

> at all stages of the audit, that is, from planning, examination to report writing, the auditee needs to be involved. One reason for non-compliance (with) the audit objections or observation is the non-involvement of (the) auditee in the audit process. Such a proposition may seem ridiculous to many who believe that audit is something quite pious and untouchable.[4]

---

[4] Md. Shahad Chowdhury (2003), 'The Importance of Audit in a Limited Resources Environment', *Asian Journal of Government Audit, 2003*, Asian Journal of Government Audit, New Delhi, India, pp. 97–102.

Ideally, different paths to reform should be canvassed during the audit rather than appear only at its end. Consensus between auditor and auditee management is more likely where different ideas of reform are discussed as they appear. Then, the chance that auditee management will accept and implement the recommendations is greater. The framing of audit recommendations must balance expectations of the auditor's client that the audit opinion and findings are accurate and complete with the audit's function to affect change and reform. All management is sensitive to its image and reputation. An auditor can express the opinion and recommendations to satisfy the client's expectations, but upset the auditee because of the way in which the opinion and recommendations are expressed. To affect change, the auditor must be sensitive to how the opinion and recommendations are worded.

This discussion highlights how auditors have two masters. The first is the audit's client, and the second is the auditee. These two masters may have the same expectations of the audit, or they may diverge.

Possible relationships between the expectations of the auditor's client and the auditee are shown in Figure 13.1. In the first example, the expectations of the SAI's client and the SAI's auditee are the same. An identity of expectations, and possibly of interests, simplifies the SAI's focus. The second and third examples in the figure show varying degrees of overlap in expectations of the SAI's client and auditee. The fourth example in the figure is the most difficult for the SAI. It is where the client and the auditee have different expectations of the audit.

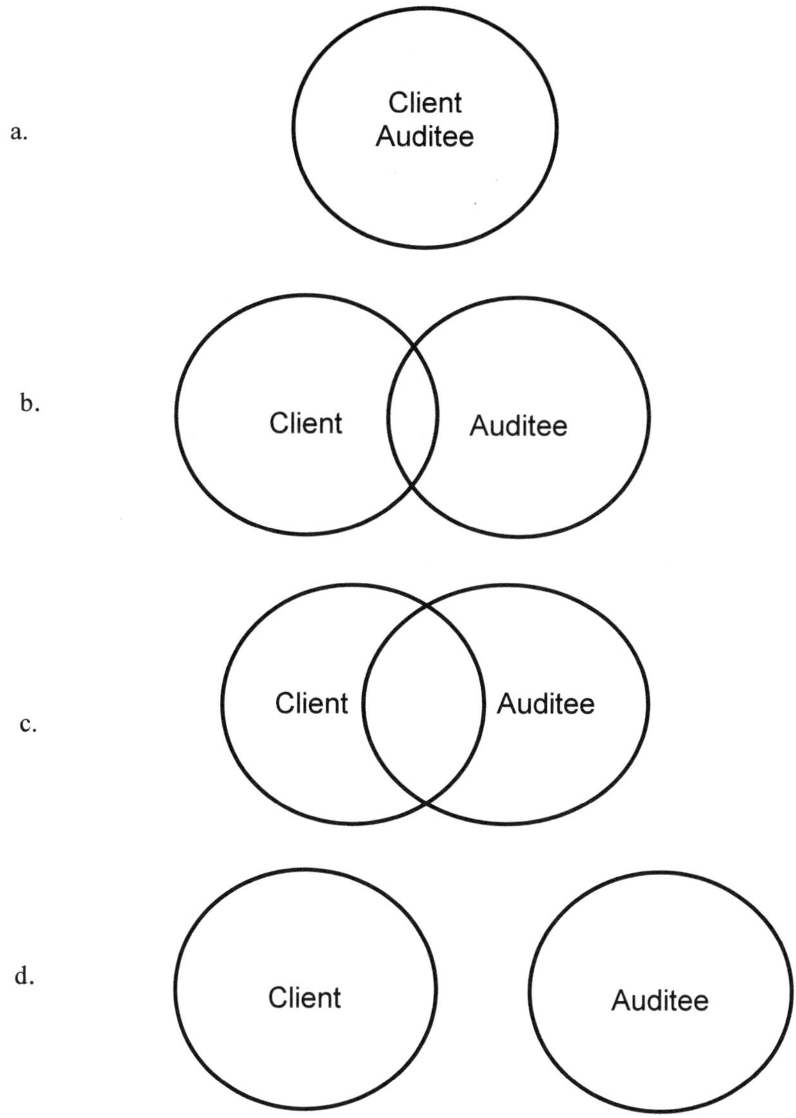

Figure 13.1 Possible Relationships between Expectations of the Auditor's Client and Auditee

Conclusions

Audits are likely to achieve change and reform when they satisfy the expectations of at least one of the two major groups of stakeholders. Change is more likely when the expectations of the audit's client are met. But, unless the client has strong control and power, the expectations of management of the activity audited must also be at least partially met for change and reform to occur. Possibly, the conditions for administrative reform are most favourable when the expectations of the two major groups of stakeholders – the client and the auditee – are met simultaneously.

Because audit expectations are often created before the auditor arrives, many audits are conducted where the expectations of the two major groups of stakeholders are different. Therefore, the reality for most audits is that the most favourable conditions for administrative reform will not exist. Notwithstanding, the auditor can take initiatives to help shape those expectations. Earlier we discussed the purposes of audit. We have returned to that issue since the existence of different audit expectations points to multiple understandings of the purposes of audit. Even when legislation states clearly the purposes of audit, the reality will be the continued existence of different expectations.

PART III

WHAT AUTHORITY DOES THE SAI NEED FOR ITS WORK?

What Authority Does the SAI Need For Its Work?

Part II explored the question of what is an SAI. It was necessary to answer this question before considering what provisions there should be in public sector audit law for the SAI to perform its role.[1] In Part III, we ask what authority the SAI needs for its work. We address this question, first, by posing and answering the question of what freedom should the legislature permit the SAI to have; second, by examining three critical aspects of an SAI's work, which are audit planning, the conduct of audits, and audit reporting; and third, by describing how the SAI can reduce costs and increase its impact when it conducts both regularity and performance audits, which are the two main kinds of audits.

[1] The Comptroller and Auditor-General of India has analysed the attributes of INTOSAI's members, Appendix 1.

Chapter 14

What Freedom Should the Legislature Permit the SAI to Have?

As mentioned earlier, the legislature has primary responsibility for devising law or laws that determine the SAI's role. No legislature can determine every circumstance or eventuality that an SAI will confront. Therefore, the need for an SAI to resolve issues during an audit results in the SAI interpreting audit law. In light of this inevitability, the legislature must consider how much freedom it will provide to the SAI for its interpretation of audit law.

There are a number of issues where the boundaries of audit law appear and where the SAI will need to make decisions unless the legislature has made them for it. Those threshold issues include:

- Who should decide how much money to spend on different kinds of audits, and on different SAI roles?
- Who should set audit standards?
- Who should decide whether the SAI can contact the media?

Who should decide how much money to spend on different kinds of audits and on different SAI roles?

As described earlier, an agency can administer funds in compliance with the law, and it can administer funds efficiently, effectively and economically. The objectives for each audit will determine whether the SAI provides an audit opinion on agency compliance with the law, and/or provides an opinion on other aspects of organisational behaviour such as an agency's efficiency. Knowing this, a first task is to decide how many resources should be spent on different kinds of audits.

Resource allocation to different kinds of audits

An option is for the legislature to prescribe the proportion of resources that the SAI must allocate to the two kinds of audit. The legislature can consider this desirable where, for instance, there are major problems with fraud and corruption in the public service, and where the SAI is seen as an ally in combating them. Generally, regularity audits play a more prominent role in identification of fraud and corruption than do performance audits. Where the latter identify such dysfunctional individual or organisational behaviour, usually it is as a secondary result of an audit.

If fraud and corruption are major problems, the SAI's strategic planning of its own work should lead it to identify these as important future audits. Consequently, the SAI may decide to allocate resources to regularity audits that address fraud and corruption. Agreement between the legislature and the SAI will reduce the legislature's interest in mandating the SAI to allocate resources to certain kinds of audits.

Unless the legislature has prescribed the audit objectives, these will be determined by the SAI. The latter can determine audit objectives on a case-by-case basis. Retrospectively, such as at the end of the year, the legislature or the SAI can analyse the entire set of objectives to determine whether the SAI gave more prominence to regularity than to performance matters in its work, or vice versa. The results of this analysis become baseline data for the legislature, the SAI, or both to consider what proportion of resources should be allocated to different kinds of audits in future.

Historically in many countries, regularity, or compliance, auditing has preceded performance auditing. Therefore, it would be expected that many SAIs would devote more resources to regularity than to performance audits. In general, this resource allocation probably has been consistent with priorities of local legislatures. Performance audits are relatively new tools for administrative reform. To exploit them as agents of change, the question of the percentage of audit resources to be devoted to them must be addressed in light of that knowledge. If an SAI has little knowledge of how to conduct them and limited success in their execution, then a cautious approach is warranted to maintenance or expansion of the numbers of such audits. Extensive and thorough training in performance audit is necessary before the numbers of such audits are increased significantly. Decisions on the proportion of resources to be allocated to different kinds of audits can only be answered with knowledge of the capacity of the SAI to conduct those audits. If its capacity is limited, then decisions about resource allocation should take those limitations into account.

Another factor affecting the resources allocated to different kinds of audits is any regulation of the frequency of audits. Audits can be planned for different intervals: for instance, monthly, annually, or every few years. A requirement in some countries is for financial audits, especially financial statement audits, to be conducted annually, and for performance audits to be planned at wider intervals. No SAI will have sufficient resources to conduct performance audits annually of every government program and initiative. Choice will be necessary. Audit planning based on what choice, if any, the SAI has over the frequency of audits, is essential to allocate resources to regularity and performance audits.

Over time, in order to maximise the contribution of the SAI to administrative reform, the proportion of resources for performance audits should increase if there is a small base of such work presently. Therefore, it would be reasonable for the SAI, possibly working with the legislature, to develop a medium or long-term plan for enhancement of staff skills in performance auditing. A medium or long-term option is for the SAI to divide its resources equally between regularity and performance audits. Achievement of this longer term goal will depend on the pace of reform in the wider public sector, of which the SAI is only one part.

In Australia, as described in Chapter 4, in 2004–2005 the ANAO proposed allocating 37 per cent of its resources to performance audits and 63 per cent to financial statement audits. Therefore, even more than twenty years after the introduction of performance auditing in that country, the SAI had not achieved an approximate parity of resources between regularity and performance auditing

Resource allocation to different SAI roles

Earlier we described how the SAI can audit and advise government agencies. Customarily, audits offer insights into how management can improve. That insight is profered through suggestions and recommendations arising from an audit and contained in issues papers and in the audit report. Provision of such advice is how the SAI assists in public sector reform. Agencies will also request advice on management and administrative matters when they are not being audited. The number and nature of those requests determines how frequently the SAI performs this other role of adviser.

As we have shown, the SAI has a possible conflict of interest when it audits agencies that have requested, accepted and implemented the SAI's advice where that advice is given outside an audit. There are steps that it can take to reduce the risk of conflict of interest. Let us assume that those steps have been taken and the SAI has found avenues whereby it can both audit and advise outside of individual audits. The next question is to determine the proportion of the SAI's resources that should go to this new role. The first step in answering the question is for the SAI to monitor the amount and kind of resources it allocates currently to its advisory role. Collection of such data will inform either the legislature's or the SAI's decision on resource allocation. It is necessary for the SAI to establish data systems to capture information on all of its work. This is an SAI task that does not require legislation.

If the advisory role is demand driven, then the number and nature of those demands will determine how many and what kinds of resources are allocated to the general advisory role. Resource allocation would then be set by the government agencies that request its advice and which are its clients. This is a passive role for the SAI in resource allocation to major functions. It may be the only role that the legislature permits the SAI to have on such matters. Carried to an extreme, it would mean that government agencies' requests shaped the amount of resources available for advice. In turn, this would point to how government agencies' requests would also be determining the SAI's resources available for audit, which is its primary role. Financial and human resources allocated to SAIs are limited. Where they are applied, if the resources available for advice are outside the SAI's control, then so are the resources available for audit. It can be seen that, in light of the SAI needing to maintain its independence, it is unwise for its provision of advice to be driven only by the strength and nature of the demand for assistance from government agencies. It is far better for the SAI to estimate its preferred resource use for both audit and general advice, because then it, and not government agencies, determines the relative priority of different tasks.

Who should set audit standards?

The third threshold issue discussed here is audit standards. An SAI uses audit standards as frameworks for the establishment of procedures and practices to be followed in the conduct of audits.[1] Auditing standards are guides in determining the steps and procedures that should be applied in audits. Auditing standards constitute the criteria or yardstick against which the quality of the audit results is evaluated. INTOSAI argues that these standards consist of:

- basic principles of auditing;
- general standards;
- field standards; and
- reporting standards.

INTOSAI points out that its recommended audit standards should be viewed in the particular constitutional, legal and other circumstances of the SAI. Determination of which auditing standards should apply in the public sector is primarily a responsibility of the SAI. However, consultation with the legislature and with government prior to setting those standards provides the SAI with information about matters that will arise in their implementation. Consultation over draft standards can lead the SAI to amend or affirm its proposals, with the SAI making the final decision. INTOSAI encourages all SAIs to consider compliance with INTOSAI's auditing standards in all matters that are deemed material. It recognises that certain standards may not be applicable to some of the work done by SAIs, including those organised as courts of account, nor to the non-audit work conducted by SAIs. It encourages each SAI to determine the applicable standards for such work to ensure that it is of consistently high quality. It is very important to note INTOSAI's view that each SAI should apply its own judgement to the diverse situations that arise in the course of government auditing. In other words, the legislature should withdraw from participation in individual audits.

---

[1] INTOSAI (2001), *Auditing Standards*.

Chapter 10 addressed the question of whether the SAI should lead the private sector in accounting and auditing. This question is important in answering who should set audit standards. It will be remembered from Chapter 3 that in Australia, public sector audit and accounting were proceeding in the same direction and at the same speed as in the private sector, but with significant exceptions for audit.

Who should decide whether the SAI can contact the media?

The Introduction to this book argued for comparative research into the visibility of SAIs in different nations and societies. Research data would assist in exploring whether high or low profile SAIs have the greater impact in reform of public administration. The profile of an SAI was evident in political and societal knowledge of its role.

An SAI's contact with the media is a determinant of its visibility. An SAI that uses the media increases the probability that its audit opinions and judgements are known in relevant circles. The most relevant circles include those of elected representatives and government, and, beyond those, customers and clients of government programs, citizens and taxpayers. Targeted dissemination and knowledge of opinions and judgements is a step towards achieving the public sector reform that the SAI's work argues for. The risk to an SAI that disseminates through the media its opinions, judgements and reports is of being seen to be party political or a political player. Where the SAI has the authority and discretion to disseminate its work through the media, it has to weigh the advantages of drawing attention to its findings against the possible disadvantages of being seen to criticise the government publicly. The adequacy of protection of the SAI's independence will influence the SAI's choice or behaviour in this matter. Chapter 6 described how the British, Canadian and New Zealand SAIs have regular contact with the media and issue media releases. Each of those SAIs has a legislative base for its independence and work, maintaining credibility with their respective legislatures, governments, media and public.

Where an SAI uses the media as one avenue for disseminating its work and increasing the likelihood that its findings are used in public sector reform, it can take steps to gain or maintain the confidence of legislators and government by preparing and using guidelines for media contact.

In some political systems, it is possible that the SAI has no authority to disseminate through the media. Acknowledging this as another area for comparative research, in those systems it is likely that the government is very influential over the elected legislature.

Overall, the answer to the question of who should decide whether the SAI should have contact with the media depends on the nature of the political system, and the relationship between the government and the elected legislature.

Conclusions

This chapter has explained why, unless the legislature has determined how much money should be spent on different kinds of audits, the latter is a decision for the SAI. Similarly in regard to settling on resources available for any SAI advisory role for government agencies, it will be a matter for the SAI to decide unless the legislature has made the decision. The SAI will require expenditure and other resource data on its own activities in order to be best placed for any advisory or decision-making role on these matters. Audit standards are primarily the SAI's decisions. However, it is advisable for it to consult first with the legislature and government on issues of this kind that can have wide effects in the public sector. The characteristics of a political system will influence who determines whether the SAI can use the media to disseminate its work and accelerate public sector reform.

Chapter 15

The Planning, Conduct and Reporting of Audits

The planning, conduct and reporting of audits are discussed in turn.

A. Planning

Previously we have discussed the importance of the SAI having:

- the legal mandate to conduct various types of audits;
- sufficient resources; and
- at least some flexibility in moving resources between different kinds of audits, such as regularity and performance work.

Let us assume that these conditions for a successful SAI have been met. The next challenge for the SAI is to determine which audits it should conduct. This question, which is addressed in this chapter, is part of audit planning. The question is raised so that the authority the SAI needs for its work can be determined. This issue of authority is the subject of Part III of this study.

The legislature may reserve the right to decide which audits the SAI should conduct. This would be a very tight control over the SAI, suggesting a difficult relationship between the legislature and executive government. Alternatively, where executive government dominated the legislature, the latter's selection of all audit topics neutralises the independence of public sector audit, since – in effect – the government would determine what the SAI examined. A legislature that determined all audits the SAI should conduct would have little confidence in the SAI to choose audit topics that maximised the legislature's definition of the public interest. Possibly the legislature is impatient with the rate and direction of change in executive government, and uses the SAI to speed and to redirect change. In total, there are various reasons why a legislature may wish to control audit planning. The validity of those reasons can only be tested in individual countries where this situation exists.

A legislature that controlled audit topics so tightly would be interested firstly in receiving and using the SAI's reports. This is a legitimate use of the latter. Potentially, every SAI can foster change and improvement in all aspects of its work. A caution is that a heavy and exclusive focus by the legislature on receipt of audit reports can raise doubts within government agencies about the SAI's interest in working with them. Ideally, the SAI, including when it is a court of accounts, is a creation of but separate from the legislature, and it is separate from government. The SAI is between government and the legislature, accommodating the interests and expectations of both in forming audit opinions. Consequently, a risk for the SAI is that the very close association between the legislature and the SAI – marked by the legislature's selection of all audit topics – reduces the confidence of government agencies in the independence of audit opinions formed in this context. The result is that the credibility of the audit opinion is questioned.

INTOSAI advises that the SAI should give priority to any audit tasks which must be undertaken by law and assess priorities for discretionary areas within the SAI's mandate.[1] This description suggests that the SAI will have at least some discretion over the selection of audit topics. How much discretion will depend, as discussed before, on circumstances within each country. Audit law should specify the SAI's freedom to select topics for audit. The SAI is advised to set auditing standards to guide its audit planning.

An SAI considered successful by its legislature is likely to be subject to increased requests by legislators for audits. Possibly the number of requests for audit will be greater than the SAI's resources available to address them. Then, either the legislature must set the SAI's audit priorities, or the SAI must select which of the topics proposed by legislators it will pursue. Both situations are defensible since both will result in the SAI conducting audits that match its financial and other resources.

All SAIs will have more audit topics than there are resources available to address them. In its planning to decide which audits it will commence, the SAI requires criteria for determining the range of audit activities which will give the maximum practicable assurance regarding performance of public accountability obligations by each audited entity.[2] Strategic planning gives effect to this task.

Where the SAI has freedom to select its audit topics, it will be of value to consult with the legislature over its selection. It can do so by preparing a draft strategic plan for audit, and by explaining it and consulting with the legislature. This arrangement signals that the SAI has primary carriage of strategic audit planning, and that it is advisable for the SAI to consult with the legislature. The latter will contribute to strategic planning by commenting on the proposed plan, where those comments can indicate agreement or disagreement, and nomination of alternative topics for audit. As mentioned before, this dialogue between the two parties suggests that the SAI's relationship with the legislature is like a dance with a partner.

---

[1] INTOSAI (2001), *Auditing Standards*, p.51.

[2] INTOSAI (2001), *Auditing Standards*, p.38.

B. Conduct of audits

The conduct of audits requires SAI staff to have the legal powers necessary to pursue their audits efficiently and effectively. A selection of those powers is introduced here and discussed in turn.

Those powers encompass:

- the authority to audit all aspects of government;
- appointment of its own staff, including specialist staff;
- access;
- audits of the sales of government enterprises and of government contracts;
- audit methodology; and
- the gathering and retention of audit evidence.

The audit mandate

For the SAI to provide an assurance to the legislature and to taxpayers that executive government is managing public moneys legally and successfully, it requires a mandate to audit all government agencies. Where it has such a mandate, it is able to plan an audit program to encompass all major areas of risk of illegal, inefficient or ineffective use of public moneys, and to select audits accordingly. If it cannot audit all government agencies, then there will be some parts of the executive that have a limited accountability to the legislature.

Government agencies include government companies. Therefore, for the SAI to provide the assurance wanted by the legislature, it will audit commercially and non-commercially oriented entities. Government companies include their subsidiaries into which assets and liabilities can be moved. Local accounting standards indicate whether the accounts of subsidiaries must be consolidated with accounts of the parent company. Whether they are or are not consolidated, the legislature confronts a risk of limited and partial information being available on the performance of government companies when it has different auditors for different parts of government companies. Therefore, it is advisable for the SAI to be the auditor of the host government company as well as auditor of its subsidiaries. Depending on the SAI's resources, one option is for the SAI to employ a private sector audit firm to audit subsidiaries.

Many developing countries have passed or are passing through a process of selling government assets, such as state banks, railways and telecommunication organisations. Once they are sold, the government can move to regulate the activities of these former assets within, for instance, the finance, transport and telecommunications industries. Regulation is a critical area of public and private sector contact.

The extent and nature of regulation is a manifestation of the government's role in promoting stability and in influencing the degree of competition in particular parts of the economy. Government regulation is external regulation of an industry. SAIs can reinforce a government's interest in the promotion of industry stability and competition where SAIs have mandates to audit government regulatory bodies.[3] The ANAO has pointed out that:[4]

> The avoidance of further failures (in the private sector) is also crucial to continuing public confidence in the new regulatory regime and a prime example that privatisation and deregulation do not necessarily diminish the public interest inherent in the operation of certain businesses. Accordingly, governments may see that the regulation of privatised companies or of industries in which privatised companies compete is in the public interest. In this case, Auditors-General can perform an important function by examining and reporting on the public sector's performance in regulating privatised businesses and/or administering government contracts with these businesses. The regulators themselves have to be accountable as well as being reasonably independent – a suitable balance is often difficult to achieve.

This analysis focuses on the SAI's work with national governments. In some jurisdictions, the SAI is responsible for auditing the national and all other levels of government. Other levels of government are provincial, state, local or municipal governments. An SAI with such wide responsibility requires more resources and has a wider mandate than does an SAI which focuses only on the national or central government. All SAIs have limited resources. An SAI with a mandate to audit all levels of government and with insufficient resources for this task is in a difficult situation. It will have to decide on the best way to use its limited resources. In these circumstances, it will be especially important for it to have the support of the legislature for deciding where to apply its resources. The Auditor-General of Pakistan has reminded us that very little guidance is available for planning SAI-wide or government-wide audits.[5]

---

3 The Brazilian Court of Accounts has collected in one publication some of the Court's main findings about regulation of the energy sector. The publication had the objective of improving the quality of debate and of regulatory activity in public administration in that country. Tribunal de Contas da União (2003), *O Controle Externo das Agências Reguladores. Questões relevantes sobre o sector eléctrico e de petróleo e gás natural*, Tribunal de Contas da União, Brasilia, <Isc@tcu.gov.br>

4 18th Commonwealth Auditors-General Conference (7–9 October 2002), Kuala Lumpur, Malaysia, *Re-engineering Auditing in the Public Sector. Privatisation of State Activities – The Role of SAIs*, the National Audit Department of Malaysia, p.12.

5 Auditor-General of Pakistan (October 2003), 'Quality Management in Public Audit. Pakistan's Perspective', *9th ASOSAI Assembly*, Manila, Philippines.

Appointment of staff

The head or heads of the SAI require tenure to protect their independence. The latter has little meaning if they can be removed readily from office either by the legislature or by government. There are particular dangers where a government can remove SAI personnel in this way because such authority threatens the integrity of the audit opinion. SAIs are critical of government. If it is easy for a government to replace SAI personnel because of negative findings on the adequacy of government administration, then the SAI's willingness and capacity to form critical audit opinions is threatened. An associated concern is the need to limit and prohibit government selection of which SAI staff will conduct particular audits. Although the government is not the main client, where it can choose which auditors it wants, it is acting as if it is the SAI's principal client. For these reasons, audit law should protect the terms and conditions of employment of SAI personnel. This can be done through reference in the national constitution, or in particular laws, such as general administrative or audit law.

For some audits, the SAI will need specialist staff. The SAI is best placed to decide which specialist staff it needs. For example, the SAI audits the national telecommunications company. This engages in foreign currency transactions to purchase equipment and to facilitate international calls both to and from the country. The great majority of the SAI's work does not require knowledge of foreign currency transactions since it is domestically focused. For the SAI to audit the national telecommunications company, it will need outside expertise, which it will employ on contract. If it cannot recruit specialist staff, then it will have difficulty in doing the audit or perhaps it will not be able to audit at all.

Another area of expertise where the SAI will require the skills of contractors will be in performance audits of highly specialised agencies. For example, a performance audit of a government insurance company will probably require engagement of an actuary. A performance audit of a major construction project can require engagement of a quantity surveyor or a civil engineer. A performance audit of a meteorology bureau may require employment of a meteorologist. The conditional nature of most of the above statements is because the SAI will make the final decision on whether it needs to engage subject matter specialists in light of the objectives for each audit.

Access

Auditors require access to premises to do their work. They also need access to personnel of agencies they audit, and access to agency documentation. Access is necessary in order for SAI personnel to interview agency staff, and to find and study computer-based and other documentation on aspects of agency management relevant to an audit's objectives.

An SAI may have the authority to audit all parts of government. However, if it is denied access to agencies, their records and staff, then its authority is meaningless because it cannot do its work. The best way for a legislature to provide the right of access to SAI staff is through audit law. A majority of auditors have met agency personnel who were reluctant to permit them to enter and commence work. Knowledge that audit law provides public sector auditors with the legal right of access leads to auditors collecting the written and other forms of information they need despite continuation of this reluctance.

At some time in the work of every SAI, auditors' right of access will be challenged by agency personnel. Grounds for the challenge can include national security and protection of the political nature of decision-making. In order for the SAI's staff to access information relevant to national security, the SAI will need staff with the right level of security classification. Anticipation of this need points to the importance of the SAI preparing before it commences audits with national security implications. Preparation involves acknowledging that only a minority of audits addresses national security matters, and ensuring that staff have adequate levels of security clearance, preferably before they commence auditing. All staff should be trained in the importance of maintaining the confidentiality of audit information that becomes audit evidence. Circumstances in each country determine whether each auditor needs an individual security clearance, or whether the SAI's auditing standards requiring maintenance of the confidentiality of material collected during audits are sufficient. Where national security is involved, a general power of access will be insufficient unless staff have appropriate security clearances. It should be kept in mind that arguments limiting the access of SAI staff to premises and personnel can be spurious. Pursuit of the audit is one way to determine if they are.

A second major difficulty in access is where agencies wish to protect the political or partisan nature of their decision-making and service delivery. For instance, the objective of an environmental program is to distribute funds for remedial action on a needs basis nationally. Administrators distribute funds according to the wishes of the minister, who wants public moneys spent in electorates that her party controls. In order to conduct the audit, the SAI will require access to the agency's documentation and personnel. It may also require access to the minister, including to her material. This is an instance of where circumstances in each country shape whether the SAI's access powers extend to ministerial offices.

Audits of sales of government enterprises

For various reasons, governments in many countries are selling their assets. These can be fixed assets such as land and buildings. They can also be government entities providing services to the community as a whole or to parts of it. The integrity and execution of the sales process are of great importance to government policies. That is because where the sales processes are concealed from public view, the public can become concerned about the intent of sales. The public can also be concerned about asset sales if the grounds for selling are structured such that only some parts of the private sector benefit. A worse case is when a government sells its assets to parties believed to be very close to it. A government will have difficulties if popular opinion is that certain assets should not be sold or if the sales process is poorly executed, with allegations of loss to the state and favouritism amongst purchasers. The New Zealand Audit Office has pointed out that because a number of enterprises that were sold were strategic or were infrastructural assets to the New Zealand economy, the privatisation through trade sale did not necessarily mean that the government was free of any future risks that may arise in these entities.[6]

Audit can assist governments to maintain confidence in the asset sales process. It can do so by reviewing the process to determine whether it was legal and fair. In order for the SAI to assist the government, it needs access to information on the sales process. Assets sales are controversial in many countries. Therefore, an audit of one, some or all of them will involve the SAI in controversy.

Earlier it was argued that the SAI should invite the legislature to comment on its strategic plan, which identifies prospective audit topics and how the SAI will allocate its resources. An SAI decision on whether to audit asset sales should take account of the financial and other materiality of those sales. That is, if a government sells few assets and gains little from them, then audits of sales may not be justified compared to other topics. But if the SAI conducts a preliminary review of financial and other data and concludes that the topic is important nationally and includes it within its plans, it would be advisable to seek the legislature's views on the importance it attaches to the topic. The SAI will be strengthened if the legislature supports its intention to audit asset sales. However, if executive government dominates the legislature, then the latter may not comment favourably on the SAI's plans because it does not want the sales audited. At this point, the SAI will have a difficult decision. If it audits some – such as the largest – sales or if it audits all of them, it will be opposed by the government and possibly by the legislature. On the other hand, if the SAI does not audit asset sales, then it is excluding from public and legislative view one of the most active areas of contemporary government, and not contributing to strengthening the accountability of those involved.

Privatisation, whether by trade sale or public share offer, has impacted on the financial statement business of Auditors-General and Presidents of courts or chambers of accounts through participation in the activities associated with the due diligence process, which ensures the accuracy and completeness of information

---

6 18th Commonwealth Auditors-General Conference (2002), *Privatization of State Activities – The Role of SAIs*, p. 74.

provided to prospective purchasers.[7] Information disclosed to prospective purchasers typically includes financial performance data for a five year period as well as for the most recent audited financial statements, where these are routinely prepared. Availability of accurate information on these matters emphasises the importance of comprehensive and sound financial audit practices.[8]

The ANAO has pointed out how one of the key outcomes from privatisation audits has been identification of opportunities for significant improvement to the process of tendering and managing sales advisers' contracts with government. Adoption of these opportunities can lead to improved overall value for money and project management quality in subsequent sales. Audit reports have examined the key factors that affect the success of public share offers, such as:[9]

- the level and structure of fees paid to stockbrokers and advisers as these fees significantly influence the motivation for these firms to act in the vendor's interests;
- the process of determining a final price for the sale of the asset; and
- the logistics of the settlement process.

Audits of the sale of government assets can lead to strong conclusions. One such instance was the ANAO's performance audit of the sale of Australian Government property and the latter's lease back to government agencies. The audit concluded that sale of properties for which the government had an ongoing interest in the form of long-term leases exposed it to future liabilities that, over time, effectively

---

7 The Department of the Auditor-General of Pakistan has defined the scope of its audits of privatizations as follows:

- whether the fair value and/or reserve/reference price of a business unit was established in accordance with professionally acceptable criteria;
- whether the procedure adopted by the Commission for disposal of the business units conformed to the principles of competitive bidding;
- whether prescribed procedure in regard to invitations for bids and their evaluation was observed in letter and spirit;
- whether the approved sale price was in line with the fair value/reserve price fixed and if not whether there were cogent reasons for any deviations; and
- whether the decision of the authority in acceptance or rejection of an offer or instance taken during the disposal proceedings was in conformity with the general principles of probity and propriety.

18th Commonwealth Auditors-General Conference (2002), *Privatization of State Activities – The Role of SAIs*, p.86.

8 18th Commonwealth Auditors-General Conference (2002), *Privatization of State Activities – The Role of SAIs*, p.23.

9 18th Commonwealth Auditors-General Conference (2002), *Privatization of State Activities – The Role of SAIs*, p.26.

negated the sale proceeds. To be able to support such conclusions requires a secure public sector audit mandate.

Where governments sell part of a government business to the private sector, auditing is still required. However, there can be different views on whether or not audits of partially privatised entities are core SAI tasks. For instance, the Australian SAI argues that they are not core tasks, while the Canadian SAI believes that they are.[10]

Audits of government contracts

Another major change in government is its increasing reliance on the private sector to provide goods and services to implement government policies. For example:

- a government once had a network of offices to assist unemployed persons find jobs. Now, those services are provided by a private sector company under contract to the government;
- a government once constructed naval ships. Now the ships are built by a private sector firm under contract;
- a government once owned and operated hospitals to provide services to the community. The hospitals were sold and the new private sector owners provide those services on the government's behalf under contract; and
- government agencies once employed their own computer staff and purchased computers and computer software. Now, agencies lease their computers and software, while computer maintenance and data entry are services provided by private firms under contract.

This is a small number of examples of a growing trend in government. Provision of government services by contract is a controversial move, despite governments' increasing reliance on them. An SAI must accommodate to this major change in public administration by being prepared to audit the government's contracts. Ideally, it should work to ensure that it has sufficient legal authority for this purpose. In fact, it should work with the legislature to develop audit law to cover its work in all new and emerging areas of government, of which this is one example.

Since these contracts involve entities from both the public and private sectors, there will be opposition from either or both kinds of entities to audits of contracts. This increases the need for audit law to provide for this kind of audit.

The latter can include contract design, the award of contracts, contract administration and contract services. Countries differ in their experience in these

[10] Refer to the discussion in the 18th Commonwealth Auditors-General Conference (2002), *Privatization of State Activities – The Role of SAIs*.

fields. Probably, the SAI must borrow skills from the local private sector since it will require staff with skills and expertise in these areas. The need for the SAI to have the authority to recruit and employ specialist staff was introduced earlier, and this is an opportunity for the SAI to use those powers.

In its strategic planning, an early step for the SAI is to evaluate the relative importance to public administration of the delivery of government services by contract. The same decision rules apply as in all audit planning. That is, if the SAI assesses that the government has few service contracts and the amount of money involved is small, then audits of contracts may be relatively unimportant.

Notwithstanding, the SAI should prepare for growth in numbers of contracts and eventual audits by employing and training staff with skills necessary for this work. If the number and value of contracts is large, then the SAI should consider whether to include at least some such audits in its strategic plan. As before, it is advised to consult with the legislature over its plans. Assuming that the legislature is interested in audits of contracts, the legislature may assist the SAI through recommending which contractual arrangements should be reviewed.

Audits of the award of contracts will necessitate audit staff accessing commercial information provided by private sector companies. To maintain confidence in the audit process, prospective tenderers should be advised before they tender that the SAI will access their contract proposals. The grounds are that their proposals are the property of the government, and the SAI has the authority to audit all government documentation. Private sector tenderers will be surprised, and some shocked, unless they are advised beforehand of who will read their material. Communication of this advice is the responsibility of the tendering authority, which is the relevant government agency. To increase the probability of private companies being informed early in the tender process, the SAI and the government agency must liaise.

Audits of contracts involve the standard dimensions of public sector audit, which are to provide an assurance of compliance with the law in the tendering process, and to find ways to improve public administration through constructive criticism of agencies' management of the process. This constructive criticism involves finding out whether the government agency managing the contract has sufficient information to affirm that the objectives of contracting have been achieved. Those objectives can include more economical services than those provided previously and directly by government, and more efficient and effective services than before. Such broad purposes of contracting can be gathered together under the heading of whether agency management has sufficient information to know whether it receives value for money from the contracted services.

Assessment of whether agencies have sufficient information to know whether the purposes of contracting have been achieved is simpler where those agencies have systems to capture financial and performance data on previous and current service delivery. Earlier we highlighted how a condition of public sector reform and modernisation is for government to specify what agencies should do in order to reform. One of those acts is for agencies to establish financial and performance data management systems. Clearly, it will be very difficult for agencies to demonstrate that the purposes of contracting have been achieved if they do not have the supporting data. The audit opinion would reflect agencies' lack of data to establish whether the new contracted services are better than those offered previously. In light of such an audit finding, the SAI may be required to assess, or take the initiative to assess of its own accord, whether contractual arrangements achieve their purposes. The caveat is that an SAI that poses this audit objective risks commenting on government policy. Whether this is a legitimate role for an SAI varies between jurisdictions.

A sound government contract permits the government agency purchasing private sector services to require documentation and other information from the supplier to substantiate the supplier's invoices and statements of performance achievements. The need for this information is evident in the following example. A government agency purchases information technology services from a private sector firm. The contract specifies performance targets for the information technology that the firm provides, with financial penalties if performance targets are not met. The firm makes information available to the government agency showing that it has achieved its performance targets.

The problem for the agency is to determine whether the firm's performance information is correct. What should it do? It can accept the assurance of the firm as sufficient. However, if the assurance is incorrect, then it will pay public moneys for services not provided according to the contract. It can request supporting documentation and, after analysis, this can satisfy the agency. Especially if a large sum of money is involved, the agency may wish to see primary documentation and even to conduct its own tests of the provider's systems. This will necessitate access to the provider's premises, staff and documentation. The provider will permit this access by the purchaser of its services if such access is provided for in the contract. If no such access clause is in the contract, then the provider will be unlikely to permit the agency's staff to enter its premises for the purpose of verifying financial and performance data in its invoice. Mediation could result – if mediation or another form of dispute resolution is included in the contract. If not, the agency will have a messy task in deciding whether to pay the invoice, since it will have placed itself in a situation wherein it has incomplete information.

The SAI's access to the provider's premises, documentation and personnel is built on the access rights of the government agency purchasing the provider's services. Ideally, a contract between a government agency and a service provider should provide for the agency's access to the contractor's premises and to other data for the purpose of verifying statements in invoices. In practice, such access clauses are most important in large contracts, since in smaller contracts it may not be worth the effort for the government agency to seek such separate verification. Inclusion of such clauses at the insistence of government is another example of how government can support public administration's evolution. Also ideally, the contract should provide for the SAI to have the same access rights as the agency. If this is not done, then the SAI must rely on its own legislation to access the premises, documentation and personnel of service providers.

This is likely to be a controversial practice which many, if not most, contractors will resist. Private sector knowledge of such contractual provisions, together with knowledge of the SAI's general powers of access, will encourage private sector service providers to government to ensure that their invoices are correct and that the performance data they provide to government are accurate. Potential use of these powers will suffice in the great majority of cases. Elsewhere, the SAI may need to use its powers after making sure that it has a solid legal foundation for their use and sufficient reason as well. This last step should include the SAI confirming that it has the legal authority to report its findings on the accuracy and completeness of the financial and performance data that the private firm gives to the government agency buying its services.

Audit methodology

There is a range of questions, issues, approaches, and concerns that distinguish auditing from other occupations and professions. This set of concerns and body of knowledge includes the methodology or methodologies of auditing. Every SAI develops expertise in methodology. This expertise is an essential resource for the SAI, with the latter having ownership and, hopefully, mastery of it. It is an area of expertise that legislators and government administrators may know something about, but unless they have been trained as auditors their knowledge will be limited. Therefore, it is logical for the SAI to determine which methodology it applies to each audit.

Were legislators to determine the methodology, they would be infringing on the professionalism of SAI staff. A government agency that set audit methodology would be controlling audit. Such control is inconsistent with the role of audit. Notwithstanding, there is an indirect way in which either or both the legislature and government can influence selection of audit methodologies. That is when the SAI consults with them on the audit objective. The SAI does not have to consult with them, but may choose to do so. Audit objectives are powerful but not the only determinants of audit methodologies. So by sharing proposals on audit objectives, the SAI is opening its audit methodologies to scrutiny. Here the role of the legislature and government agency is consultative and advisory, not one of control. Consultation and advice maintains the SAI's independence while acknowledging the importance of the views of the legislature and government. In this environment, the legislature and agency can give their views on audit methodology, either directly or indirectly, while respecting the SAI's right to accept or reject their views.

Of note is that INTOSAI encourages each SAI to establish and maintain policies and procedures for the professional development of audit staff regarding the audit techniques and methodologies applicable to the range of audits it undertakes.[11] [12]

Audit evidence

The audit opinion, findings and recommendations must be based on evidence gathered during the audit. Because in most audits SAI personnel will have time to collect information about only some aspects of the administration or management of the agency or program audited, information gathered will cover only part of the administrative phenomenon reviewed. The audit objective and methodology will set which information will be collected.

Audit evidence can include records of interviews with agency personnel, data analysis, systems documentation and computer records. It is the SAI's task alone to determine what information is necessary for the audit opinion. If the SAI is not free to collect the information it considers necessary, then audit law constrains its work. This information becomes audit evidence. It must be protected and retained by the SAI since its existence is of fundamental importance to the conduct of each audit. The SAI will require auditing standards and administrative systems to ensure that audit evidence is sufficient to form audit opinions. Audit records must be maintained for the period in which findings, conclusions and recommendations remain relevant. This can be for some years.

C. Audit reporting

The last area discussed where the SAI requires strong legal authority is that of audit reporting. This consists of draft judgements, draft findings in management letters, issues papers, draft reports and opinions, and final reports and opinions. Consequently, this section could be described as an account of the powers that the SAI needs to communicate good and bad news. Before proceeding, it is worth affirming the importance of audit information to a well-informed legislature. The SAI of Iran has emphasised the importance of the dissemination of audit

---

[11] INTOSAI (2001), *Auditing Standards*, p.36.

[12] One important area of methodology is IT auditing. British Commonwealth Auditors-General have explored this area and published their advice on IT audit methodology, for instance, in the following publications: 18th Commonwealth Auditors-General Conference (7–9 October 2002), Kuala Lumpur, Malaysia, Sub-Theme 111, *SAI's Involvement in System Development: Opportunities and Risks*, National Audit Department of Malaysia; and in ASOSAI (October 2003), 6th Research Project, *IT Audit Guidelines*, <www.asosai.org>

information, since with that information, citizens, through their legislature, can find answers to questions such as:[13]

- How are economic and financial resources obtained and spent?
- What has been the managerial and financial performance of each individual agency?
- Have expenditures exceeded the allocations approved or not?

As affirmed earlier, it is necessary to adapt to the local reality the principles and concerns discussed below. The SAI, for example, may prepare neither draft judgements, opinions, issues papers nor draft reports for discussion with auditees. Instead, it may reach its judgements in isolation without further involvement of auditee agencies, and then publicise its opinion and remedial action. With this in mind, the three issues discussed are:

- draft judgements, opinions and issues papers;
- draft opinions and findings to more than one government agency; and
- the final audit opinion and report.

Draft judgements, opinions and issues papers

Issues papers summarise audit observations, findings, opinions, conclusions and recommendations. All of these are in draft form. That is because they are provided as matters for discussion with the agency under audit. The auditee is provided with the issues paper and draft opinion so that it can consider these matters. This is so that the SAI can take account of any further perspectives that the auditee brings forward when the issues paper or draft judgement is discussed. In those discussions, the auditee is given the opportunity to identify errors of fact or unbalanced interpretation of events. Those discussions take place in interviews or meetings with staff of the agency under audit.

Wider circulation is not warranted because of the draft and contestable nature of the matters raised by the SAI in the issues papers and early opinion. Since the main audience is the agency being audited, there is less reason to provide issues papers and draft opinions to the primary client, which is the legislature. There is also less need to provide these to other interested parties, such as other parts of the agency being audited, the ministry, or to other parts of government.

It may appear contradictory to limit the readership of issues papers and draft opinions to the agency being audited. The possible contradiction is because the SAI's primary client is the legislature, not the agency that is part of government. However, limitation of the readership of the issues paper or papers

[13] SAI Iran (April 2004), 'The Concept of Governance: by SAI-Iran', *Asian Journal of Government Audit*, ASOSAI, pp. 80–106.

and draft opinion to the agency being audited is a means to subject preliminary findings to critical scrutiny. Critical scrutiny by the agency being audited will lead to the sharpening and validation of preliminary opinions, findings and recommendations. Once these are sharpened and validated, the SAI will have a stronger basis to report them to the legislature and to other interested parties, such as other parts of government.

It is worthwhile reviewing an SAI's current legislation and charter that describe current provisions for circulation of draft opinions, findings and recommendations.

Draft opinions and findings to more than one government agency

Circulation of issues papers and draft opinions occurs within relationships long established between government agencies. For instance, two government agencies can be involved in an audit, with the issues paper and draft opinion relevant to both. Therefore, the SAI must consider whether it provides the issues paper and provisional opinion to one or to both agencies.

An example is where the two agencies involved in an audit are a government department and a national research funding organisation, whose moneys come from government through the department. The audit is of the adequacy of the national research funding organisation's administration. The issues paper and/or draft opinion should be provided to this organisation. However, since its moneys come from the government department, the latter has an interest in the audit's findings and can claim that it should receive them as well.

In these cases where more than one government agency is involved in the audit, the SAI must determine what its legislation provides, permits or requires in regard to the circulation of draft findings. The SAI has a simple course of action where the legislation prescribes to whom it must provide a draft opinion or issues paper. However, since it is impossible for legal provisions to anticipate every circumstance, legislation may be suggestive rather than prescriptive. Then, the SAI must use its discretion in determining whether the department receives all or part of the draft opinion or issues paper.

The SAI will have an easier choice if both agencies agree that the draft opinion and issues paper should be distributed to the two agencies. It will have a more difficult choice if one agency believes that it should receive the draft, and argues that the other should not receive it at all or should receive only part of it. This situation could arise if the national research funding organisation did not want the government department to know of the draft audit opinion and findings, at least until it discussed them with the SAI. On the other hand, the government department would want to know about those audit findings so that it could engage with the national research funding organisation. By providing the issues paper and the draft opinion to the national research funding organisation and not to the government department, the SAI will satisfy the former body and upset the latter.

However, by giving the draft to both bodies, the SAI will be criticised by the national research funding organisation but satisfy the government department.

As indicated earlier, the SAI will need legal advice to ensure that its decision is soundly based. If the law is suggestive rather than prescriptive, leaving the decision on distribution of the draft audit findings to the SAI, then the latter has to find new grounds for decision-making. Those grounds are in the purposes of audit. Assuming that the audit has identified areas for administrative improvement in the national research funding organisation, the SAI could determine which option for circulating the draft audit findings is most likely to lead to the underlying administrative problems being addressed. In other words, the SAI's decision would be based on its goal of improving public administration. However, it could give priority to its assurance role, and provide a copy of the draft audit findings to both bodies.

The final audit opinion and report

Once the SAI has discussed the draft opinion and findings and considered the content of those discussions, it is now ready to prepare its final report, opinion or judgement. Without doubt, the SAI will require legislative authority to formulate and to report its final audit opinion.

Circulation of a final opinion or report will depend on local arrangements. It is possible for the final report or judgement to be released by the SAI only to those sections of government audited. Then, no other body receives the final opinion or report. Where this is standard practice, the SAI is closer to the government than to the legislature. The latter does not use public sector external audit as an instrument to maintain the government's accountability to the legislature.

Local arrangements may require provision of the final opinion or report to the legislature and not to any part of government, including not to the agency audited. This points to a different relationship between the SAI and legislature than in the previous example. It suggests that the SAI is required to work principally with the legislature rather than with executive government. Evaluation of different arrangements for release of audit opinions and reports is based on local resolution of the best use of audit to provide assurances of good administration and to advance reform where this is warranted.

The Philippines Commission on Audit provides an example of local resolution of the above issues as follows:[14]

> One significant development resulting from the Commission's organizational restructuring is the preparation of a single, unified and integrated audit report for each government agency. Prior to this, an agency with a central office in Metro

[14] Chairman Guillermo N. Carague, Commission on Audit (2003).

Manila and branch offices in each of the country's fifteen regions, did not have a single set of audited financial statements. Instead the central office and each of the fifteen regional branches were treated as sixteen different and independent agencies, each with its own independent audit report.

An effective way to maximise the impact of audit opinions, reports and judgements is for the SAI to release them publicly. Public information through audit reports about the performance of government is a powerful accountability tool. There are various options for the SAI. It can provide the final opinion, report or judgement to the government, legislature and to the public at the same time, or at different times. In some countries, general administrative law requires agencies to include the auditor's financial statement opinion in their annual or other public reports. Release of the final report to the legislature increases the likelihood that it will become available to the public.

Once audit reports become public, the relationship of the SAI with the government agencies audited alters, depending on whether the reports are critical or not. The SAI must be aware of the likelihood of change.

The SAI can provide the entire report to the auditee and extracts to other parts of government, such as to the ministry, to the legislature and to the public. Attention is drawn to one kind of audit where the implications of releasing some but not all of the audit report are far-reaching. That is audit of an agency's internal controls. Management is responsible for establishing an effective system of internal controls to ensure compliance with laws and regulations. In designing steps and procedures to test or assess compliance, auditors should evaluate the entity's internal controls and assess the risk that the control structure might not prevent or detect non-compliance.[15]

The SAI's auditing standards will require it to audit agencies' internal controls. Auditing standards will guide the SAI on whether it releases all of its reports on internal controls to the legislature and publicly, or only extracts from them.

National private sector auditing standards are predictors of the SAI's decisions on this matter. Where these require private sector auditors to provide shareholders with reports on private companies' internal controls, then the SAI can adopt the same practice for the public sector. Commonly, and as explored in earlier chapters, private sector auditors provide internal control reports to management and boards, where the latter function, and not to shareholders. These receive less information in the form of a copy of the auditor's financial statement audit opinion. The SAI can follow that model, resulting in the boards and management of government agencies receiving the internal control reports, and possibly the ministries receiving them as well. The legislature will receive the financial statement audit opinion and it may also receive a summary of the main points in the internal control report.

---

[15] INTOSAI (2001), *Auditing Standards*, p.56.

By definition, a legislature that does not receive copies of internal control reports from the external public sector audit is less well informed about the government's money and program management than legislatures that receive them. It is a matter for the legislature to decide whether to ask for them. Where a legislature has delegated this decision to the SAI, then the latter must make this public interest decision based on its role of providing assurance and finding how public administration can improve – when it has these twin roles. Its decision can take into account the materiality of its internal control findings and report only the most significant of these. If an SAI can decide what it reports publicly or to the legislature, it is advised to specify beforehand the criteria it uses to decide what it will report. That is unless the legislature has specified those criteria for it. The SAI's decisions will be informed by auditing standards and by its understanding of its role.

Public release leads the SAI to open the question of whether its findings should be worded for the public to understand them. Extensive use of legal, accounting and other specialist terminology in publicly released audit reports reduces public impact, as well as contributing to misunderstandings of audit findings.

The timing of provision of final audit reports to stakeholders also affects the use of those reports by others. For instance, distribution of a final report immediately after an audit gives the audit immediacy. Local convention can be that final audit opinions and findings are released in an omnibus report at set periods, such as biannually or annually. The advantage of this approach is that readers of the omnibus report will be able to see findings of all audits at the same time. This simultaneous release may assist users and readers of the final report to come to their own views on the relative importance of particular audits. Choice of the style of language in audit reports and on the timing of the latter's release can be considered in light of the needs of users of audits.

Since a principal purpose of public sector audit is to assist in reform, a readership that is informed about all audit findings, and which uses the information to make its own judgements on what aspects of public administration must change, is an ally in the reform and modernisation process. The public has two bases for wanting to know the SAI's final views on particular programs such as in health, education and defence. The first is that the public funds those programs through national revenue raising, and the second is that the members of the public are the clients of programs.

Local conditions will also determine whether the final report from the SAI criticises government policy. The charters of some SAIs permit them to criticise government policy where the latter does not demonstrate efficient and effective use of public moneys. There is a difference between subject matter policy and administrative policy. For example, subject matter policy refers to government intentions in specific areas such as health, education and foreign affairs. Administrative policy refers to the government's preferred administrative arrangements for delivering the subject matter policies. The SAI must be aware of the difference between these categories. Audit law may permit the SAI to comment on either form of policy, on one form – which would usually be administrative policy – or on neither form.

Conclusions

We have argued that the SAI's mandate must specify which kinds of agencies it has the authority to audit. This is specification of the audit mandate. One of the more discussed areas of mandate is in regard to the authority to audit government companies and business enterprises, including whether the mandate extends to these entities' subsidiaries. The SAI requires security of employment of staff. If these can be removed because they form or may form opinions critical of government, then the SAI's exercise of its mandate is weakened. The SAI requires the authority to employ specialist staff for particular kinds of audits. Since the work of government continues to evolve, the specialist skills that an SAI requires also will continue to change. These can include, for instance, the skills and training necessary for audits of foreign currency transactions. Because auditors require access to the premises and documents of government agencies in order to work, audit law must clarify the SAI's access powers. A contentious area for government is the sale of public assets. Independent audits can assist government to maintain public confidence in the sales process. Whether the SAI has the authority to audit asset sales is another area for legal clarification. Increasingly in many countries, governments are employing private firms to deliver public services. Ideally, for the SAI to provide an assurance to the legislature on government's purchase of those services, the audit mandate would include the authority to audit those private sector entities from which the government purchases its services. This is another area for much discussion and debate. Finally, the SAI must have the authority to determine its own audit methodology without interference from other parties. This includes the legal authority to settle on what evidence it needs to form an audit judgement or opinion.

The chapter has put the point of view that the SAI requires the authority to distribute or disseminate draft judgements, opinions and findings to those entities it is auditing or to those on which it is passing judgement. This authority is consistent with the principle of natural justice. It also requires the SAI to have the authority to amend its draft conclusions in light of further discussions with those entities. Lastly, the SAI will need a legal base to provide its final judgement, opinion, findings and report to those which it considers are affected by or have an interest in those matters. That authority includes decisions over the timing of release of final judgements and opinions, and the authority to disseminate these more widely, even publicly, where such general distribution furthers the SAI's role of providing assurances of sound public sector management or of improving the latter.

Chapter 16

How Can the SAI Reduce Costs and Increase its Impact When it Conducts Two Kinds of Audits?

This chapter explores how an SAI can reduce costs and increase its impact in reviewing the management of government operations by linking regularity and performance audits. The SAI's effectiveness is increased because both regularity audits, particularly financial and financial statement audits, and performance audits offer insights into management. When these two kinds of audits are combined, audit planning is better informed, the conduct of audits more focused, and the findings more comprehensive.

Before exploring how an SAI can increase its impact through linking or combining financial and performance audits, we will outline the reasons for regularity audits offering rich material for performance audits. The chapter's structure is as follows:

- Why are financial reports, especially financial statements, prepared?
- Examples of links between the two kinds of audits.

Why are financial reports, especially financial statements, prepared?

In the great majority of organisations, management requires financial reports to fulfil their responsibilities for the care and future of their organisation. Where reports are produced for internal purposes, management specifies their form and content, and determines requirements for their accuracy. Management can require these financial reports to be approximately accurate or completely accurate. These two levels of accuracy have different costs because more effort is required to produce data with a high degree of accuracy rather than data with a lower level of precision. Management can be satisfied with an approximate degree of correctness. Where it is so satisfied, it will still indicate to the preparers of those reports the degree of approximate accuracy it wants. It can do this by specifying the extent of acceptable and unacceptable error, such as by stating that a one per cent error in the accuracy of data in the reports is acceptable, or a ten per cent error is acceptable and so on.

A special challenge for management is where it prepares financial reports for others. These can be the owners of the organisation, whether the latter is in public or private ownership. They can also be the market where the organisation is in the private sector, and the general public where it is wholly or partially government owned. Those others may accept any financial reports that management produces. However, it is more likely that the other interested parties, including the owners, will specify what kinds of financial reports they require. Those specifications will cover the form and content of financial reporting, and the degree of accuracy the external interested parties will accept. The specifications of reporting requirements point towards the reasons for financial reports, including financial statements, being prepared for external audiences. The ability of those external stakeholders to specify their requirements is a manifestation of the accountability of the management which provides the reports. In some cases, those external requirements can be mandated.

Thus, there are two sets of financial reporting requirements: those required by management and those required by interested others outside the organisation. The latter may require or ask for general or specific purpose financial statements. General purpose financial reporting provides a mechanism to enable managements and governing bodies to discharge their accountability. Managements and governing bodies are accountable to those who provide resources for planning and control of the entity. In a broader sense, because of the influence reporting entities exert on members of the community at both the microeconomic and macroeconomic levels, they are accountable to the public at large.[1]

Stakeholders will ask themselves whether the information in the financial reports is correct. Management will assert that the data are correct, and stakeholders can accept those assertions. However, in many cases, stakeholders or the law will require independent verification of data. As we know, independent verification is a task for the auditor. In testing and verifying the accuracy of management's assertions about the accuracy of its financial reports, the auditor works for the stakeholders. This puts into practice the separation, described earlier, of the auditor's client from the auditee, which is the body being audited.

Financial statements summarise key information about the organisation, and they are integral components of financial management. That is because an organisation that cannot produce accurate financial statements cannot claim that it has adequate systems to manage its operations. For instance, accurate financial statements provide a correct account of assets and liabilities, cash flows, revenue and expenses, and operations for the year. Errors in any of these suggest that financial information provided to management by its own staff is flawed. This affects the soundness of management's decisions on the use of resources.

---

[1] Australian Accounting Research Foundation (December 2002), *Objective of General Purpose Financial Reporting*, Statement of Accounting Concepts, CPA Australia, Members' Handbook, <www.cpaaustralia.com.au>

Management that overestimates operating results and assets, or underestimates liabilities, is ill-placed to make decisions on the short – and long – term future of the organisation.

Financial statement audits offer insights into an organisation's financial management capacity. That is because well-managed organisations are more likely to produce accurate financial reports than ill-managed entities.

In Australia, audit opinions provide reasonable assurance that statements are materially free of mis-statement. A financial statement audit opinion that verifies the accuracy of the financial data provided by management provides assurance to stakeholders outside the organisation. The assurance is nothing more than that the data are accurate. Production of accurate financial statements is a necessary but not a sufficient indicator of sound financial management. That is because, for example, accurate financial statements can point to management problems. The financial statement data can also point towards the influence of factors outside management's control.

The INTOSAI definition of regularity audits includes audits of internal controls. Examples of these are account reconciliation processes, appropriate segregation of duties and delegations, correct classification of expenditure, monitoring of obligations under funding agreements, and ensuring appropriate access to banking facilities.

The regularity auditor's reports on financial or internal controls are of value to management. They are a springboard and an opportunity for management to improve those controls and their management. However, reporting of financial control weaknesses does not necessarily lead to their correction. That is because management may not be aware of reasons for the weaknesses. All that it sees are financial or internal control problems.

Examples of links between the two kinds of audits

Links between regularity and performance audits can be created in specific audits, and in annual planning of audit programs. Examples of both connections are described here. Also, we consider the utility of shared analyses of the business risks that audited agencies face, and the importance of training both groups of auditors in the approaches and concerns of the other.

Links between specific audits

The first example is of an audit where the regularity auditor identifies problems in access to the organisation's computers. The possibility of unauthorised access problems cast doubt over the accuracy of financial information the organisation or agency reports from those computers. Management can investigate the causes of the problem so that it can issue instructions for access to be tightened. Unless it knows why access control was inadequate, those instructions will not necessarily lead to improvements. Consequently, the auditors of next year's financial statements may find the same problems.

In these cases, performance audits can probe the reasons for financial and internal control weaknesses such as:

- management may never have issued instructions over those controls. This is a fundamental problem that the regularity audit possibly identified;
- management issued instructions but these were not followed. They were not followed because not all staff received them, which is a circulation and communication problem;
- staff did not understand management instructions. This is a communication and training problem;
- staff did not understand the importance of financial controls. Again, this is a training deficiency;
- computers did not have appropriate security software, so that staff could not implement management's instructions; and
- the nature of the contract between the organisation and the firm that provides information technology services to it, where such an arrangement exists. The contract permitted any of the supplier's staff to access the organisation's computers at any time and for any purpose.

Management may take action in response to the regularity auditor's report on the organisation's financial reports and internal controls. The rigour and certainty of the external requirements influence the adequacy of management's response. In order to speed this, to inform management and to inform external stakeholders, the SAI can conduct a performance audit. Taking the results of the regularity audit as the starting point, the SAI's performance auditors would identify reasons for the control weaknesses. Ideally, this identification would be done with management in those cases where management has not acted or where management action has not succeeded. Reporting would be to management and externally, and it would be on aspects of financial management relevant to production of the financial statements.

In this example, the regularity auditor completes his or her work, and the performance audit follows. The SAI must permit regularity and performance auditors to be informed about the other's work and to encourage them to share information. There can be practical difficulties. These include the regularity audit's objective and timetable. The regularity auditor, when conducting financial statement audits, is tightly focused on forming an opinion on whether information in the financial statements is correct, true and fair. The focus is not on improving management, but on financial accuracy. As we have seen, preparation of financially accurate reports is a necessary but not a sufficient condition for sound financial management. By coming to a view on the financial reports or financial statements, the regularity auditor is contributing to improvements in administration. The performance auditor can take the next steps by examining in more detail the reasons for financial management problems.

Another example is of a national government's funding of public health services in state and provincial governments. The national government provided very large sums annually to the other levels of government for public hospitals. Annual funding was within a five-year agreement between the national and state and provincial governments. The national government used a funding formula to distribute its funds. The formula took account of the population distribution, the fiscal capacity of other levels of government, and of health needs. It was a complex formula that the national government did not share with the other governments.

The regularity audit tested annually the accuracy of the national government's payment records. Testing involved:

- determining the consistency of the national government's payments to the other governments. This required the auditor to confirm whether the amounts paid by the national government were the same as those described in the national government's letters informing the other governments of how much money they would receive; and
- confirming that the total amount paid by the national government was the same as the total amount in the law.

These steps permitted the regularity auditor to affirm the accuracy of the single amount included in the agency's financial statements.

Performance auditors extended this work in two ways through:

- reviewing the controls over payments; and,
- attempting to confirm the accuracy of the sum of payments over the five yearly length of the agreements.

Performance auditors found problems with payment controls. They also found that the national government's payment agency did not maintain a copy of the funding formula used in each year. Therefore, the payment agency had a limited ability to confirm the accuracy of payments it made in previous years. The large size of the national government's payments resulted in small percentage errors in payments being significant amounts of money. Other levels of government would complain about the accuracy of national government's payments only if the latter decreased from year to year. The payment agency's difficulty in reconstructing previous year's payments, the invisibility of the funding formula to other governments, combined with the other governments' silences if they were overpaid, resulted in the risk of the national government paying more than necessary under its agreements. These matters were included in the performance audit report.[2]

In this case, of note is that the performance auditors employed the regularity auditors to conduct extra testing at the same time as their work on the financial statement audit. This may not always be possible. The SAI's creation of conditions for cooperation between the two kinds of audits must consider the practical problems of synchronising the audits' timetables. The benefits of cooperation between the two audit teams – and the additional audit findings from cooperation – appear only when the SAI addresses such practical problems.

The example above is of how regularity and performance audits can bring different perspectives legitimately to the audit of one government activity. The result is a more comprehensive account of the strengths and weaknesses of relevant management activities.

Links in annual audit planning

An SAI can increase its effectiveness in reviewing government operations by utilising the work of regularity and performance audits in annual audit planning. The latter identifies audit topics for the following year. It also requires the SAI to decide how many resources it will allocate to the two types of audits.

Each regularity audit is of a particular government activity or program. Ideally, each audit will lead to a report, although individual reports can be amalgamated for convenience. The SAI's analyses of trends and patterns in those audits and reports will inform its planning of regularity audits. Also, such analyses have the potential to inform the planning of a program of performance audits.

An example is of a regularity finding that financial management information systems in government agencies had inadequate internal controls. If these were serious problems, the SAI would bring them to the attention of the agencies audited. The SAI could make a more general observation in an omnibus or annual report to the legislature and to the government. In addition, the SAI could commission a performance audit or audits that identified the reasons for such widespread problems in agencies' financial management information systems. Potential reasons are inadequate systems development, inappropriate tendering and lack of user training.

Just as a review of the main findings from regularity audits can add to annual performance audit planning, a review of the main findings of performance audits can inform annual regularity audit planning.

There are obstacles to sharing of information and results between the two teams of audits. The obstacles can include:

- legal barriers to sharing information between audits and audit teams;

---

[2] ANAO (2002), *Performance Information in the Australian Health Care Agreements, Department of Health and Ageing*, Report No.21 2002–2003, ANAO, Canberra.

- each group of auditors' limited understanding of the purposes, conduct and findings of the other's audits;
- associated with this limited understanding is often found a very strong focus on the professionalism of each group of auditors. This professionalism can work against cooperation;
- differences in the relative priorities of both groups of auditors; and
- a belief that there are insufficient resources to share information between audit teams.

In order for the SAI to optimise the effectiveness of its work in reviewing government operations, the SAI's management must find ways to address these obstacles. Regularity auditors usually must complete their work within a set period after the financial year. Often, performance auditors have more control over their timetable. This gives them the flexibility to plan a comprehensive audit around the regularity audit timetable, accommodating the latter.

From the auditee's perspective, there appear two groups of auditors. The auditee agency may not understand why two groups of auditors are necessary, and why they are in the agency at the same time. The two groups of auditors must share information to avoid the agency providing the same information twice to SAI personnel. Potential problems in agency understanding of the reasons for two different audits, and any difficulties in the audit teams sharing information, must be addressed by the SAI if it is to gain from the work of both kinds of audits. Tight deadlines for the conduct of audits and for reporting can complicate this task.

Staff from the two audit teams can pursue different audit objectives. For instance, in an audit of an agency's financial management, financial auditors will emphasise the importance of agency staff preparing accurate and timely financial statements for audit. Performance auditors can focus on whether the agency's financial management framework, systems and reports assist agency personnel to utilise public resources efficiently and effectively.

Shared risk analyses

Regularity and performance auditors customarily engage in an analysis of the business risks that audited agencies encounter or will encounter during the year. Those business risks are the basis for audit planning.

Each group of auditors can share its risk analyses with the other. Regularity auditors will identify factors affecting the performance of agencies, but will be unable to address them because of the scope of their audits. Those agency business risks can be shared with the SAI's performance auditors. Conversely, the latter can identify particular agency business risks that may not be visible to the regularity auditors, and bring them to their attention. The most comprehensive and balanced agency business risk assessment will involve perspectives of both sets of auditors.

Training

To further augment the SAI's capacity, the SAI can provide training for its regularity auditors in performance audit, and vice versa. Instruction and training in the nature of both kinds of audits will inform staff of how and why they can learn from their peers. In this way, the SAI will enhance the consistency of its work, and encourage each group of auditors to support the work of the other, where this encouragement and reinforcement is based on knowledge.

Conclusions

This chapter has asked why management prepares financial reports including financial statements. Answers point towards the results of regularity audits being a potential source of ideas for performance audits. Two approaches to cooperation and the sharing of ideas between regularity and performance audits were raised. The first was cooperation in individual audits; the second was cooperation in audit planning. The chapter described some obstacles to cooperation between audit teams. There are limits on the resources of all SAIs which increase reasons for cooperation between staff involved in different kinds of audits. However, those resource limits also appear as obstacles to joint work. The chapter has argued that the SAI's capacity to draw on all its resources manifests where regularity and performance auditors share their agency business risk analyses, leading to a more comprehensive SAI description of the major business risks confronted by agencies it audits. Finally, the chapter has drawn attention to how the SAI's capacity can be enhanced where it provides each of its main groups of auditors with some training and exposure to the approaches and methodologies of the other.

An SAI that encourages discussion and debate between staff from regularity and performance audits is well placed to benefit from the perspectives of both in improving public administration and in holding executive government to account. In the absence of legal barriers to cooperation between the two groups of auditors, this is an imaginative approach by the SAI to its role.

PART IV

WHAT ARE THE NEXT STEPS IN REFORM OF AN SAI'S LEGAL FRAMEWORK?

What Are the Next Steps in Reform of An SAI's Legal Framework?

This final part summarises the legal base for public sector audits. It is necessary since such a large number of issues has been canvassed. Lastly, we consider the next steps to establish or reform public sector audit law.

Chapter 17

The Legal Basis for Audits Summarised

A legal basis for audits is necessary because:

- legislation can safeguard the SAI's independence;
- legislation is essential for defining the purposes of audit;
- legislation can ensure that the SAI has adequate resources;
- access to officials and to official records can be difficult;
- legislation supports the SAI's freedom to form, and to report publicly, its audit judgements and opinions.

These are summarised in turn.

Legislation can safeguard the SAI's independence

INTOSAI's 1977 Congress affirmed that the orderly and efficient use of public funds was essential for proper handling of public finances and the effectiveness of the decisions of the responsible authorities. To achieve this objective, it was necessary for each country to have an SAI whose independence was guaranteed by law.[1]

INTOSAI stated that SAIs accomplish their tasks objectively and effectively only if they are independent of the audited entity and are protected against outside influence. It affirmed that establishment of SAIs and the necessary degree of their independence should be laid down in a country's constitution, with details set out in legislation. Adequate legal protection by a supreme court against any interference with an SAI's independence and audit mandate should be guaranteed. SAIs should be provided with the financial means to enable them to

[1] INTOSAI (1988), *The Lima Declaration of Guidelines on Auditing Precepts*.

accomplish their tasks. They should be entitled to use the funds allocated to them as they see fit.

The independence of SAIs provided under a country's constitution and law provides for a high degree of initiative and autonomy, even when they act as an agent of the legislature and perform audits on its instructions. Therefore, the relationship between the SAI and the legislature and the government should be laid down in the law.

SAIs audit governments and their instrumentalities. This does not mean that these are subservient to SAIs. That is because governments retain responsibilities for acting in accord with mandates they have from electorates. A consequence is that governments are responsible for considering SAIs' recommendations, and for implementing them where they agree. It is up to each government to decide how to respond to the external auditor's recommendations, meaning that the latter may not be implemented if there is no consensus between the auditor and auditee. Where the external auditor's recommendations are not implemented, then the administrative problem that they addressed will remain. Continuation of that administrative problem is also a government responsibility.

Ideally, an SAI is independent of both the legislature and government. The legislature and the government may identify major public administration problems as audit topics. The SAI requires the independence to be able to accept or reject proposals for audits.

The SAI's audits are ways to keep the executive government accountable to the legislature. Legislative independence, particularly from executive government, means that the latter cannot select and reject topics and issues for audit. Where executive government controls the SAI, there is a risk that the government will not permit:

- audits of particular topics;
- certain audit approaches and methodologies; and
- unbiased reporting.

In some jurisdictions, the SAI has more authority for regularity, including financial statement, auditing than it does for performance auditing. The former can be mandatory for the SAI, while the latter is optional or discretionary. As indicated earlier, the combination of regularity and performance auditing is a strong means of ensuring a government's accountability to the legislature. Clearly, when only one of these kinds of audits is conducted, the legislature has fewer means to ensure accountability.

Another sign of government control or dominance of the SAI is where the latter is permitted to audit some agencies and not others. For instance, government departments and secretariats can be subject to external audit, but not government companies. A governmental justification for the exclusion of its companies from the mandate of an SAI is that those companies are subject to the discipline of the market. The argument continues that market forces are sufficient to ensure the performance and accountability of government companies and business enterprises.

The persuasiveness of this position is dependent on whether a government company or business enterprise has a market monopoly or is the dominant presence in the relevant part of the economy. If so, market forces are unlikely to ensure the strongest financial and service performance. With a government trading monopoly, it will be especially important for the legislature and for taxpayers to obtain accurate financial and service performance information on the government company. An SAI is one of the few sources of such information, as long as it has a mandate to audit it.

The plausibility of a government view that its companies and business enterprises should be exempt from the SAI's mandate is also partially dependent on the requirements of the country's accounting and auditing standards. These may not require any company, even a private sector firm, to have an external audit for regularity or other purposes. Shareholders in unaudited private firms and citizens in countries where government companies are not audited have no independent means of assessing the finances and service performance of such enterprises. Legislative reform is to be encouraged in such jurisdictions.

Accounting and auditing standards may require all private and public sector firms to have an external auditor. This requirement is favourable to the interests of shareholders and citizens. The interests of these two groups are further fostered where auditing standards require the external auditor to give an opinion on the adequacy of private and public sector firms' financial and service controls. In some countries, auditing standards require such opinions. A smaller number of countries require those opinions to be reported publicly.

Another government argument for the exclusion of the SAI's mandate from government companies and business enterprises is because of different reporting requirements of private and public sector auditors. Many government companies do not have a monopoly. They function alongside private sector firms, acquiring and disposing of assets and providing services. Where the SAI's auditing standards and reporting requirements are stronger than those in the private sector, then the government can claim that its company is disadvantaged by the SAI's mandate. It wants the same audit reporting and accountability requirements as private sector firms. In practice, were private sector audit reporting and accountability requirements to apply to the government firm, often there would be a reduction in the amount of financial and service performance information available publicly. Therefore, a government's argument for exclusion of its firms from the SAI's mandate is an argument for either a lesser form of accountability, or an argument for application of private sector audit standards to its enterprises. Where such views are expressed in legislation, citizens will have less information about the performance of government enterprises than were the SAI to audit these.

Legislation is essential for defining the purposes of audit

Part II of this study emphasised the need for clarity in defining the purposes of audit. To achieve clarity, a process of vigorous community and political debate may be necessary. The essence of public sector auditing is its utility in assisting the legislature to ensure the accountability of the government and its agencies. That is because an SAI is an instrument of the legislature, whose application demonstrates that it is a tool by which the government and its agencies show their accountability for the management of resources provided to them by the legislature on behalf of citizens. Therefore, the work of the SAI is a mark of the government's external accountability. Expressing this in legislation communicates the SAI's accountability role, leaving no ambiguity about its purpose.

The SAI's accountability role is evident in both its regularity and performance audits, judgements and opinions.

Legislation can ensure that the SAI has adequate resources

There are many ways for executive government to control an SAI where the latter's independence is not guaranteed by law. A particularly effective way is through control of the SAI's resources. An SAI can have legal authority to select topics and issues for audit. However, if it has insufficient resources to address them, then its independence is hollow.

As emphasised earlier, few if any governments have sufficient resources to implement all their policies and to respond to all demands of their electorates. The great majority of governments have resource constraints for many policies. In light of this, it is the responsibility of the SAI to estimate carefully the resources necessary for its work. Estimation must take account of the country's and the government's financial situation. The SAI can discuss its resource needs with the legislature and with the government. The nature of those discussions depends on each country's political customs and traditions.

A government will have a view on the amount of resources necessary for the SAI, including resources for performance audits, and it is appropriate that the government inform the SAI of its view. Ideally, the legislature should have the authority to decide on the amount of resources the SAI should receive. The legislature should take account of the SAI's and the government's estimates in reaching its decision.

Legislators will consider the SAI's previous audits when deciding on its resource allocation. Amongst their considerations will be the impact of earlier audits on public administration and public policy. Legislators may also consider the political effects of those audits. It can be seen that it is almost inevitable for political considerations to influence decisions on the amount of resources available to an SAI.

Another form of government influence on an SAI is by control over appointment of personnel to the SAI. The latter should be able to appoint its own staff. Where a government decides on who will work for the SAI, it is controlling the latter's resources. Such control prejudices the SAI's independence.

Access to officials and to official records can be difficult

INTOSAI's *Lima Declaration of Guidelines on Auditing Precepts* affirms that SAIs should have access to all records and documents relating to financial management and should be empowered to request, orally or in writing, any information considered necessary by the SAI.[2]

Access powers are necessary for the SAI to obtain the information it needs to form audit opinions. These legal powers must include the authority to interview government officials, including officials of government companies and business enterprises where these are within the SAI's mandate.

Since so many government documents are stored on computers, those legal powers must include the right of SAI personnel to access them. INTOSAI gives special reference to the audit of electronic data processing facilities. It affirmed that the considerable funds spent on electronic data processing facilities called for appropriate auditing. Such audits should be systems-based and cover aspects such as planning; economical use of data processing equipment; use of staff with appropriate expertise preferably from within the administration of the audited organisation; prevention of misuse; and the usefulness of the information produced.

Legislation supports the SAI's freedom to form and to report publicly its audit judgements and opinions

An SAI can have the legal authority to select and commence audits, and to form an audit judgement or opinion as it wishes, but it may not have the legal authority to report the judgement or opinion. The public nature of the SAI's audit opinions is a powerful means of maintaining executive government's accountability to the legislature. That is because publication of audit results provides credible information about the performance of government entities. Citizens and taxpayers are the market for such credible information, as is the legislature which they elected.

Many audit opinions are and will be critical of government. Since these are not in their interests, there is a risk that a government will seek to suppress or limit their release. Only when the SAI has the legal authority to form and release its judgements and opinions is government influence over audit reports controlled.

---

[2] INTOSAI (1988), *The Lima Declaration of Guidelines on Auditing Precepts.*

Conclusions

We have discussed reasons for the SAI having a legal basis for regularity and performance audits. The discussion highlighted the various means of government influence and control of an SAI. It also described how this influence and control can restrict, channel and suppress audit judgements and opinions, and their communication to the public. The amount and kind of information available to the public about the performance of its government is an indicator of the strength of a country's democracy.

At some time, SAIs in every nation refer to the legal basis of their authority when explaining the purposes of audit, selecting issues for audit, conducting audits, and when forming judgements and opinions and releasing reports. An SAI is perhaps most accepted by government agencies when it seldom or rarely uses its legal powers to conduct audits. That is because its legal powers are kept in reserve, and not exercised obviously on a daily basis.

Chapter 18

The Next Steps

The purpose of this study has been to establish a basis for review of an SAI's role and legal framework where the SAI operates in a mixed economy with an emerging market. The basis was the Australian model of public sector audit. It was the beginning of an exploration and examination of those issues that affect an SAI's performance. While the Australian model has sound characteristics, the critique in Part I highlighted some problems with it. The critique identified principal issues for review of an SAI's role. A benefit of confronting those principal issues is creation of a more favourable environment for a mixed economy. The twist is that to confront them necessitates a vigorous democracy that may not exist, while success in addressing them strengthens democratic institutions. In a mixed economy, sustained public sector reform is enhanced when participants in the reform understand and develop the relationship between public and private sector auditing.

Consequently, for an SAI and those associated with it, a starting point for reform is to introduce perspectives and techniques to strengthen the accountability of the government to the legislature through audit, while acting as an agent of wider public sector reform. In particular, this starting point emphasises the importance of audit reports in the accountability of the government to the legislature.

As soon as the SAI and interested parties such as legislators and administrators interested in and committed to creation or reform of public sector audit law have commenced their task, several complex issues appear. To confront these issues refines the purposes of reform and widens the potential of the SAI. Brazil is an example of a country that has commenced reform of its SAIs, and is refining the purposes of reform.[1]

Legislative authority

A legislature with authority over public sector audit has a means of keeping executive government accountable for the implementation of legislation. A legislature can use public sector audit for this end once it is aware of where lies the

---

[1] Nicoll, Paul (2004), 'A Reforma Da Lei De Auditoria Pública Na Austrália e No Brasil – Aspectos Comparativos', *Revista Ibero-Americana De Direito Público*, Volume XV, Rio de Janeiro, Brazil.

authority for selection of audit topics, and where lies the authority for deciding what will be reported and how. A government that decides which matters will be audited and how results are reported would have reduced accountability to the legislature for its actions in spending taxpayers' funds.

Information about agency use of funds and agency change

The need for the SAI to generate knowledge about government agencies' use of taxpayers' funds must be balanced with the need for change. The latter need will necessitate that audit reports explain why improvement in public administration is necessary, and also indicate how audited agencies must change. The difficulty is that by describing accurately what government is doing, the SAI risks alienating the agencies being audited, and generating opposition within them to change.

Limits to an SAI's influence

Although the SAI has a very important role in modernisation of the public sector, it can never be the principal agent of change. If it is the only agent of change, or considered to be the major agent when in reality there are several, the speed of reform will be slower than otherwise, and there will be a greater risk than necessary of the direction of reform being controversial and contested. Understanding what the SAI can do leads to acknowledgement of what it cannot do and what is not its role. Ideally, the principal agent of reform is government, not the entity that sits between the legislature and government.

Expectations

Audits are likely to achieve change and reform when they satisfy the expectations of at least one of the two major groups of stakeholders – clients and auditees. Change is more likely when the expectations of the audit's client are met. But, unless the client has strong control and power, the expectations of management of the activity audited must also be at least partially met for change and reform to occur. Possibly the conditions for administrative reform are most favourable when the expectations of the two major groups of stakeholders the client and the auditee – are met simultaneously. At the national level, the principal client is the elected legislature and the secondary client or auditee is executive government. Therefore, the environment for change and reform is most favourable when the expectations of both the legislature and government are met.

Reform of administrative law

Reform of public sector audit law must be accompanied by reform of administrative law for the sector. In particular, this means consideration of the adequacy of current financial and program management legislation, and its possible extension to ensure that key managers have responsibility for the economic, efficient and effective delivery of government programs and services. The legislative task is larger than how it first appeared, since the two sets of laws are open to review.

Relationship with private sector audit law

The other limitation on the success of reform of public sector audit law is the status of audit legislation and requirements for the private sector. Reformers must be aware of whether public sector audit law reform is behind, at the same level, or in front of reform of audit legislation for the private sector. They must consider the critical decision of where they want public sector audit law to be in comparison with its private sector equivalent.

Resources

The legislature should have the authority to decide who should pay for audits. However, the legislature can be advised by the government and by the SAI. An SAI with the authority to determine its own resources would be maximising its independence. Only a small number of SAIs is in this situation. Disclosure of audit costs is an incentive for the SAI to operate efficiently. In the public sector, there are risks where audited agencies pay fees directly to the SAI because the latter can then confuse the identity of its principal client, the elected assembly, with that of its auditee, which is the government and its parts. Unless the legislature has determined how much money should be spent on different kinds of audits, the latter is a decision for the SAI. Similarly in regard to settling on the audit resources available for any SAI advisory role for government agencies, it will be a matter for the SAI to decide unless the legislature has made the decision. The SAI will require expenditure and other resource data on its own activities in order to be best placed for any advisory or decision-making role on these matters.

Reports

The SAI can experiment with the form and content of audit reports, reviewing strengths and weaknesses in their communication. Audit reports evolve in every jurisdiction and country. With knowledge of this, there are opportunities to develop new forms of reporting and communication of audit opinions, and to trial them with representatives of the SAI, the legislature and the government. It could take a considerable time to develop a new form of reporting satisfactory to these and to any other important stakeholders.

Mandate

The SAI's mandate must specify which kinds of agencies it can audit. One of the more discussed areas of mandate is the authority to audit government companies and business enterprises, including whether the mandate extends to these entities' subsidiaries. The SAI requires security of employment of staff. If these can be removed because they form or may form audit opinions critical of government, then the SAI's exercise of its mandate is weakened. The SAI requires the authority to employ specialist staff for particular kinds of audits. Since the work of government continues to evolve, the specialist skills that an SAI requires will also alter. They can include, for instance, the skills and training necessary for audits of foreign currency transactions. Auditors require access to the premises and documents of government agencies in order to work. Therefore, audit law must clarify the SAI's access powers. A contentious area for government is the sale of public assets. Although independent audits can assist government to maintain public confidence in the sales process, whether the SAI has the authority to audit asset sales is another area for legal clarification. Increasingly in many countries, governments are employing private firms to deliver public services. Ideally, for the SAI to provide an assurance to the legislature on government's purchase of those services, the audit mandate would include the authority to audit those private sector entities from which the government purchases its services. This is another area for much discussion and debate.

Standards, methods and evidence

Audit standards are primarily the SAI's decisions. However, it is advisable for it to consult first with the legislature and government on such issues that can have wide effects in the public sector. The SAI must have the authority to determine its own audit methodology without interference from other parties. This authority includes the legal authority to settle on what evidence it needs in order to form an audit judgement or opinion. It also includes the authority to permit its regularity and performance auditors to share their approaches and findings.

Judgements and reports

The SAI requires the authority to distribute and disseminate draft judgements, opinions and findings to those entities it is auditing or to those on which it is passing judgement. This authority is consistent with the principle of natural justice. It also requires the SAI to have the authority to amend its draft conclusions in light of further discussions with those entities. Lastly, the SAI must have the authority to provide its final judgement, opinion, findings and report to those which it considers are affected by or have an interest in those matters. That authority includes decisions over the timing of release of final judgements and opinions, and the authority to disseminate these more widely, even publicly, where such general distribution furthers the SAI's role of providing assurances of sound management or of improving the latter in the public sector.

Where an SAI uses the media as one avenue for disseminating its work and increasing the likelihood that its findings are used in public sector reform, it can take steps to gain or maintain the confidence of legislators and government by preparing and using guidelines for media contact. Answers to the question of who should decide whether the SAI should have contact with the media depends on the nature of the political system, and the relationship between the government and the legislature.

What next?

Many developing countries confront major difficulties in reforming public administration. To find a way to address these major difficulties can involve an emotional or nationalistic as well as a detailed response. I was struck by this when, while reading a Philippine publication titled *Performance and Accountability: Central Pillars of Democracy*,[2] the author quoted from a poem by the great Indian poet, Tagore.[3] Another example of the wider implications of reform of public administration using audit is in Brazil. In that country, a program of modernisation

---

2 Tantuico Jr., Francisco S. (1994).

3 Let My Country Awake!
Where the mind is without fear and the
Head is held high;
Where knowledge is free;
Where the world has not been broken up into fragments by narrow domestic walls;
Where tireless strivings stretches its
Arms towards perfection;
Where the mind is led forward by thee
Into ever-widening thought and action –
Into that heaven of freedom, my father, let my country awake.
Gitanjalai, Rabindra Nath Tagore.

of the Federal Court of Accounts is associated with the Brazilian Government's campaign to reduce hunger in the population.[4]

An assumption on which this report is based is that the law can and should protect the integrity of the audit opinion. Next steps should separate matters that will lead to amendment of current audit law if it exists, from matters on which the SAI can act within the constraints of current law. This last action sets out an agenda for change in the SAI's charter within present unamended legislation. It highlights the value of development of a plan to initiate or reform the legislation with both short- and long-term objectives. Such a plan would specify the content of initial or reformed audit law. Figure 18.1 suggests components of an action plan.

In a number of places, we have highlighted the importance of research, especially comparative and longitudinal research, into factors affecting the efficacy of SAIs. Research projects in independent institutions, such as universities, can assist an SAI in understanding the effects of its interpretation of its role, while being another affirmation of the conditions necessary for the SAI to function with a minimum or absence of political control.

This book's introduction referred to the importance of decisions on the pace of change in reform of public sector audit law, especially when there are significant changes in the economy and in market regulation. Decisions on what to change will overlap with decisions on how to create or amend the law. Once there is agreement on those matters, the new law can be implemented. It is at this point that the challenge of reform becomes even greater.

---

4 Tribunal de Contas Da União (2004), *Fome Zero*, <www.tcu.gov.br>

Essential components would include clauses on:

- the SAI's main functions, powers and independence;
- the SAI's mandate, for instance, whether it includes government companies and business enterprises as well as non-commercial government agencies;
- specification of the kinds of audits that the SAI must conduct, and the authority to conduct regularity and performance audits;
- clarification of whether the SAI must evaluate government programs as well as audit them;
- identification of the SAI's role in combating corruption, and the limits to the SAI's capacity in this area;
- clarification of whether the SAI can advise government agencies, and conditions on which advice can be given;
- identification of the general legal powers necessary for public sector auditors to conduct their audits efficiently and thoroughly, and to report results in a balanced and well-supported way;
- appointment of permanent, specialist and temporary members of the SAI, and protection of their terms and conditions of employment to minimise political interference;
- the SAI's authority to employ private sector audit firms to audit under contract;
- the SAI's responsibility for audit standards;
- selection of topics for regularity and performance audits and audit planning;
- the authority to determine audit objectives, and the scope and conduct of fieldwork;
- the authority to request and to conduct interviews and meetings with government officials, and access to government ministers and individual legislators;
- information gathering powers and confidentiality of audit information;
- powers of access to agencies and private firms delivering government services, including the authority to access, copy and remove all documents that the auditor considers important; and
- reporting to agencies, the government and to the legislature in draft issues papers and judgements, and the authority to determine the content and circulation of final reports and judgements.

Figure 18.1 Items for Review in Public Sector Audit Law

Appendix

Attributes of SAIs

The Comptroller and Auditor-General of India has identified 22 attributes of SAIs' statutes, including independence, jurisdiction and powers, both auditorial and administrative.[1] The attributes are shown below.

Independence

- Legal basis
- Mode of appointment and qualifications
- Tenure
- Mode of removal
- Conditions of service

Jurisdiction

- Federal
- Provincial
- Commercial
- Expenditure
- Receipts
- Exchequer control
- Reporting procedure
- Others

Powers

- Requisitioning records
- Testimonals
- Search and seizure
- Physical verification
- Punitive action
- Others

Powers – Administrative

- Budget allocation
- Appointment of staff
- Others

---

1 Comptroller and Auditor-General of India, <www.cagindia.org/mandates/index.htm>

Bibliography

Relevant Internet website addresses are shown below when known or available. With some exceptions, the Internet website is given for the first reference where there are multiple references to the same author.

9th ASOSAI Assembly (October 2003), *Quality Improvement of Public Audit, National Report: the Chamber of Accounts of the Russian Federation*, Manila, Philippines, <www.asosai.org>

18th Commonwealth Auditors-General Conference (7–9 October 2002), *Proceedings*, National Audit Department of Malaysia, Kuala Lumpur, Malaysia.

ANAO (1996), *Building Better Cities. Department of Transport and Regional Development*, Report No.9 1996–97, ANAO, Canberra, <www.anao.gov.au> All ANAO publications are available on this website.

ANAO (1997), *Audits of the Financial Statements of Commonwealth Entities for 1996–97. Summary of Results and Outcomes*, Report No.22 1997–98, ANAO, Canberra.

ANAO (1998), *Evaluation Processes for the Selection of Hearing Devices. Department of Health and Family Services*, Report No.49 1997–98, ANAO, Canberra.

ANAO (1998), *OGIT and FedLink Infrastructure. Office of Government Information Technology, Department of Finance and Administration*, Report No.11 1998–99, ANAO, Canberra.

ANAO (1998), *Annual Report 1997–98. The Auditor-General*, ANAO, Canberra.

ANAO (1999), *The Management of Performance Information for Specific Purpose Payments – The State of Play*, Report No.31 1998–99, ANAO, Canberra.

ANAO (1999), *National Aboriginal Health Strategy – Delivery of Housing and Infrastructure to Aboriginal and Torres Strait Islander Communities. Aboriginal and Torres Strait Islander Commission*, Report No.39 1998–99, ANAO, Canberra.

ANAO (1999), *Energy Efficiency in Commonwealth Operations. Department of Industry, Science and Resources, Australian Greenhouse Office*, Report No.47 1998–99, ANAO, Canberra.

ANAO (2000), *Implementation of Whole-of-Government Information Technology Infrastructure Consolidation and Outsourcing Initiative. Cross Agency*, Report No.9 2000–2001, ANAO, Canberra.

ANAO (2001), *Internet Delivery Decisions. A Government Program Manager's Guide*, ANAO, Canberra.

ANAO (2001), *Internet Security Within Commonwealth Agencies*, Report No.13 2001–2002, ANAO, Canberra.

ANAO (2002), *ANAO Auditing Standards May 2002*, ANAO, Canberra, <http://www.anao.gov.au/Website.nsf/Publications/744C7f82DE39D37C4A256DGEO>

ANAO (2002), *Performance Information in the Australian Health Care Agreements, Department of Health and Ageing*, Report No.21 2002–2003, ANAO, Canberra.

ANAO (2003), *Survey of Fraud Control Arrangements in APS Agencies*, Report No.14 2003–2004, ANAO, Canberra.

ANAO (2003), *Annual Report 2002–2003. The Auditor-General*, ANAO, Canberra.

ANAO (2003), *Control Structures as part of the Audit of Financial Statements of Major Commonwealth Entities for the Year Ending 30 June 2003*, Report No.61 2002–2003, ANAO, Canberra.

ANAO (2003), *Audits of the Financial Statements of Australian Government Entities for the Period Ended 30 June 2003*, Report No.22 2003–2004, ANAO, Canberra.

ANAO (2004), *Annual Report 2003–2004*, ANAO, Canberra.

ANAO (2004), *Audit Work Program 2004–2005, July 2004*, ANAO, Canberra.

ANAO (2004), *Comparison Between Pre-2005 Australian Standards and Australian Equivalents to International Financial Reporting Standards*, ANAO, Canberra.

ANAO (2004), *Control Structures as part of the Audit of Financial Statements of Major Australian Government Entities for the Year Ending 30 June 2004*, Report No.58 2003–2004, ANAO, Canberra.

ANAO (2004), *Opinions*, ANAO, Canberra.

ANAO (2005), *Interim Phase of the Audit of Financial Statements of General Government Sector Entities for the Year Ending 30 June 2005*, Report No.56 2004–2005, ANAO, Canberra.

ASOSAI (2003), *ASOSAI Guidelines for Dealing with Fraud and Corruption*, <http:www.asosai.org/fraud_guidelines/index.htm>

ASOSAI (October 2003), *IT Audit Guidelines*, 6th Research Project.

ASOSAI (April 2004), *Asian Journal of Government Audit*, <www.asosai.org>

Attorney-General's Department (2004), *Audit Act 1901*, Attorney-General's Department, Canberra, <http://scaleplus.law.gov.au> All Australian Government legislation is available from this website.

Attorney-General's Department (2004), *Australia. The Constitution – as in force on 1 June 2003*, Attorney-General's Department, Canberra.

Attorney-General's Department (2004), *High Court of Australia Act 1979*, Attorney-General's Department, Canberra.

Attorney-General's Department (2004), *Inspector-General of Intelligence and Security Act 1986*, Canberra.

Attorney-General's Department (2004), *Ombudsman's Act 1976*, Canberra.

Attorney-General's Department (2004), *Public Accounts and Audit Committee Act 1951*, Attorney-General's Department, Canberra.

Audit Office of New South Wales (2003), *Annual Report 2002–2003*, Audit Office of New South Wales, Sydney.

Auditor-General (1987), *Annual Report of the Australian Audit Office 1986–87*, AGPS, Canberra.

Auditor-General Australian Capital Territory (2003), *Annual Management Report for the Year Ended 30 June 2003*, ACT Auditor-General's Office, Canberra.

Auditor-General of Pakistan (October 2003), 'Quality Management in Public Audit. Pakistan's Perspective', *9th ASOSAI Assembly*, Manila, Philippines.

Auditor-General Victoria (2003), *Annual Report 2002–2003*, Auditor-General Victoria, Melbourne.

Auditor-General Victoria (2004), *Version No.043, Audit Act 1994. Act No.2/1994*, Victorian Auditor-General's Office, Melbourne, Victoria, S3A.

Auditor-General's Department South Australia (2003), *Annual Report on the Operations of the Auditor-General's Department for the Year Ending 30 June 2003*, Auditor-General's Department South Australia, Adelaide.

Australian Accounting Research Foundation (AARF), (2002), *AUS 104 Glossary of Terms, AUS 202 Objective and General Principles Governing An Audit of a Financial Report, AUS 206 Quality Control for Audit Work, AUS 306 Materiality and Audit Adjustments, AUS 806 Performance Auditing, AUS 808. Planning Performance Audits, AUS 810 Special Purpose Reports on the Effectiveness of Control Procedures*, AARF, Melbourne, <www.aarf.asn.au>

Australian Accounting Research Foundation (December 2002), *Objective of General Purpose Financial Reporting*, Statement of Accounting Concepts, CPA Australia, Members' Handbook, <www.cpaaustralia.com.au>

Australian Accounting Research Foundation (13 January 2003), *Auditing and Assurance Standards Board (AuASB) Policy on Harmonisation and Convergence with International Standards on Auditing (ISAs)*, AARF, Melbourne.

Australian Accounting Standards Board (1995), *AAS 5 Materiality, AASB 1031 Materiality*, Australian Accounting Research Foundation, Melbourne.

Australian Capital Territory (1996), *Auditor-General Act 1996*, ACT Government, Canberra.

Blake Dawson Waldron (2004), *The BDW Guide to CLERP 9. Practical Guide to the Corporate Law Economic Reform Program (Audit Reform and Corporate Disclosure) Act 2004*, Blake Dawson Waldron, Sydney, <http://www.bdw.com/frameit.asp?page=/news/clerp9guide.pdf>

Buchanan, Robert (April 2004), *The Independence of the Supreme Audit Institutions of New Zealand and other Pacific and Asian States*, Paper prepared for the 17th UN/INTOSAI Seminar, Symposium on the Independence of Supreme Audit Institutions, <www.oag.govt.nz>

Business Credit, (February 2004), Volume 106, No.2, 'The Sarbanes-Oxley Act of 2002: Understanding the Independent Auditor's Role in Building Public Trust', <www.pwc.com>

Chairman Guillermo N. Carague, Commission on Audit (2003), *COA Directions During Critical Times in the Philippine Economy*, Conference of the Philippine Computer Society (PCS), and Philippine State Universities and Colleges Computer Education and System Society (PSUCCESS), AIM Conference Center, Manila, Philippines, 2 October 2003.

CNAO, 'Applicable Model for Audit Testing', *Asian Journal of Government Audit 3*, ASOSAI, New Delhi, India, pp. 86–96.

Comptroller and Auditor-General of India, <www.cagindia.org/mandates/index.htm>

CPA Australia Audit Centre of Excellence (1999), *A Guide to Understanding the Audit of a Financial Report*, <www.cpaaustralia.com.au/05_about_cpa_aust/06centres_of_excellence/docs/audit_0999_final_of_fr.pdf>

Department of Finance and Administration (2004), *Finance Minister's Orders. Schedule 1: Requirements for the Preparation of Financial Statements of Australian Government Entities*, Department of Finance and Administration, Canberra, Policy 1B, http://www.finance.gov.au

Department of Parliamentary Services (12 December 1996), *House of Representatives Hansard*, Parliament of the Commonwealth of Australia, Canberra.

Department of Parliamentary Services (7 October 2003), *Hansard, House of Representatives*, Parliament of the Commonwealth of Australia, Canberra, p.20729.

Department of Parliamentary Services (11 May 2004), *Hansard, House of Representatives*, Parliament of the Commonwealth of Australia, Canberra, pp.28163–28164.

Department of Parliamentary Services (2004), *Parlinfo Web*, <http://paralinfoweb.aph.gov.au>

Department of Prime Minister and Cabinet (2004), *Prime Minister and Cabinet Portfolio. Portfolio Budget Statements 2004–2005*, Department of Prime Minister and Cabinet, Canberra, <http://www.pmc.gov.au/pbs_paes/2004-2005/docs/pbs_2004-2005.pdf>

Do Binh Duong (April 2004), 'Corruption in Public Sector Investment Projects: Preventive Role of the Office of the State Audit of Vietnam, SAV'. *Asian Journal of Government Audit*, ASOSAI, pp. 43–48.

Funnell, W. (2001), *Government by Fiat. The Retreat from Responsibility*, UNSW Press, Sydney.

General Accountability Office (2004), *Strategic Plan 2004–2009*, GAO, Washington, <http://www.gao.gov>

Hopper, T. and Hoque, Z. (eds) (2004), *Accounting and Accountability in Emerging and Transition Economies*, Research in Accounting in Emerging Economies Supplement 2, Elsevier, Oxford.

Houghton, K. and Jubb, C. (November 2003), *Auditor Selection: What Influences Decisions by Listed Companies?* Australian Accounting Review, Vol.13, No.3, pp. 67–72.

Institute of Directors in Southern Africa (2002), *Executive Summary of the King Report 2002*, Institute of Directors in Southern Africa, Parktown, South Africa, <www.iodsa.co.za>

INTOSAI (1988), *The Lima Declaration of Guidelines on Auditing Precepts*, INTOSAI, Vienna, Austria, <www.intosai.org/2_LIMADe.html>

INTOSAI (1992 and 1995), *Accounting Standards*, INTOSAI, Vienna, Austria, <www.intosai.org>

INTOSAI (1998), *Code of Ethics and Accounting Standards*, INTOSAI Auditing Standards Committee, Vienna, Austria.

INTOSAI (2001), *Auditing Standards*, INTOSAI, Vienna, Austria.

INTOSAI (2002), *Implementation Guidelines for Performance Auditing Standards, Exposure Draft*, INTOSAI, Vienna, Austria.

Joint Committee of Public Accounts (1989), *The Auditor-General: Ally of the People and Parliament, Reform of the Australian Audit Office*, Report No.296, AGPS, Canberra.

Joint Committee of Public Accounts (1994), *An Advisory Report on the Financial Management and Accountability Bill 1994, the Commonwealth Authorities and Companies Bill 1994 and the Auditor-General's Bill 1994, and on a Proposal to Establish an Audit Committee of Parliament, Report 331*, AGPS, Canberra, <http://www.aph.gov.au/house/committee/jpaa/index.htm>

Joint Committee of Public Accounts (1996), *Guarding the Independence of the Auditor-General, Report 346*, AGPS, Canberra.

Joint Committee of Public Accounts and Audit (2000), *Review of Auditor-General's Reports 1999–2000, Report 376*, Parliament of the Commonwealth of Australia, Canberra.

Joint Committee of Public Accounts and Audit (June 2002), *Report 388. Review of the Accrual Budget Documentation*, Parliament of the Commonwealth of Australia, Canberra.

Joint Committee of Public Accounts and Audit (August 2003), *Report 395. Inquiry into the Draft Financial Framework Legislation Amendment Bill*, Parliament of the Commonwealth of Australia, Canberra.

Joint Committee of Public Accounts and Audit (2003), *Review of Auditor-General's Reports 2002–2003: First, Second and Third Quarters, Report 396,* Parliament of the Commonwealth of Australia, Canberra.

Joint Standing Committee on Foreign Affairs, Defence and Trade (11 April 2001), *Completed Inquiry: Rough Justice? An Investigation into Allegations of Brutality in the Army's Parachute Battalion*, Parliament of the Commonwealth of Australia, Canberra.

Joint Standing Committee on Foreign Affairs, Defence and Trade (8 May 2002), *Official Committee Hansard. Joint Standing Committee on Foreign Affairs, Defence and Trade, (Defence Subcommittee). Reference: Review of Defence Report 2000–2001*, Parliament of the Commonwealth of Australia, Canberra.

Joint Standing Committee on Foreign Affairs, Defence and Trade (13 October 2003), *Review of the Defence Annual Report 2001–2002*, Parliament of the Commonwealth of Australia, Canberra.

Joint Standing Committee on Foreign Affairs, Defence and Trade (2003), *Review of the Defence Annual Report 2001–2002*, Parliament of Australia, Canberra, <http://www.aph.gov.au/house/committee/jfadt/defence_report2001-2002/report.htm>

Joint Standing Committee on Foreign Affairs, Defence and Trade (11 August 2004), *Review of the Defence Annual Report 2002–2003*, Parliament of the Commonwealth of Australia, Canberra.

Kornish, L. and Levine, C. (2004), *Discipline with Common Agency: The Case of Audit and Nonaudit Services*, The Accounting Review, Vol. 79, No.1, pp. 173–200.

Main, Andrew (2003), *Other People's Money. The Complete Story of the Extraordinary Collapse of HIH*, Harper Collins Publishers, Sydney.

Md. Shahad Chowdhury (2003), 'The Importance of Audit in a Limited Resources Environment', *Asian Journal of Government Audit, 2003*, New Delhi, India, pp. 97–102.

Mulgrave, R. (2003), *Holding Power to Account. Accountability in Modern Democracies*, Palgrave Macmillan, Hampshire, UK.

National Audit Office (2002), *State Audit in the European Union*, NAO, London.

National Audit Office, NAO, (undated), *Co-operation Between Internal and External Auditors. A Good Practice Guide*, NAO, London.

National Audit Office (2004), *Financial Management of the European Union. A Progress Report*, Report by the Comptroller and Auditor-General, HC 529 Session 2003–2004, 6 May 2004, NAO, London.

New South Wales Consolidated Acts (1983), *Public Finance and Audit Act 1983*, <http://www.aaustlii.edu.au/au/legis/nsw/consol_act/pfaaa1983189/>

Nicoll, Paul (2004), 'A Reforma Da Lei De Auditoria Pública Na Austrália e No Brasil – Aspectos Comparativos,' *Revista Ibero-Americana De Direito Público*, volume xv, 2004, Rio de Janeiro, Brazil.

Northern Territory Auditor-General's Office (2003), *Annual Report 2002–2003*, Northern Territory Auditor-General's Office, Darwin.

Northern Territory of Australia (2002), *Audit Act*, Northern Territory Government, Darwin.

Office of the Auditor-General of Canada (2003), *Performance Report for the period ending March 31, 2003*, Office of the Auditor-General of Canada, Ottawa, <http://www.tbs-sct.gc.ca/rma/dpr/02-03/OAG-BVG/OAG-BVG03D01_e.asp>

Office of the Auditor-General for Western Australia (2003), *Annual Report 2002–2003*, Office of the Auditor-General for Western Australia, Perth.

Office of the Comptroller and Auditor-General of Bangladesh (2003), *Enhancing Management for Quality Audit*, Dhaka, Bangladesh.

Parliament of Tasmania (2003), *Auditor-General. Annual Report 2002–2003. September 2003*, Government Printer, Tasmania.

Parliament of the Commonwealth of Australia (1989), *Audit Act 1901*, Attorney-General's Department, Canberra.

Parliament of the Commonwealth of Australia (September 1990), *Not Dollars Alone – Review of the Financial Management Improvement Program*, Report of the House of Representatives Standing Committee on Finance and Public Administration, AGPS, Canberra.

Parliament of the Commonwealth of Australia, House of Representatives (1996), *Auditor-General Bill 1996. Explanatory Memorandum (Circulated by authority of the Minister for Finance, the Honourable John Fahey, MP)*, S25, <http://scaleplus.law.gov.au>

Parliament of the Commonwealth of Australia (1996), *House of Representatives Hansard*, Thursday, 12 December 1996, Canberra, pp.8342–8344.

Parliament of the Commonwealth of Australia (1997), *Auditor-General Act 1997*, <http://scaleplus.law.gov.au/>

Parliament of the Commonwealth of Australia (1997), *Commonwealth Authorities and Companies Act 1997, No.153, 1997*, Attorney-General's Department, Canberra, <http://scaleplus.law.gov.au/>

Parliament of the Commonwealth of Australia (1997), *Budget Strategy and Outlook 1997–98, 1997–98 Budget Paper No.1*, AGPS, Canberra.

Parliament of the Commonwealth of Australia (2000), *Financial Management and Accountability Act 1997. Act No.154 of 1997 as amended,* Attorney-General's Department, Canberra, <http://scaleplus.law.gov.au/>

Parliament of the Commonwealth of Australia, Senate Finance and Public Administration Legislation Committee (2000), *The Format of the Portfolio Budget Statements. Third Report*, Canberra, November 2000.

Parliament of the Commonwealth of Australia (2002), *Report 391. Review of Independent Auditing by Registered Company Auditors. Joint Standing Committee on Public Accounts and Audit*, Parliament of the Commonwealth of Australia, Canberra, <http://www.aph.gov.au/house/committee/jcpaa/indepaudit/execsum.htm>

Parliament of the Commonwealth of Australia, Joint Committee of Public Accounts and Audit (2002), *Report 388. Review of the Accrual Budget Documentation*, Canberra, June 2002.

Parliament of the Commonwealth of Australia (2004), *Committees*, <http://www.aph.gov.au/committee/committees_type.htm>

Parliament of the Commonwealth of Australia (2004), *Budget Strategy and Outlook 2004–2005. Circulated by the Honourable Peter Costello MP, Treasurer of the Commonwealth of Australia, and Senator the Honourable Nick Minchin, Minister for Finance and Administration, For the Information of Honourable Members on the Occasion of the Budget 2004–2005. Budget Paper No.1*, Parliament of the Commonwealth of Australia, Canberra, <www.budget.gov.au>

Parliament of the Commonwealth of Australia (2004), *Corporate Law Economic Reform Program (Audit Reform and Corporate Disclosure) Act 1994. No.103, 2004*, <http://scaleplus.law.gov.au/html/comact/browse/TOCN.htm>

Parliament of the Commonwealth of Australia (2004), *Federal Financial Relations 2004–05. Circulated by the Honourable Peter Costello MP, Treasurer of the Commonwealth of Australia, and Senator the Honourable Nick Minchin, Minister for Finance and Administration, for the Information of Honourable Members on the Occasion of the Budget 2004–05, Budget Paper No.3*, Department of the Treasury, Canberra.

Parliament of the Commonwealth of Australia, House of Representatives (2004), *Standing Committee on Family and Community Affairs*, <http://www.aph.gov.au/house/committee/fca/reports.htm>

Parliament of the Commonwealth of Australia, Parliamentary Library (2004), *Parliamentary Handbook of the Commonwealth of Australia*, <http://www.aph.gov.au/library/handbook/index.htm>

Queensland Audit Office (2003), *Annual Report 2003*, Queensland Audit Office, Brisbane.

Queensland Electoral and Administrative Review Commission (1991), *Report on Review of Public Sector Auditing in Queensland*, Electoral and Administrative Review Commission, Brisbane, Australia.

Raghunandan, K. and Rama, D. (September 2003), *Audit Committee Composition and Shareholder Actions: Evidence from Voting on Auditor Ratification*, Auditing: A Journal of Practice and Theory, Vol.22, No.2, pp. 253–263.

Report by the Independent Auditor of the Australian National Audit Office on the Results of a Performance Audit of 'Value for Money' Provided by the Australian National Audit Office, (June 2004), Canberra, ANAO, <www.anao.gov.au>

SAI Iran (April 2004), 'The Concept of Governance: by SAI-Iran', *Asian Journal of Government Audit*, ASOSAI, pp. 80–106.

Sarbanes-Oxley Act of 2002, S404, FindLaw, <www.findlaw.com>

Semple, J. (Fall 2002), *Accountants' Liability after Enron*, FDCC Quarterly, Vol.53, No.1, pp. 85–98.

Shergold, Peter (3 July 2003), *Administrative Law and Public Service*, Australian Institute of Administrative Law Opening Address, <www.pmc.gov.au>

Shergold, Peter (23 June 2004), *Once was Camelot in Canberra? Reflections on Public Service Leadership*, Sir Roland Wilson Lecture 2004, Canberra.

Tantuico, Jr., Francisco S. (1994), *Performance and Accountability: Central Pillars of Democracy*, Fiscal Administration Foundation, City of Mandaluyong, Philippines.

TCE RJ Noticia, Ano 2, No.19, Dezembro 2003, <www.tce.rj.br>

Tendero, Avelino P. (2000), *Theory and Practice of Public Administration in the Philippines,* Fiscal Administration Foundation, Inc., Manila, Philippines.

Tribunal de Contas da União (2003), *O Controle Externo das Agências Reguladores. Questões relevantes sobre o sector eléctrico e de petróleo e gás natural*, Tribunal de Contas da União, Brasilia, <Isc@tcu.gov.br>

Tribunal de Contas da União (2003), *Plano Estratégico 2003–2007*, Março de 2003, Tribunal de Contas da União, Brasilia.

Tribunal de Contas da União (2004), *Fome Zero*, <www.tcu.gov.br>

Tribunal de Contas do Estado do Rio de Janeiro (2000), *Lei Complementar 101 de 4 de Maio de 2000, Lei De Responsabilidade Fiscal*, Tribunal de Contas do Estado do Rio de Janeiro, Brazil.

Tribunal de Contas do Estado do Rio de Janeiro (March 2003), *Relatório de Atividades, Exercicio de 2002*, Rio de Janeiro, Brazil.

United Kingdom Parliament (24 February 2004), *Public Accounts Commission*, <http://www.parliament.uk/documents/upload/TPACtscript24024.pdf>

United Kingdom Parliament (2 October 2004), *Public Accounts Commission*, <http://parliament.uk/parliamentary_committees/public_accounts_commission.cfm>

Victorian Auditor-General's Office (1996), *Building Better Cities. A Joint Government Approach to Urban Development, Special Report No.45, November 1996*, Victorian Government Printer, Melbourne.

Victorian Legislation and Parliamentary Documents (1994), *Version No.043. Audit Act 1994. Act No.2/1994.*

Internet Sites

The following websites contain a large number of documents relevant to reform of an SAI.

Asian Organisation of Supreme Audit Institutions, ASOSAI	<www.asosai.org>
Australian Council of Auditors-General	<www.acag.org.au>
Australian National Audit Office (All ANAO publications are available on this site)	<www.anao.gov.au>
International Organisation of Supreme Audit Institutions, INTOSAI	<www.intosai.org>
National Audit Office of the United Kingdom	<www.nao.org.uk/home.htm>
New Zealand Office of the Auditor-General	<www.oag.govt.nz>
Office of the Auditor-General of Canada	<www.oag-bvg.gc.ca>>
United States General Accountability Office	<www.gao.gov>

Index